Currently Ava

Forthcoming

ALSO BY PETER GREEN

Armada from Athens: The Failure of the Sicilian Expedition, 415–413 B.C.

A Concise History of Classical Greece to the Close of the Classical Era

Alexander to Actium: The Historical Evolution of the Hellenistic Age

Alexander of Macedon, 356–323 B.C.: A Historical Biography

The Greco-Persian Wars

THE HELLENISTIC AGE

PETER GREEN

THE

HELLENISTIC AGE

A SHORT HISTORY

A MODERN LIBRARY CHRONICLES BOOK

THE MODERN LIBRARY

NEW YORK

2008 Modern Library Paperback Edition

Copyright © 2007 by Peter Green

Published in the United States by Modern Library, an imprint of The Random
House Publishing Group, a division of Random House, Inc., New York.

MODERN LIBRARY and the TORCHBEARER Design are registered
trademarks of Random House, Inc.

Originally published in hardcover in the United States by Modern Library,
an imprint of The Random House Publishing Group,
a division of Random House, Inc., in 2007.

LIBRARY OF CONGRESS CATALOGING-IN-PUBLICATION DATA
Green, Peter
The Hellenistic age: a short history / Peter Green.
p. cm.—(A Modern Library chronicles book)
Includes bibliographical references and index.
ISBN 978-0-8129-6740-1
1. Mediterranean Region—History—To 476. 2. Greece—History—
To 146 BC. 3. Greece—History—146 BC–323 AD.
4. Hellenism. I. Title.
DE86.G74 2007   938'.08—dc22   2006046657

Printed in the United States of America

www.modernlibrary.com

4 6 8 9 7 5 3

The abiding importance of Alexander lies more in the field of moral and philosophical debate than in practical politics.... The debate over legitimacy lasted a mere generation. After that Alexander was a symbol and nothing else. For subsequent ages he typified the world conqueror, and his territorial acquisitions were a standing inspiration and challenge to successive dynasts.

A. B. Bosworth

It is now impossible to consider the Hellenistic period in Greece as a uniform, essentially static epoch.

Susan E. Alcock

Preface and Acknowledgments

It is now seventeen years since my study *Alexander to Actium: The Historical Evolution of the Hellenistic Age* first saw the light of day (and well over twenty since the original text was first delivered to my publisher: I had a copy editor who specialized in minutiae). Since then the outflow of work on the Hellenistic age, already voluminous, has become a torrent. No scholar can master it all, and I have not, sensibly, attempted to do so. As those who compare the earlier work with this one will see, my essential views have not changed all that much; but I have learned a good deal from what I have read in the past two decades and am very glad of this opportunity to review, update, and where necessary modify my original arguments.

Once again, I study the three centuries of the Hellenistic age in a continuous ongoing diachronic narrative embracing the entire scene, rather than, like most writers on this subject, leading off with a condensed (and generally bewildering) political history in vacuo, followed up with a series of more or less static theme-park essays, first on the major kingdoms (Ptolemaic, Seleucid, Antigonid, Attalid) and then on a variety of topics ranging from the monarchy to economics, from Alexandrian literature to the visual arts, from urban planning to military science, from philosophy to piracy. The trouble with this approach is its kaleidoscopic disjunctiveness (which can make for severe confusion) and its inevitable tendency to subsume, under loosely generalizing labels, disparate trends or groups widely separated in both place and time.

My alternative method has, of course, its own built-in difficulties (as ancient universal historians were well aware), chief among them being the difficulty of maintaining what might be described as a polyphonic narrative with too many competing voices and the undeniable need to digress on certain specific themes as they arise in context. But I still believe that, in historiographical terms, this represents the most rational compromise, with the least amount of generic distortion and the best chance of conveying to an interested reader some sense of the complex, many-faceted, continually evolving, in ways revolutionary, in ways eerily familiar, social, political, and religious flux—the upshot of Alexander's disruptive eastern legacy—that we call, for want of a better label than Droysen's (see p. *xvi*), the Hellenistic age.

The curse of historiography in the Greco-Roman period was the increasingly prevalent taste for digests, epitomes, and abridgments that ousted fuller and more serious texts, which as a result, on the principle of Gresham's law, fell out of demand and were lost. It is not my intention, in this concise treatment, to encourage a similar process. *The Hellenistic Age* is not a substitute for those larger investigations that the period demands, but rather an introduction, offering readers just enough information to enable them to pursue the subject in greater detail. This must be my excuse for a fairly lengthy excursus on the sources (especially in translation), linked to a bibliography pointing the way toward further reading. Those who want just the narrative can always skip the introduction altogether.

Since I am writing for an anglophone general audience, my recommendations are not only (with a few special exceptions) to works in English, but also to those in print and thus easily available. For the same reason, I have for the most part avoided articles in learned periodicals, runs of which tend to be held only by academic libraries. Last, though I am on principle in favor of transcribing Greek names as near as possible to their original forms, I have in this book retained the Latinized versions throughout (for example, Cassander rather than Kassandros), since these are—like it or not—far more widely recognized.

The published work of many scholars, past and present, and personal acquaintance and discussion with more than a few, have enriched my knowledge of Alexander and the Hellenistic period more than I can say. Among them I owe an especial debt to Ernst Badian, Gene Borza, Brian Bosworth, Pierre Briant, Elizabeth Carney, J. K. Davies, Peter Derow, W. S. Ferguson, my old Cambridge teacher Guy Griffith, Erich Gruen, Christian Habicht, N. G. L. Hammond, Waldemar Heckel, Amélie Kuhrt, Geoffrey Lloyd, Jon Mikalson, Claire Préaux, Graham

Shipley, Andrew Stewart, Frank Walbank, and Édouard Will. As always, my work has been sustained by the rich holdings in ancient history, backed up by the highly professional Interlibrary Loan Service, of the University of Iowa. At Random House I am particularly indebted to the support, practical efficiency, and cooperative professionalism of Will Murphy, Matt Kellogg, and Dennis Ambrose. Last but very far from least, what I owe to my wife, Carin, both personally and professionally, she knows better than I do.

My grateful thanks to those friends and colleagues, in particular Professor Paul Cartledge, who reported errors in the first hardcover edition. Needless to say, for any still remaining, the responsibility is mine.

CONTENTS

INTRODUCTION

BACKGROUND AND SOURCES

·

BACKGROUND

What do we mean by the "Hellenistic age"? Answers may vary in detail,[1] but there is a broad general consensus as to its genesis and political dimensions, while the phrase itself and the concept behind it are recognized as the brainchild of a nineteenth-century German historian, Johann Gustav Droysen. It begins with the shattering impact of Alexander's conquest of the Persian Achaemenid empire (334–323) and follows the history, first, of the power struggle engendered among Alexander's marshals by his premature death, and then of the several dynasties founded by the victors (the so-called Diadochoi, or Successors) in that struggle, most notably Ptolemy in Egypt and Seleucus in Asia. Its end is most commonly defined—a definition that I accept in this volume—by Octavian's victory over Antony and Cleopatra at Actium in 31 BCE, which eliminated the last of these dynasties, that of the Ptolemies.[2]

As late as the mid–nineteenth century, in the preface to his *History of Greece* (1846–1856), George Grote, a liberal historian (and banker), could still write that "as a whole, the period between 300 B.C. and the absorption of Greece by the Romans is of no interest in itself, and is only so far of value as it helps us to understand the preceding centuries."[3] Though quite a few ancient writers (Polybius and Plutarch among them) saw that Alexander, knowingly or not, had transformed the Mediterranean world, while others (for example, Diodorus Siculus) attributed a similar role to Julius Caesar, there is no clear evidence that anyone at the time, or even in late antiquity, visualized the three centuries between them as a coherent and definable entity.[4] For that perception, Droysen must get the credit. In his history of the Successors

(Droysen, 1878) he promoted, as the key factor of the period, the adoption of the Greek language and Greek culture by non-Greeks in territories previously ruled by the Achaemenids. To express this concept, he used the term *Hellenismus,* based on the Greek term ἑλληνισμός (*hellenismos*), in its biblical sense of imitating or acquiring Greek language—specifically, the common Attic dialect adopted by Philip II of Macedon for official use—and culture. For Droysen, this demonstrated the working of providence to facilitate the dissemination of Christianity. The adjective "hellenistic"—not, significantly, existing in any Greek original—was first coined, in its French form *hellénistique,* by J. B. Bossuet in 1681, as a term for the Greek of the Septuagint, the "hellenized" version of the Old Testament.

As has long been realized, Droysen's definition is unsatisfactory on several counts. By concentrating on aliens, it paradoxically ignores Greeks. While its theological basis encapsulates a major, if indirect, consequence of Alexander's eastern conquests, this remains one factor only among many in the historiography of the period. Further, developments in archaeology, epigraphy, papyrology, social anthropology, and numismatics (to name only the most important disciplines) have opened up the immense complexities of the Hellenistic era in a way inconceivable to Droysen, Grote, and their contemporaries. Far from being a mere link between classical Greece and the nascent imperialism of Rome, as Grote supposed, those three centuries reveal themselves as a politically violent and variously creative epoch in their own right, and it is as such that they are studied today.

Why did Grote so despise this period? Ever since the reestablishment, from the beginning of the nineteenth century, in England in particular, of the primacy of Greek culture over that of Rome,[5] it has been the Periclean age of fifth-century Athens that has received constant and largely exclusive praise as representing, in virtually every area—literature, drama, historiography, architecture, sculpture, philosophy, and above all the democratic ideal of the city-state—an unprecedented, never to be repeated summum bonum of original creative achievement. With this benchmark in place, it was inevitable that what followed—especially given Athens' crushing military setbacks at the hands of Sparta (404) and Macedon (338)—should be widely regarded as a period of decline, a falling off from an unmatchably high standard.

Modern students of the Hellenistic era argue that the benchmark of Periclean achievement is meaningless in terms of cultural evolution, an apples-and-oranges comparison, and this in ways is plausible. Yet it remains true, and less often emphasized, that most writers *at the time* likewise mourned the end of an incomparable era; many saw no further scope for great achievement and looked to the past for help rather than to bold new innovation. Toward the end of the fifth century, Choerilus of Samos, an epic poet who had treated the Persian Wars, could write:[6]

> *Lucky the man of those times who was skilled in song-making,*
> *the Muses' servant, when the meadow was still untrodden:*
> *But now that it's all shared out, when the arts have their boundaries,*
> *we're the last left there on the road, and there's nowhere for the poet,*
> *search as he may, to steer his fresh-yoked chariot.*

Even allowing for the fact that Choerilus' main complaint is directed at Homer, the general sense of creative exhaustion is unmistakable. An age was over, and known to be over. As we shall see, one of the main functions of the great Library at Alexandria was to recover and edit all that that age had produced. The past, in the Hellenistic age, became crucial as a stepping-stone into the future.

A related problem that has much preoccupied scholars in recent decades is the survival of the classical city-state, or polis, under the ultimate authority of various royal dynasties. The general consensus here has been resolutely meliorist: despite inevitable curbs on their liberty, the cities, we are told, flourished. Some enjoyed greater democracy than before. Being subordinate to a king—that is, enjoying merely municipal freedom to make public decisions—was no worse than being governed by Athens or Persia.[7] The attitude is very much that of Plutarch to Roman rule: "Of freedom the townships have as a great a share as those in power dispense, and perhaps more would not be beneficial."[8] Yet Plutarch was very much at heart a man of the polis. For him, Greek freedom died with Demosthenes (*Dem.* 3), and much of his work can be seen as a nostalgic obsession with Athens' lost and glorious past. His cautious attitude to Rome may well have been induced by his knowledge of the number of times—desperately, always in the face of overwhelming odds, and never with success—the Athenians had rebelled against foreign overlordship. This dogged pursuit of *eleutheria* (freedom) was both passionate and significant. The difference of outlook, and confidence, in a powerful independent naval stronghold such as Rhodes, which remained free from the dictates of royal bureaucracy, is unmistakable.

The emphasis on personal rather than public relationships that stamps the Hellenistic age applied, essentially, to a leisured minority, which depended for its existence on the unremitting toil of others. When we examine the art, the literature, the town planning and architecture, the advances in science and scholarship, the religious developments, the administrative patterns, and the political and military practices that between them offer an evolutionary profile of the three centuries between Alexander and Augustus, it is that minority—cultured, colonialist, well-off, actively or indirectly exploitative—whose actions and beliefs, by and large, shape our picture. Courtiers and mercenaries, merchants, entrepreneurs and bureaucrats, artists and artisans, scholars, poets, scientists, historians, and philosophers, whether living off private incomes or patronage: it is their world, rather than that of the near-invisible majority, for which we have the evidence, such as it is. But then the same is true of Periclean Athens. It is the articulate who change history, who record those changes for posterity.

The social strata of any society evolve historically at different speeds and in different ways. For the Hellenistic era, as for many other periods, a safe rule of thumb is "The lower, the slower." For the fellahin of Egypt, or the peasantry of Greece and Anatolia, very little changed over these three centuries except the identity and, sometimes, the severity of their (mostly alien) oppressors, whose unswerving aim was to extract as much tax-money and labor from them as could be done without provoking mass revolution. Virtually ceaseless local warfare, together with uncontrolled brigandage, laid waste much of the countryside, disrupting both agriculture and trade. This in turn worsened the situation of both the rural and the urban poor. The latter group, always at greater risk of famine in a crisis, could at least—as the Alexandrian mob frequently proved—have some real influence on political events. The nearest the peasantry came to doing so was by joining a would-be rebel leader under arms: pretenders to the Macedonian or the Attalid throne, the priests and the *machimoi* (trained native troops) in Egypt. Above that level, the bureaucracy, the merchant class, the police, and the army all had good financial reasons—and indeed ingrained ideological motives—for upholding the status quo.

Thus real change, in the last resort, had to come from the top, and more often than not from the outside, whether the agent was Alexander, one of the Successors, or, finally, Rome. This must be my justification for presenting the Hellenistic age in the now unfashionable form of a narrative (though interspersed with general reflections). The current emphasis on cultural anthropology and populist demographics at the expense of narrative history has, inevitably, encouraged a curious sense of timelessness in studies of the Hellenistic world, compounded by the concomitant tendency to treat the period thematically rather than diachronically.

Sometimes, especially when summing up the cumulative impact of a major historical event such as Alexander's conquest of the East, this is inevitable (see chapter 3). Yet to view those three kaleidoscopic centuries as a monolithic cultural block—even in a laudable effort to retrieve "the illiterate, the rural, the poor, the inhabitants of regions beyond the scope of our textual accounts"[9]—must inevitably obscure both historical change as such and the powerful individuals whose actions brought that change about. The fashion today is to downplay those dynastic upheavals and characters that figure so prominently in my account, in favor of the abstractions of underlying trends and theoretical economics or the voiceless life of the common people as revealed by landscape archaeology. But power dictates still, the abuses of untrammeled power are as ugly today as they were in the lifetimes of Alexander or Ptolemy VIII, and now and again we need to remind ourselves of that basic (if unpalatable) fact.

———

These three *mouvementé* centuries cover some of the most crucial and transformational history of the ancient world, played out on an unprecedentedly large stage (see map, pp. 150–51). The changes are lasting and fundamental. Chief among them has to be the final demise—always with the occasional odd exception, like Rhodes—of the so-called polis mentality, the city-state as the normative political institution in international affairs. The parochial weaknesses of the system, glaringly apparent during the first half of the fourth century (Buckler, 2003, passim), led directly, in mainland Greece, to the diplomatic, political, and, finally, military supremacy of Philip II of Macedon. The cumbersome democratic process met efficient autocracy and failed. Too many cooks (of necessarily low quality) not only spoiled the broth, but tended to disagree on the recipe.

In Athens or Alexandria, Pella or Pergamon, when every allowance has been made for local or cultural variations, the same characteristic profile emerges. The traditional collective claims of the polis, progressively loosened from the late fifth century onward, are now restricted to local civic and municipal activities shorn of genuine power. Pericles' despised private individualist (*idiôtês*) has become the norm. That powerful binding force, the citizen militia, has now been largely replaced by hired mercenaries, while rising incomes allow many other activities, previously the responsibility of citizens, to be performed by slaves. In both cases, the idea that you can buy your way out of anything unpleasant—that perennial mantra of the nouveaux riches—must have been hard to escape. The propaganda of Panhellenism, an ingrained contempt for eastern *barbaroi*, and the carving up of the Persian empire by Alexander and the Successors, between them created an ideal atmosphere for confident de haut en bas colonialism, on a basis of justified exploitation, in the "spear-won" conquered territories.

Yet the shift to huge kingdoms and central royal authority was no innovation, but in essence a reversion to something very old, long familar in pharaonic Egypt and the Fertile Crescent, and by no means unlike that Achaemenid empire that Alexander had just dismembered so ruthlessly. As in the Alexandrian Library, so among the new dynasties of the Successors, the vision of the future could not shake off an enduring obsession with the past. If one thing united the multifarious members of this huge new diaspora, it was a search for roots, for justification and identity in the form of ancestral myth. That the process was (as we can see) in essence one of self-invention deterred no one and in all likelihood never occurred to them. But the great advances it engendered in every branch of culture are with us still, and constitute a major reason for studying the period.

SOURCES

Our sources[10] for the career and lifetime of Alexander and the three Hellenistic centuries that followed (in themselves two sharply distinguished categories) are various, often fragmentary, hard to assemble, and in part inaccessible to nonspecialists, most often through being untranslated from Greek or Latin and available only, even then, in foreign-language collections seldom to be found except in major university research libraries. Since the aim of this section is primarily to point the interested general reader to texts in English translation, I have omitted much that is normally consulted only by scholars fluent in Latin and Greek and used to reading commentaries in German, French, or Italian. This applies especially to articles in periodicals. On a very few occasions, when the exact meaning of a citation is crucial (for instance, Plutarch discussing the proper limitations on freedom, pp. *xvii*, 181), I give the original Latin or Greek text in an endnote.

The reader should also note that the term "fragment," though useful shorthand, can be misleading. Genuine fragments abound: they may be written on scraps of papyrus or a loose page of a medieval manuscript or be quoted verbatim by some ancient author or commentator (scholiast): Athenaeus (fl. c. 200 CE) is an especially rich source for such material. But all too often what we have are not direct transcriptions, but summaries and digests of material from lost works (for example, those prepared by Photius, the ninth-century CE patriarch of Constantinople). Such "fragments" give us, at best, the *gist* of what a lost author wrote and can never be guaranteed not to have omitted material in the original text or not to have reinterpreted or otherwise distorted what they transmit. Justin's *Epitome* of Trogus Pompeius (see following) is one such complete summary; substantial portions of Polybius and Diodorus survive only as summarized extracts.

———

The sources for Alexander are for the most part literary. Papyrus finds have been negligible, fragmentary, and controversial. There are comparatively few inscriptions that deal directly with his reign, and these have been well edited by Heisserer (1980). A wider fourth-century selection (translations included) is available in Rhodes and Osborne (2003). The numismatic evidence, on the other hand, is both rich and plentiful: Alexander tended to replace local currency with his own issues, both gold and silver, of which, as he progressed, he acquired an ample supply, aiming (Bosworth, 1988a, 244) "to produce an empire-wide coinage declaring his universal monarchy." Self-promoting propaganda was a prominent feature of his career. Here the key work, amply illustrated, is Price (1991). Earlier surveys that remain useful are Price (1974), Bellinger (1963), and Oikonomides (1981). Still by far the best—and best-illustrated—general introduction to Greek coinage overall is Kraay (1966).

With the literary sources, we have to deal with a different kind of problem. Though numerous writers at the time, including senior officers who had served under him, dealt in detail with Alexander's career, of their works there survive only random excerpts, citations, and allusions preserved, like flies in amber, by later historians. They include Alexander's fleet commander Nearchus of Crete, used extensively by both Arrian (see following) and the Augustan geographer Strabo; the campaign's official historian Callisthenes, Aristotle's nephew by marriage, who wrote up the *Deeds of Alexander* (a running narrative of the Persian expedition as it advanced) in fairly hyperbolic terms but nevertheless by 330 had fallen out of favor and was subsequently executed; Onesicritus of Astypalaea, Cynic by training and Alexander's chief helmsman, the source for fascinating snippets on Indian gurus; and Chares of Mytilene, court chamberlain, who provides valuable detail on, among other things, the famous mass marriages at Susa. Slightly later come two semiautobiographical accounts of the campaign, both consistently eulogistic of Alexander and both, because of their alleged factual accuracy, main sources for Arrian: the first by the self-promoting Ptolemy, veteran commander and founder of the Lagid dynasty in Egypt; the second by Aristobulus, a relatively junior officer, who composed his memoirs in old age after the Battle of Ipsus (301). All these, it goes without saying, while ostensibly offering objective accounts, had a variety of drums to beat, axes to grind, and scores to settle.

Last, but by far the most influential—I omit many minor titles and authors that are little more than names to us—we have Cleitarchus of Alexandria, probably just too young to serve in Asia but whose vivid, romanticized, and by no means overflattering account of Alexander's reign was in circulation by about 310. Cleitarchus' work formed the main source for a critical, often bitterly hostile approach to Alexander's achievements, morally based, especially popular with Stoic intellectuals, and in direct and deliberate opposition to the eulogistic tradition praising Alexander's glorious achievements and supposed quest for universal concord. Both traditions, as we shall see, are variously reflected in the accounts that survive intact and still constitute the fundamental historiography of Alexander studies today. The surviving fragments of all these lost texts, and of others that I have not mentioned, have been translated in Robinson (1953). Selections are now available, again translated, in two recent collections: Worthington (2003) and Heckel and Yardley (2004). Items from Alexander's lifetime are also included in two works dealing mainly with the Hellenistic era: Harding (1985), 98–122; and Austin (2006), 18–61.

Callisthenes and Cleitarchus provided the earliest material for an extraordinary farrago of legend, fairy tales, and fabulous storytelling, the so-called *Alexander Romance*, falsely attributed to Callisthenes, which in the course of time ousted all more serious accounts, was translated into over thirty languages, and became the sole version of Alexander's life and achievements generally known in the Middle Ages. Stoneman (1991) provides a suitably deadpan translation of this fascinating work, together with an excellent introduction on its history. The worst result of the *Romance* was to discourage medieval scribes from preserving the more sober early factual accounts, so that by the time of the Renaissance every one of them, even Cleitarchus, had been lost.

Most, nevertheless, survived long enough to be used in our five extant accounts of Alexander: that is, until about the end of the second century CE. Even the earliest of the latter, that by the Sicilian Greek universal historian Diodorus Siculus, is a product of the late Roman Republic, c. 40 BCE, and thus postdates the events it describes by three full centuries. This is rather as though our earliest source for the age of Voltaire was volume IX of Will and Ariel Durant's *Story of Civilization,* since Diodorus, though systematically underrated by modern scholars, remains a secondary and second-class historian valuable primarily for his much-maligned chronological system and for information (for instance, on Philip II of Macedon and Alexander's Successors) nowhere else available. His account of Alexander—though marred by a textual lacuna covering some of the most crucial events in the conqueror's career—fills the whole of one exceptionally long book (XVII) of the *Bibliotheke.* There is a general consensus that one of Diodorus' chief sources was Cleitarchus. His text is thus relegated to the so-called vulgate tradition, as opposed to the "court tradition" of official eulogists, primarily Arrian's authorities Ptolemy and Aristobulus. The only English translation currently available is that of Welles (1963), which has some sensible, though sometimes dated, notes; readers with French are recommended also to consult Goukowsky (1999).

The Roman Quintus Curtius Rufus probably wrote his *History of Alexander* in the middle or late years of the first century CE, under Claudius or Vespasian: see Baynham (1998) for a judicious discussion. Long underrated because of his rhetorical excesses and supposed reshaping of his material to suit Roman politics, Curtius is now recognized as providing a great deal of useful factual material, not only from Cleitarchus and the vulgate tradition, but also from Ptolemy and Trogus (see following). Rolfe (1946) offers a parallel-text translation. More up-to-date, with useful introduction and notes, is Yardley-Heckel (1984). Curtius is especially valuable for the material lost in Diodorus (see earlier).

Justin (more fully Marcus Junianus Justinus) is known only as the (? late-second-century CE) abbreviator, excerptor, and adapter of the *Philippic Histories* of Trogus Pompeius, a Romanized Gaul of the Augustan age. Alexander is covered in books IX.8 and XI–XII. Like so many ancient students of history, Justin was first and foremost concerned "to point a moral or adorn a tale," and this, too often for our taste, dictated his selections from Trogus. English readers are exceptionally lucky to have Yardley and Heckel (1997), a separate translation of the chapters concerning Alexander, with a full running commentary on the text, ample bibliographic references throughout, and a critical introduction on the background and historiography. The complete text of Justin, annotated, is also now available in English (Yardley and Develin, 1994) and covers—however inadequately—more than a few gaps in the Hellenistic period (see following).

Plutarch of Chaeronea (c. 45–c. 120 CE), essayist, moral biographer, amateur Platonist, and Delphic priest, lived peaceably under Roman rule but (like other Greek writers of the period, known as the Second Sophistic) was soaked in the history, oratory, and elegant Attic Greek of classical Athens. The prime aim of Second Sophistic writers was skill in rhetorical display piece, or epideictic, speeches, in which historical action (praxis) served only to illustrate or explain individual character (ethos). This is particularly true of Plutarch's two substantial (and probably early) essays on "Alexander's luck (*tyche*) or innate skill (*aretê*)" and only partially less so of his biography, paired with that of Julius Caesar. Rhetoric in fact colored all ancient historiography to a greater or lesser degree, and we need always to take it into account when assessing our sources: see Oliver in Bugh (2006), 113–135. The essays (*Mor.* 326D–345B) can be most conveniently read in English in

Babbitt (1936), 382–487. For the *Life* of Alexander, see either Perrin (1919), 224–439, or Scott-Kilvert (1973), 252–334, and Hamilton (1969).

The sources Plutarch refers to most often (over thirty times) are various alleged letters by or to Alexander. The authenticity of these has been questioned (and cannot be proved), but the bulk of them—some, clearly, from a collection—may well be genuine.[11] Apart from these, he names twenty-four authorities, including Callisthenes, Aristobulus, Onesicritus, and Cleitarchus, who seem to have been his chief sources. Ptolemy is conspicuous by his absence. Plutarch alone preserves almost all our evidence concerning Alexander's youth (assessing the impact of education, *paideia,* was one basic ingredient when judging a man's ethos) and is essential for such events (lost in Diodorus) as the murder of Cleitus and the Pages' conspiracy. But this biography takes little interest in military matters and badly underestimates (even for Alexander's ethos) the conqueror's sheer drive and ruthlessness from the very beginning of his career.

Finally, Arrian, whose *Anabasis of Alexander,* closely modeled on Xenophon and composed in a pastiche of Thucydidean Attic, is the longest, most detailed, and in many ways the best account of Alexander's eleven-year campaign to have survived. Lucius Flavius Arrianus (to give him his full Romanized nomenclature) was born about 85 CE, a wealthy Bithynian Greek who studied under Epictetus, was admitted to senatorial rank by Hadrian, held the consulship in 129, served as legate of Cappadocia (131–137), as military commander repelled a barbarian incursion by the Alans, and finally retired to Athens, where he was elected archon in 145/6 and died c. 162, early in the reign of Marcus Aurelius.

Arrian's career is of importance when considering his attitude to Alexander, which is largely laudatory: he was, by both nature and training, on the side of officialdom. (So, for various reasons, were his chosen sources, Ptolemy and Aristobulus.) Like Plutarch, he was more interested in ethos than praxis and in fact had little originality or critical skill as a historian. It was, of course, his adulatory verdict on Alexander at least as much as his undeniable wealth of authentic detail that caused historians such as Tarn to greatly overestimate his overall value as a source. This attitude is now in process of revision (as is the overdismissive treatment of Diodorus and Curtius). Interested readers should consult Brunt (1976, 1983), which offers not only an up-to-date translation of the *Anabasis,* but also a detailed and excellent introduction, together with running notes and some highly stimulating appendices. Shorter, cheaper, and still good value despite more recent scholarship is de Sélincourt (1971), with a characteristically acute introduction by J. R. Hamilton.[12] Bosworth (1980, 1995) offers a first-class commentary, but requires a detailed knowledge of Greek.

—

The problems presented by the evidence for the three centuries following Alexander's death are of a strikingly different nature. Where Alexander's campaigns have no fewer than five continuous narrative sources—late and derivative though they may be—the Hellenistic period as a whole has one only, the "sketchy and confusing"[13] abridgment of Trogus by Justin (see earlier), which nevertheless offers glimpses of many events otherwise unknown. On the other hand, from 229 to 145/4 we have what for Alexander is missing: a first-class contemporary witness, Polybius, an Achaean politician deported after Pydna (167) to Rome, where he became an intimate of Scipio Aemilianus and set himself to explain Rome's astonishing rise to world power in a mere fifty-three years.

This bonus is less than might at first appear, since in fact from Polybius' history only the first five books out of forty survive intact. Even so, his value for historians is enormous: he was preserved because, like Thucydides, whom in many ways he resembles, he was highly and rightly esteemed by ancient critics. Two English versions are now available: the six-volume Loeb edition (Paton, 1922–1927) and Shuckburgh (1889, repr. 1960). Shuckburgh (1980) and Scott-Kilvert (1979) offer selections only. An excellent critical introduction, distilled from his great commentary (Walbank, 1957–1979), is to be found in Walbank's Sather Lectures (Walbank, 1972).

The major historians of the third century BCE are all lost, surviving only in scattered fragments, excerpts, and citations: unlike the Alexander historians, they have not been systematically translated. For a succinct survey, see Sacks in *OCD*3 (1996), 715–716. Hieronymus of Cardia, Duris of Samos, Timaeus of Tauromenium (the modern Taormina), Phylarchus of Athens or Naucratis, Aratus of Sicyon's *Memoirs,* and the local Attic historian Philochorus: it is these who are generally agreed to have shaped and characterized the tradition of the early Hellenistic period; and of them, the most important—despite the paucity of his surviving fragments—is undoubtedly Hieronymus.

His history of the Successors, from 323 to the death of Pyrrhus in 272, was based on firsthand material and personal experience. Its quality can be gauged from Plutarch's *Lives* of Demetrius, Eumenes, and Pyrrhus and above all from books 18–20 of Diodorus, covering the period down to the Battle of Ipsus in 301, which use it extensively. The best study of Hieronymus is still Hornblower (1981).

Duris (c. 340–c. 260), tyrant of Samos as well as historian, wrote a lengthy and somewhat hostile history of Macedonian affairs from 370 to Corupedium (281), which incurred Hieronymus' criticism. Timaeus (c. 350–260) wrote a *Sicilian History* that became the dominant account of western Greece for the ancient world, though Polybius, predictably, savaged his military ignorance and lack of autopsy. Timaeus also was responsible for a chronological system reckoning by the quadrennial Olympian Games (Brown, 1958). Phylarchus followed the convenient Hellenistic convention of starting his own work where a predecessor—in this case Hieronymus—had left off, in 272: his *Histories* ended in 220/219, with the death of Cleomenes III, the revolutionary Agiad king of Sparta, thus linking up chronologically with Polybius. Polybius attacked him for sensationalism, but the animus of his criticism was clearly due to Phylarchus' pro-Spartan, anti-Achaean bias (Africa, 1961). By the same token, Polybius placed too much confidence in the *Memoirs* of Aratus, the architect of the Achaean confederacy. The loss of the last eleven books of Philochorus' *Atthis*, covering Athenian history from 320 to 260, is especially tantalizing.

For the later period, the greatest historical loss is that of the great polymath Posidonius of Apamea (c. 135–c. 51), who wrote a fifty-two-book *History* taking up where Polybius left off, at the fall of Carthage and Corinth in 146, and carried the story on to some point in the 80s. A Stoic moralist, Posidonius favored the Roman *nobilitas* while at the same time giving sympathetic treatment to the first-century BCE slave revolts (material on which Diodorus drew). His cosmic universalism was already pointing toward the identification of Roman imperium with the world order. Edelstein and Kidd (1989) and Clarke (1999), appendices A and B, update the historical fragments; Kidd (1999) provides a translation of them, to which Kidd (1988) adds a full and detailed commentary.

After Aristotle, whose works are largely preserved and available in good English translations (for instance, Barnes, 1984), and, to a far lesser extent, his successor Theophrastus, mainly of interest to nonspecialists for his *Characters* (Ussher, 1960; Rusten and Cunningham, 2002; Diggle, 2004), the philosophical tradition, though of immense richness and variety, has fared no better than that of the historians. Original fragments are very sparse; otherwise we are forced to rely on late citations and summaries, often hostile and generally out of context. However, the English reader now has a full and well-annotated sourcebook of this material available in translation (Long and Sedley, 1987, vol. 1, with the original texts, plus contexts and technical commentary, in vol. 2).

Several of the surviving texts, most notably that of Polybius (covering 229–146/5, mostly in excerpts), have already been discussed earlier. Justin's selective abridgment of Trogus Pompeius, as we have seen, is the sole surviving narrative to span all three centuries. For the period of the Successors, from Alexander's death to the Battle of Ipsus (323–301), we have books 18–20 of Diodorus Siculus (Geer, 1947, 1954; Bizière, 1975; Goukowsky, 1978), which use much crucial material from Hieronymus of Cardia. The remaining books of Diodorus (21–40), down to 60/59 BCE, are represented only by fragments and excerpts, translated by Walton (1957) and Walton and Geer (1967). Appian of Alexandria (fl. second century CE; White, 1912–1913) wrote on Rome's Syrian, Mithradatic, and civil wars: much of his material sheds light on the history of the later Hellenistic kingdoms. The late Republican litterateur Cornelius Nepos (Rolfe, 1929) wrote a series of biographies, of which three—his *Eumenes, Phocion,* and *Timoleon*—are relevant to the period, though markedly inferior to those of Plutarch.

As Walbank says,[14] Plutarch's importance as a source is hard to overvalue. He likes the odd men out: Aratus, Cleomenes III, Timoleon, the Roman Sertorius; idiosyncratic individualists such as Demetrius the Besieger and Eumenes.[15] He also deals unforgettably with Roman warlords in Greece: Flamininus, Aemilius Paullus, Sulla, Pompey. For a classic translation of the *Lives,* Dryden et al. (2001) now offers cheap and handy access; Perrin (1914–1926) has the advantage of a parallel Greek text. The *Lives* of Demetrius the Besieger, Pyrrhus, Phocion, and Timoleon are included in Scott-Kilvert (1973). Of almost equal interest is the huge range of material covered by the essays in the *Moralia* (Babbitt et al., 1927–2004), including numerous scattered historical facts and revealing anecdotes (Waterfield, 1992; and Russell, 1993, offer selections only). Similar miscellanies by Tiberius' contemporary Valerius Maximus (Shackleton Bailey, 2000) and the second-century CE essayists Aulus Gellius (Rolfe, 1927–28; cf. Holford-Strevens, 2003) and Aelian (Wilson, 2000) add random items of value amid much rhetorical dross.

The three most important, primarily nonhistorical, literary sources for the Hellenistic era are the Augustan geographer Strabo of Amaseia, the second-century CE travel writer Pausanias, and his near-contemporary Athenaeus of Naucratis (fl. c. 200). Strabo's seventeen-book *Geography* (Jones, 1917–1932; cf. Clarke, 1997, and 1999; Dueck, 2000) surveys the full extent of the Roman empire in his day, using both autopsy (for example, for Alexandria) and earlier Hellenistic sources now lost. His text is a huge mine of variegated information. Pausanias (Levi, 1979; Jones, 1918–1935; cf. Habicht, 1985; Arafat, 1996; Hutton, 2005) in effect does for central mainland Greece what Strabo does for the wider Mediterranean periphery: though his sympathy, like Plutarch's, is for the classical era, he still manages to provide, over and above his guide to the monuments, a remarkable amount of historical information. In Athenaeus' one work, the *Deipnosophists*, neatly translated by Basil Gildersleeve as *The Gastronomes* (Gulick, 1927–1941; cf. Braund and Wilkins, 2000; Olson, series in progress, 2007), we get fifteen books of well-read table talk about, literally, cabbages and kings: food, drink, scurrilous eavesdropping on celebrities, endless quotations (mostly from Middle and New Comedy).

Because of the ultra-fragmentary nature of most of this evidence, nonspecialists will find it most convenient to rely on the various selective sourcebooks, all of high quality, now widely available in paperback. Excerpts and fragments of all the lost writers discussed here are variously given—in translation, chronologically arranged, and with helpful notes—by Austin (2006), Harding (1985), Burstein (1985), and Bagnall and Derow (2004). These collections also include excerpts from the (largely untranslated) Byzantine lexica. The largest and most important of the latter, known as the *Suda* ("Fortress": tenth century CE), is currently being translated online by a vast collective consortium and can be consulted at www.stoa.org/sol. The sourcebooks also provide ample epigraphic and papyrological (though not, unfortunately but understandably, numismatic) testimonia, and it is to these that we must now turn.

Whereas for Alexander's lifetime the directly relevant inscriptions were comparatively few, during the Hellenistic era (when recording practices multiply exponentially) they can be counted by the tens of thousands and are still steadily being added to annually. Gravestones, not surprisingly, are perhaps the most numerous. The variegated civic business of the Greek cities, enacted by Council (*Boulê*) and People (*Demos*)—treaties, honorific decrees, records of arbitration, the funding of religious festivals, rewards to successful athletes and other gymnasium business, relations with royal overlords, school regulations, building accounts, grants of citizen rights or immunity—accounts for the remaining bulk of public inscriptions. The records of the major Panhellenic sanctuaries (for example, on Delos or at Delphi) illuminate their economies and social practices; royal charters, letters, and edicts tell us much about Ptolemaic and Seleucid administration on which our literary sources are silent. Because of the gaps in the literary record, inscriptions sometimes provide fleshing-out evidence for historical events that are otherwise underreported or even unknown. Private life, though not epigraphic by nature, has its graffiti (on walls and potsherds) and can show its nasty side in the inscriptions on curse tablets (Gager, 1992). Woodhead (1981) provides a fascinating hands-on introduction to the epigraphist's art, from making squeezes to deciphering numerical systems. For the inscriptions of the Hellenistic period, McLean (2002) offers an excellent general introduction.

With the innumerable more or less fragmentary texts surviving on papyrus—originally a smooth white[16] writing paper made from the *Cyperus papyrus,* a marsh plant common in the Egyptian Delta but rare elsewhere—we are confronted with a very different type of evidence. Almost all our papyrus finds—whether discarded scrolls, mummy cartonnage, or the detritus from rubbish dumps and ruined houses—come from up-country provincial sites of Middle and Upper Egypt. Thus even when finds have obvious national or administrative importance, it is dangerous to generalize from them.

That said, it remains true that the evidence from papyrus is not only richer than that offered by inscriptions, but infinitely more varied: in particular, it offers far more material in the private sector. Bills and contracts, daily rations, farm rents, tax returns, jottings of dreams, school exercises, divorce settlements, letters to wives or village officials—the list is endless. (In addition to the sourcebooks cited earlier, see Hunt and Edgar, 1932 and 1934: the first for a fine assortment of agreements, correspondence, and wills, the second for regulations, judicial orders, petitions, applications, contracts, tenders, and the endless bureaucratic minutiae governing small-town life in provincial Egypt.) There have also been literary finds. Apart from famous discoveries like Aristotle's *Constitution of Athens* or a lost play, the *Dyskolos* by Menander, there have been endless tantalizing fragments of earlier drama and lyric poetry (see, for instance, Page, 1941). For a general introduction to papyrology, Turner (1968) remains unbeatable, though updated in some respects by Bagnall (1995).

Inevitably, all these sources, being Greek-based, provide variants on a ruling-class (if not always official) outlook. The most useful (and frequently disquieting) surveys on the relationships—and hostilities—between Greek and non-Greek in the Hellenistic world are Eddy (1961), Momigliano (1975), and Isaac (2004). A good short introduction is now available: Gruen in Bugh (2006), 295–314. Material in Akkadian, Aramaic, and, above all, demotic Egyptian (which gives us glimpses into the lower echelons of Egypt's native population) exists and is slowly being made available. But for most practical purposes (even for the spreading of anti-Greek propaganda—for example, in the apocalyptic "Oracle of the Potter," Burstein, 1985, 106), Greek remained the Hellenistic lingua franca. Besides, the three centuries of Greco-Macedonian rule were a gigantic colonizing venture, and it is as such, for good or ill, that we have primarily to study them.

Few things make this clearer than the period's plentiful and varied coinage (on Hellenistic numismatics, see especially Mørkholm, 1991 and 1984); more general introductions are offered by Howgego (1995) and Crawford (1983, 185 ff.); Kraay (1966) still has the finest reproductions. The right to mint is an expression of sovereignty as well as the guarantee of economic strength (debasement of the currency, as antiquity well knew, publicizes political no less than financial weakness). In the Hellenistic period, this meant, most notably, the Ptolemaic, Seleucid, and, later, the Attalid monarchies, though numerous cities also minted, some independently, others as authorized by royal mandate; while on mainland Greece in particular, a number of limited local currencies, on various standards, continued to thrive.

The Successors, beginning with Lysimachus, sought legitimacy by using Alexander's head on their issues. Then, when his heirs were all dead and the royal Argead dynasty extinct (pp. 35–36 ff.), cautiously at first, they declared themselves kings and issued coins bearing their own image. We can see the process at work with Ptolemy. His standard issues began by carrying Alexander's head and latterly switched to his own.[17] Even so, such was Alexander's authority that for over two centuries various rulers and cities continued to use his numismatic image as validation of their authority. In some special cases (for example, the Greco-Bactrian dynasties), the coin issues, plus archaeological findings, are virtually the only historical evidence we have (Holt, 1999; a wonderful piece of detective work).

Last, archaeology: not only a source of evidence in itself, but the instrument by which most of our other sources—coins, inscriptions, papyrus texts—are discovered and contextualized in the first place (Snodgrass, 1987, and in Crawford, 1983, 137–184; Alcock, 1994). The value of excavated remains is that they "represent what somebody once did, not what some contemporary or later writer says they did."[18] In other words, they are free of antique spin. But their corresponding disadvantage is that they themselves cannot speak at all, with the result that modern archaeologists speak for them, replacing antique spin with their own. Silent testimony is thus of limited historical value. But it can modify and enhance a narrative: Greek traders and mercenaries were actually established at Naucratis in Egypt long before Herodotus thought they were.[19]

For the Hellenistic period, probably the most profitable archaeological evidence is that contributing to our knowledge of increasing urbanization throughout the Mediterranean and a good deal of the Near Eastern world. This comes primarily from Athens, Rhodes, and the already famous cities of western Asia Minor, such as Pergamon, Ephesus, and Miletus (in Alexandria, frustratingly, little has survived); yet the evidence offered by a site such as that of Aï Khanum in Afghanistan shows that the trend extended to the farthest outposts of empire. But who were the beneficiaries? Who worked out in the gymnasia, watched Greek plays in the theaters? Who had weapons buried with them, and why? What effect did mass emigration from Greece to the newly conquered lands have, in physical terms, on these old and new landscapes? Did fewer rural shrines indicate a religious crisis or simply depopulation?

What insights archaeology can offer are, not surprisingly, linked with long-term conditions: the planning and layout of cities; the beliefs and customs deducible from shrines, graves, and their contents; the preoccupations—and self-images—of those who commissioned and executed portraits; the implications of their taste in household objects, decorated floors, the arrangement of living space, the size and nature of estates. Once again, the emphasis is very much on the propertied upper classes—more often Greco-Macedonian colonists than local magnates prospering through collaboration—though the stubborn persistence of local idiosyncrasies in the vastly varied material culture of Alexander's empire is only now beginning to be fully realized. An excellent (and up-to-date) introduction is Rotroff in Bugh (2006), 136–157. One of the most interesting and valuable new techniques (but see also earlier, p. *xxxii*) is that known as landscape archaeology: the detailed contextual analysis of regional terrain in all its aspects, both man-made and natural, a process that has begun to retrieve something at least of those elements missing from the rest of our evidence.

1

ALEXANDER AND HIS LEGACY

(336 - 323)

In October 336 BCE, a much-publicized royal wedding took place in the ancient Macedonian city of Aegae (modern Vergina): King Philip II's daughter Cleopatra was marrying Alexander, king of the neighboring state of Epirus. The occasion was peculiar and ended tragically. The bridegroom, to begin with, was the bride's uncle—in fact, the brother of Philip's powerful but repudiated wife, Olympias, till recently an exile in Epirus, plotting revengeful mischief, but now back in Aegae as mother of the bride. Being on the eve of launching a major invasion of Asia Minor, then part of the Persian Empire, Philip characteristically figured that an incestuous dynastic alliance would be a cheaper and easier way of protecting his rear than a time-consuming campaign. Hence the wedding. During the ceremony, the images of the twelve Olympian gods were accompanied, in procession, by one of Philip himself. Thus when, on the second day of the festivities, Philip was assassinated by a member of his own bodyguard as he entered the theater prior to the games, many regarded this as divine punishment for unseemly royal hubris.

For others, clearly, it was an opportunity not to be missed. The assassin, Pausanias, was pursued and killed—thus precluding any interrogation of him—by friends of Philip's son and (recently dispossessed) heir, the better-known, but not yet Great, Alexander. One of Philip's most trusted senior nobles, Antipater, took immediate charge, quelled the chaos, presented young Alexander to the Macedonian army assembly, and had him confirmed as successor to the throne before his father's body was cold. From being, at unlikely best, regent in Macedonia while Philip was winning glory on campaign, Alexander now found himself, at one stroke, both king and prospective leader of the long-planned Persian invasion. Regicide, as Elizabeth Carney reminds us, "was something of a Macedonian tradition."[1]

Until the late fall of 338, the year of Philip's great victory over the Greek states at Chaeronea, Alexander remained, as he had been since adolescence, Philip's crown prince and designated successor. In 340, when only sixteen, he had acted as regent while his father was campaigning. He led the successful cavalry charge at Chaeronea, a feat that won him a public acclamation by the army. He and his mother, Olympias,

were both included among the family images—of gold and ivory, hitherto reserved for divine portraiture—in the curious circular edifice that
Philip dedicated at Olympia to celebrate his victory. Alexander was also
one of the delegates to escort the ashes of the Athenian dead back to
Athens (the only time, surprisingly, that he ever went there).

This was the last official duty he carried out during Philip's lifetime. In the late fall of 338, Philip abruptly repudiated Olympias, cast
doubts on Alexander's legitimacy, and announced his intention of
marrying a young Macedonian, Cleopatra. Not only was Cleopatra
impeccably blue-blooded and ethnic—in contrast with Olympias the
Epirot—but her uncle Attalus, a successful and popular soldier, was
married to the daughter of Parmenio, Philip's most trusted general.
With Parmenio, he was to command the force securing an advance
bridgehead in Asia Minor. Philip's formation of a safe power bloc
united by marriage surely bore some relation to the coming campaign.
Yet to disinherit, and mortally alienate, the successor he had groomed
for almost twenty years—and to do so almost immediately before his
planned crossing into Asia—was the kind of gaffe that Philip, always a
canny diplomat, would in the normal course of events never commit.
These events, clearly, were anything but normal.

What, then, were his underlying motives? The wedding feast simply
underlined their apparent lunacy. Everyone got drunk. Attalus proposed a toast, a prayer for Philip and Cleopatra to produce a *legitimate
heir.* Alexander, in understandable fury—"Are you calling us [note the
royal "we"] a bastard?"—assaulted Attalus. Philip made to attack, not
Attalus, but his own son. Drunk, he stumbled and collapsed on the
floor, giving Alexander a famous exit line: "That's the man who's going
to cross from Europe to Asia, and he can't even make it from one couch
to the next!"[2] The insulted prince, heir-apparent no longer, got his
mother away to Epirus and himself took refuge among the Illyrians.
Both, predictably, proceeded to stir up frontier trouble.

Why, with a major campaign ahead of him, should so canny a diplomat as Philip have invited palace mayhem by trashing the long-
established royal succession overnight? If we assume that he had not
taken leave of his senses but was acting on a rational basis, there is one
motive only that could explain his sudden volte-face in the fall of 338:
the conviction that Alexander and Olympias were planning his overthrow. Argead history made such a fear look all too plausible. If this

was what Philip believed, his actions make good sense: in hindsight, of course, they can be seen as not ruthless enough.

Was his belief justified? On this, certainty is impossible. But it is not hard to see how such suspicions could have been aroused: Alexander's entire upbringing, especially when assessed in light of his mother's inordinate ambitions for him, suggests a pattern of high aims, even higher hubris, and dangerous royal impatience. The boy was encouraged to think of himself as a new Achilles (from whom his mother's family claimed descent). His Homeric ideal was to be "a good king and a strong spear-fighter" and, perhaps more important, "ever to strive to be best, and outstanding above all others" (Hom. *Il.* 3.179, 6.208). Glory and fame, *kleos*, were to be won by conquest. But Philip, again and again, seemed to be anticipating him. "For me," Alexander told his tight-knit circle of friends, "he will leave no great or brilliant achievement to be displayed to the world with your aid.... What use are possessions to me if I achieve nothing?" (Plut. *Mor.* 179D 1; *Alex.* 5.2). Worst of all, it was now Philip, not he, who stood ready to invade Asia. The great venture that Alexander had thought of as his own inheritance ever since childhood seemed, like Achilles' prize, about to elude him. If he and his mother were in fact planning a coup, now was the time, and his motivation could hardly have been stronger.

———

So, literally at the eleventh hour, Alexander of Macedon—now King Alexander III—came into the full inheritance of which he and his mother had dreamed for so long. Like his father, he assumed power in dangerous circumstances: a baptism of fire. He was young, relatively unknown, and not yet haloed with that extraordinary aura of charisma and achievement that in a few short years would come to define him. His powerful opponents may well have thought they could dispose of this upstart boy without trouble. They were wrong: he showed himself absolutely ruthless from the start and had good reason to be. He knew that both his cousin Amyntas, and Cleopatra's newborn son, Caranus (named, ostentatiously, after the dynasty's mythical founder), represented a direct threat to his rule and had powerful backers.[3]

Outside Macedonia, too, the situation was volatile. The Thebans expelled their Macedonian garrison. There was trouble in Thrace and the Peloponnese. From Athens, Demosthenes wrote to Parmenio and Attalus in Asia Minor, urging them to rebel, promising Athenian help, and sneering at the new Macedonian king as a mere brainless adolescent. Attalus certainly, and Parmenio very probably, took the bait. Alexander's new kingdom was "exposed to great jealousies, dire hatreds, and dangers on every side" (Plut. *Alex.* 11.1). His older advisers, led by Antipater, were all understandably advising him to use caution: to steer clear of tangling with the southern Greek states, to appease the frontier tribes with concessions. No, he told them: if I abate my resolve one iota, all our enemies will be on us at once. The only guarantee of security is courage and daring.

This, of course (a point he probably felt it preferable not to mention), included at least one assassination mission. Attalus, with or without the support of Athens, was an obvious danger (besides having mortally insulted Alexander), and Alexander had already sent a trusted friend to army headquarters in Asia Minor, officially as a liaison officer but with secret instructions to bring Attalus back alive if possible, otherwise to kill him at the first convenient opportunity and make a deal with Parmenio. Parmenio sized up the young king's record so far, decided to switch sides, and even cooperated over the murder of Attalus, his own son-in-law. But he exacted a stiff price for his support. When Alexander's task force crossed into Asia in the spring of 334, Parmenio was his immediate deputy, and almost every crucial senior command was held by one of his friends or relatives. Not for over five years, and then only by a show trial and assassination, was this stranglehold finally broken.

Having thus summarily dealt with his domestic problems and given the Greek states a taste of what they were up against, Alexander called a meeting of the Hellenic League at Corinth, where the terms laid down by Philip after his victory at Chaeronea were all reconfirmed in the name of his son. Alexander was elected *hegemon* in his father's place and captain-general, "with unlimited powers," of the forthcoming invasion of Asia, to exact vengeance (so ran the declaration) for Xerxes' sacrilegious destruction of Greek temples a century and a half before. The alliance with Macedonia "in perpetuity" was renewed. The Greek states—a little diplomatic irony never came amiss—were to be "free and independent." Delegates vied with one another to shower honors and congratulations on their new leader.

But there were two notable exceptions. The Spartans informed Alexander that their traditions did not permit them to serve under a foreign leader (Alexander duly returned the snub after the Granicus, when he emphasized Spartan absence from the battle); and Diogenes the Cynic, visited by Alexander in Corinth for the ancient equivalent of a photo op while sunning himself outside his tub and asked whether there was anything he wanted, said: "Yes, shift over: you're keeping the sun off me." Irresistible force had met immovable object. "If I were not Alexander," the new young *hegemon* is reported as saying, "I would be Diogenes"—passive intransigence rather than active.

Alexander did rather better at Delphi, which he visited on his way back from Corinth to Pella. By now it was late November. From mid-November to mid-February, the shrine was closed on religious grounds: no exceptions. Alexander, who put great faith in oracles and badly wanted one for his Persian crusade, seized the Pythia bodily and began dragging her to the inner sanctum (*adyton*). "Young man," exclaimed the quick-witted priestess, "you are invincible [*aniketos*]!" Alexander promptly released her, saying this was a good enough prophecy for him, and thereafter assumed *aniketos* as one of his regular titles.

Impatient though he was to launch the great invasion (and for good practical reasons no less than because of his *pothos*, his passionate desire: the Macedonian treasury was almost empty, and successful conquest was a quick way of filling it), Alexander knew he had to thoroughly subdue the frontier tribes first. He spent the winter of 336/5—another lesson well learned from Philip—training his troops, especially for mountain warfare. In the spring, he conducted a quick and brilliant campaign, striking north by way of the Shipka Pass, winning two engagements, collecting much booty, and extending the frontier to the Danube. From here he moved west to a more hazardous encounter with a group of tough Illyrian tribesmen. While still engaged against them (late summer 335), he was greeted by the most alarming news from Greece.

Despite the League of Corinth's reluctant cooperation, despite all the talk of a Panhellenic crusade, no sooner had Alexander vanished into Thrace than a resistance movement, led by Thebes and Athens, went into action. What brought things to a head was a report, stage-managed by Demosthenes and delivered by a bloodstained alleged eyewitness, that Alexander and his whole expeditionary force had been wiped out in a battle against wild Thracians near the Danube. Thebes had come out in open revolt, with financial support from Athens, some of it gold supplied by Persia. In Asia, a brilliant Greek mercenary general, Memnon of Rhodes, was putting heavy pressure on the Macedonian advance force: their Hellespontine bridgehead was at risk. Amyntas, son of Philip's elder brother Perdiccas, had left Pella for southern Greece and was a predictable Greek-backed candidate for the Macedonian throne. The speed, ingenuity, and decisiveness that Alexander had displayed in Thrace and Illyria were needed as never before. They did not fail him.

First, just as he had dealt with Attalus, he now arranged for the assassination of Amyntas. With a nice touch of black humor, he offered Amyntas' widow-to-be, Philip's half-Illyrian daughter, Cynane, in marriage to Langarus, the king of his local allies, the Agrianians, a tough Balkan tribe that afterward supplied some of his best light-armed troops. He also sent a message to his mother, Olympias, requesting the elimination of his other dynastic rival, Cleopatra's new-born son. Olympias, only too glad to oblige, also for good measure did away with Cleopatra herself and her infant daughter. This act earned her a severe reprimand from Alexander, always careful of his public image: neither Cleopatra nor Europa was a threat to the succession, and their murder thus made unnecessary bad propaganda. Alexander then quickly wound up his campaign of pacification and force-marched south at a speed that shook even Philip's veterans. A couple of weeks later, having covered 250-odd miles, partly through mountainous terrain, he appeared before the walls of Thebes. It took some while, even then, to convince the Thebans that he was actually alive.

Time, and funds, were running out for Alexander: he urgently needed to get to Asia. Since the Thebans had believed him dead, he told them, and his death would have voided the treaty they had signed (because he left no issue), their revolt had been in legitimate good faith. If they now returned to their allegiance, all would be forgiven. The Thebans, however, were well prepared and saw freedom within their grasp. They stood firm. Alexander countered—as *hegemon* of the Hellenic League—with a demand for the two leaders of the revolt and an offer of amnesty for the rest, who would still enjoy the benefits of the Greek "common peace" (*koinê eirênê*). At this, the Thebans proclaimed that "anyone who wished, along with the Great King [of Persia] and the Thebans, to free the Greeks and destroy the tyrant of Greece, should come over to them" (DS 17.9.5). So much for Panhellenic propaganda and the League of Corinth.

The threat of Persian collusion was bad enough; to be called tyrant, and despised as such, sent Alexander into one of his towering rages. From that moment, Thebes was doomed. The breaching of the walls led to a bloodbath in which six thousand Thebans died and thirty thousand more were captured. Then, on Alexander's urging, the League of Corinth voted "to level the city, sell off the prisoners, declare the fugitives outlawed from all Greece, and ban the Hellenes from offering them shelter" (DS 17.14.3). This was overkill, in a very literal sense. It certainly, on the surface, had its desired effect. The Greek states, Athens included, rushed to seek clemency. Alexander, his fury appeased, had no wish to be held up yet further by the Athenians' impregnable fortifications, so canceled his blacklist (which included Demosthenes) and did a deal with them.

Yet in the long run, the destruction of Thebes was one of the worst mistakes he ever made. If Alexander had meant his invasion of Asia to be a true Panhellenic crusade (which is doubtful in the extreme), this one act doomed such a hope forever. Outwardly, the Greeks collaborated. Inwardly, their attitude became one of bitter, implacable hatred: it was to keep them, no less than the frontier tribes, subdued that a Macedonian army little smaller than Alexander's expeditionary force was left behind in Europe. Also, comparatively few Greek troops served on the expedition itself, and none in the front line; even these were got rid of as soon as convenient. No mainland Greek was ever appointed a regional governor (satrap) by Alexander. That final amalgamation of races, in the last year or two of his life, which led some idealists to talk of Alexander pursuing a Stoic brotherhood of man, was between Macedonians and Persians: the Greeks nowhere entered into it.

Some modern accounts still talk of a Greek crusade led by Greeks. These may arguably have ethnicity and linguistics—both debatable—on their side, but at the time neither Macedonians nor Greeks saw it that way. They despised each other, rightly or wrongly, as foreigners who (they claimed) spoke different languages; their xenophobia was intensified on the Greek side by intellectual contempt mixed with bitter resentment at defeat, on the Macedonian by a constant fear of bad faith and rebellion. This deeply flawed and hostile relationship—preserved as an alliance only by the needs of propaganda and manifesting itself too often as unacknowledged hostage taking to ensure good behavior—was to become a major factor in the development of the Persian invasion.

Back at Pella in October 335, Alexander recalled Parmenio from Asia to be his second in command: he needed Philip's old-guard officers, and only through Parmenio did he stand a real chance of getting them. We have already seen the (largely familial) control of key military appointments that the old marshal insisted on as his reward. Alexander then held a meeting of his commanders and Companions to plan the Persian invasion. Our sources tell us that Antipater and Parmenio both advised him to marry and beget an heir first: the advice was scornfully rejected. Was this just the young would-be Achilles speaking, impatient for heroic glory? Perhaps. But there was another, highly practical, highly unromantic reason for prompt departure: money.

The army's pay was badly in arrears. The sale of captives from Thebes had not even quite covered Philip's outstanding debts. Income from the mines, roughly 1,000 talents a year, accounted for no more than a third of the annual military budget. Worse, on his accession Alexander had, as a bid for acceptance, abolished direct taxation (modern parallels suggest themselves). By borrowing from his Companions on the security of crown lands, with the clear if unspoken assumption that the "loans" would be outright gifts, he raised 800 talents, thus making good some arrears of pay and reducing (though not eliminating) the treasury debt. But with six months' training ahead of him before the earliest possible date for the expedition's departure, he was cutting things desperately fine. Behind the brave talk of vengeance for Xerxes' crimes in Greece, much less any thought of cultural proselytization, was the urgent need on the part of Alexander and all his senior officers to turn their campaign, at the earliest possible moment, into a profit-making operation.

This was an appetite that unparalleled success, far from satisfying, merely sharpened, not least since Alexander, like Philip (a notorious spendthrift), had the Homeric pirate's mentality when it came to riches: the best way of acquiring them was by relieving less manly opponents of them in battle. Neither had any real economic sense beyond immediate needs: another legacy that Alexander's dismemberment of the Persian empire, and his uncontrolled dispersal of accumulated Achaemenid treasure, would leave to his Hellenistic successors. The figure reported by our sources, at a general estimate, is 180,000 talents (1 talent of precious metal weighed 57.5 pounds); and even that does not include the vast sums allegedly squirreled away unofficially, off the top, by the treasure's subordinate captors and guardians. Like so much of Alexander's complex heritage, the long-term consequences of these acts were neither planned nor foreseen by the conquistadors who carried them out.[4]

———

What Alexander's initial aims may have been are still debated. It is unlikely that Philip planned more than securing Asia Minor "from Sinope to Cilicia" (Isocr. 5.120); he may in fact have wanted only to complete his mastery of the Aegean—as Athens had done in the fifth century—by bringing the coastal cities of the Aeolid, Ionia, and Caria under Macedonian control. The Persians made 1,760 talents a year from the satrapies involved, and Philip could do with the money. But when Alexander reached the "Achaean harbor" of Rhoeteum, he stood, fully armed, at the prow of his ship and cast a spear ashore, to show "that he received Asia from the gods as a spear-won prize" (DS 17.17.2). This not only reminds us of the mythic justification, most often Homeric, he was to invoke at every turn, but strongly suggests that he planned the overthrow of the Achaemenid empire from the very beginning. Who, if any, of his intimates were privy to such a determination we cannot tell. Few can have anticipated the lengths to which his demon-driven *pothos* (desire, longing) drove him or would, surely, have committed themselves in advance to eleven years of virtually nonstop campaigning.

The general notion of invading Persia was not new. Ever since Aristophanes' *Lysistrata*, a dream of stasis-ridden and eternally warring Greek states uniting against the monolithic Barbarian in the East had been in the air. Xenophon's successful march to the Black Sea with what remained of an original corps of nearly thirteen thousand mercenaries, after Cyrus' failed attempt at Cunaxa (401) to usurp his brother's throne, gave a misleading impression of Persian weakness. Rhetoricians, the Athenian Isocrates in particular, played this up. Achaemenid wealth was equaled only by the empire's decadence and military *faiblesse*. Here was an El Dorado virtually inviting conquest.

The trouble was, who would bell this old tiger? Despite the rhetorical attractions of the idea, none of Isocrates' Greek nominees came up to scratch. Finally he fell back on Philip of Macedon, though making it clear that he saw him as a kind of hired condottiere who would be only too glad to carry out the job for his cultural superiors in the south. "It is fitting for you," Isocrates assured him, "to consider all Hellas your fatherland" (Isocr. 5.127). Never was advice taken more literally. After Philip's crushing defeat of Athens and Thebes at Chaeronea (338), the nonagenarian pundit, perhaps recalling his own words, committed suicide. But the damage had been done. Panhellenism gave Alexander a ready-made ideological launching pad for his own career of conquest, to be dropped as soon as it had served its purpose.

———

In the summer of 336, after a period of palace intrigue, dynastic assassination, and provincial rebellion, a collateral member of the Achaemenid royal family became Great King. He had distinguished himself by personal bravery in battle—something to remember later amid Macedonian propaganda that presented him as a cowardly usurper—and was awarded the title of Darius III in recognition of that fact. On accession, he promptly executed his grand vizier, the eunuch Bagoas, who had been the chief troublemaker and power behind the throne. Darius thus inherited the empire, now two centuries old, forged by Cyrus the Great and his successors: a territory at least as big as the United States, divided into twenty provinces (satrapies) reaching as far east as modern Pakistan, and with a population of roughly 80 million.

He then set about quelling the revolts that had broken out, particularly in Babylonia and Egypt. These took at least until the end of 335 to put down. It was thus only by the summer of 334 that his powerful Cypro-Phoenician fleet, perhaps three hundred to four hundred vessels strong, was remobilized for action in the Aegean—too late to prevent the Macedonian crossing: the first of several amazing pieces of luck for Alexander. By land, on the other hand, Memnon of Rhodes and his Greek mercenaries, working in collaboration with the satraps of Lydia and Hellespontine Phrygia, had already given the advance Macedonian force a hard time of it and may well have felt that they would be an adequate match for Alexander, too.

The Achaemenid spy network (symbolized by that butt of Aristophanes, the so-called Great King's Eye, the head of an imperial intelligence-gathering team) would surely by now have assembled a dossier on the new young Macedonian king. Its compilers had access to much information and gossip now lost to us; but the evidence is enough to suggest something of the profile they must, without hindsight, have put together. Physically, Alexander was not prepossessing.[5] Even by Macedonian standards he was very short, though stocky and tough. His beard was scanty, and he stood out against his hirsute

Macedonian barons by going clean-shaven. His neck was in some way twisted, so that he appeared to be gazing upward at an angle. His eyes (one blue, one brown) revealed a dewy, feminine quality. He had a high complexion and a harsh voice. Like most Macedonians of good family, he was a superb horseman, and the story of how, as a young boy, he broke the stallion Bucephalas became a legend in his own lifetime. Like many children reared in a political household, he was precocious. Memnon of Rhodes testified (as an eyewitness) to his sophisticated quizzing (perhaps after coaching) of Persian military visitors. This agrees with the tradition that Olympias had always encouraged him to believe it was his destiny to conquer the Achaemenid empire.

His education, while physically demanding, also set him an ideal of Homeric warrior glory (*kleos*) as his goal, to be attained through manly excellence (*aretê*). His tutors, while flattering him, still put him through a punishing regime. With symbolic aptness, he kept two things under his pillow while he slept: a dagger, and his copy of the *Iliad,* annotated by Aristotle. If his mother's family claimed descent from Achilles, Philip and the Argeads included Heracles among their ancestors, and these filiations were taken very seriously indeed. Before he died, Alexander could, and did, claim to have outstripped them both. His training under Aristotle gave him a lifelong interest in science and medicine: the experts who accompanied the expedition became the main source of information on the East for centuries. He was a voracious reader of the Greek historians, poets, and playwrights, with a retentive memory that let him quote at will. He also showed great natural talent as a lyre player.

His parents left an indelible mark on him. His harsh voice, violent temper, and reckless self-exposure in battle suggest, not natural masculinity, but relentless competition with a father whose achievements he both feared and disparaged. His lifelong intimacy with Hephaestion began early. At the same time, there is no evidence for the erotic interest in women prominent in most youths of his age and class. He was, however, to form close friendships with middle-aged maternal figures such as Ada of Caria (who actually adopted him) and the Persian queen mother Sisygambis, who is said to have become so attached to him that she pined away five days after his death.

The vigor, effectiveness, and lack of compunction he displayed on ascending the throne must have sent a warning signal to the Persians and others, but no one, clearly, yet regarded him as a serious danger, even when the invasion first got under way. He was young. He was still a comparatively unknown quantity. He had various potential rivals for the throne among the aristocracy of the highland cantons. His treasury was seriously underfunded: his troops were therefore short of pay and might well look elsewhere for a paymaster. He was inexperienced, rash, impulsive, and prone to fits of uncontrollable rage. His recent destruction of Thebes, while ensuring subservience, also meant that from then on he would never be able to trust any Greek ally in the field. If the Persian satraps of Asia Minor felt confident in their ability to handle this Greek upstart—after all, they were far better supplied with everything from cash to cavalry—that was a very reasonable assumption.

———

Alexander's conquest of the Achaemenid empire—the great military victories of the Granicus, Issus, Gaugamela, and the Jhelum; the symbolic cutting of the Gordian knot; the pilgrimage to the desert oracle of Zeus-Ammon, with its rumors of divinity; the foundation of Alexandria; the seemingly endless eastward march; the frustration of Alexander's ambitions by a full-scale sit-down mutiny of his own men when faced with the interminable Ganges plain; the death march through the Gedrosian desert; and Alexander's premature death in Babylon, just short of his thirty-third birthday, while still planning further conquests—this is a story that has been told well many times already, and I see no need to recount it in detail here. What matters for an investigation of the Hellenistic world that resulted directly from his activities (but which he himself almost certainly never foresaw or intended) is to isolate those features of the Macedonian invasion that in one way or another helped to determine the shape that this new world took. The conclusion of the present chapter will therefore examine the expedition for relevant evidence that may, in one way or another, have influenced the future course of events when Alexander was no longer there to bend them to his will.

The young man who crossed the Hellespont in the spring of 334 was still very much involved with Europe. He was king of the Macedonians and captain-general of the Hellenic League of Corinth. Macedonian territorial conquest would be presented as retribution for Xerxes' profanation of Greek shrines. To this end, Alexander's vigorous public propaganda was a nice blend of the Homeric and the Panhellenic. Before crossing, he sacrificed at the shrine of Protesilaus, traditionally the first Greek ashore at Troy. He followed Xerxes' route in reverse, making libation in mid-Hellespont just as Xerxes had done. At Ilium, he dedicated his own armor in Athena's shrine (a nod here to Athens) and was presented in return with a shield and panoply allegedly from the Trojan War. He and Hephaestion ran a race, naked, around the tombs of Achilles and Patroclus. But he also (having Trojan blood in his veins through the victor's liaison of his mythical ancestor Neoptolemus, Achilles' son) sacrificed to Priam (whom Neoptolemus had killed) and made gifts in memory of Andromache, Hector's widow and Neoptolemus' prize. Trojans (a decision aimed at the often pro-Persian Greek cities of Ionia) were to be seen as Greeks of Asia: an early and symptomatic case of Alexander's attempts to secure cooperation by being all things to all men.

All this propaganda lasted as long as it was needed—that is, until Asia Minor was secure—and then largely disappears from the record. It needs to be counterpointed against the lack of enthusiasm for the great crusade shown by those in whose name the crusade was launched. From the combined Greek states—Sparta contributed nothing—only 160 ships, seven thousand men-at-arms, and a mere six hundred cavalry crossed to Asia with Alexander: a tiny fragment of what was actually available. No one in mainland Greece opposed a war against Persia on principle: the Greeks simply had no enthusiasm for in any way aiding the hated figure who had conquered and brutalized them. This attitude, as we shall see, never changed throughout Alexander's reign, and it involved him in considerable risks during the early part of the campaign. Deprived of Greek hoplite support, unable yet to afford large-scale hiring of mercenaries (who instead flocked to Darius), and above all distrustful of his small Greek flotilla's loyalty, he found himself forced to attack ports like Halicarnassus from the landward side. Except for a small cadre of siege technicians and court favorites, the vast resources of Greek cooperation—military cooperation in particular—remained closed to Alexander throughout his eleven-year campaign; and on the news of his death, Greece promptly broke out in armed rebellion.

One significant consequence of the general absence of Greeks at command level in the expedition was, after a while, a lack of reliable Macedonians to leave in charge of steadily accumulating conquered territories. Attrition through death in action, disease, and the occasional high-level treason trial similarly took its toll on the military command structure. Consequently, much of Alexander's later integration of Persians and Macedonians, especially in army units, far from indicating ideological racial fusion, was dictated by a chronic shortage of Macedonian officers and troops: a shortage caused not only by attrition, but also, later, by mass dismissal of the old, the unfit, and the potentially mutinous. Politically, as Ernst Badian once remarked in the course of a famous assessment (Badian, 1966, 46), Alexander was "cautious, pragmatic, and opportunistic." Here is a nice, and much misinterpreted, example of his pragmatism.

Two other factors, present from the very beginning, were to have a major long-term impact on events after Alexander's death. His refusal, against advice, to marry and beget an heir before leaving Europe, combined with the built-in competitive distrust between his own group of coevals and the old-guard network set up by Parmenio, meant, inevitably, that once Alexander was gone, there was no unified structure to ensure a smooth succession. Nor is there any indication that this was a problem that bothered Alexander himself overmuch. His pursuit of Homeric glory was essentially solipsistic: it did not concern itself with the future. Dying, he was asked to whom he left his kingdom. "To the strongest," he reportedly said. Those words may or may not be historical, but they are certainly ben trovato. Let another Homeric hero try to do as well. There is no sense of continuity. *Après moi le déluge.* Augustus was struck by Alexander's lack of interest in administering the lands he had conquered. The act of conquest was all. If he had lived, Arrian surmised shrewdly, he would have gone on until he had added Europe to Asia, "in competition with himself if there was no one else."[6]

What all this meant was that the expedition was fundamentally disruptive rather than constructive in any unifying sense. It began with an urgent need for booty and ended in megalomania. It took over an empire that had lasted for two long centuries, shattered its theocratic rationale, patched a Macedonian superstructure onto its administrative system, treated its accumulated wealth as fairy gold to be poured out at will, and looked no further than the grandiose personal ambitions of its leader. Isocrates and other Panhellenists had repeatedly stressed the wealth and weakness of Persia as good reasons for invasion: the Macedonians took the hint and went all out for the fabulous loot to which Alexander himself was largely indifferent (except when he needed to buy himself out of a difficult situation by means of massive bribes, as so often with his exhausted and resentful troops). The treasuries of Susa, Persepolis, and Ecbatana made him the wealthiest man in the known world. Delusions of grandeur followed, and his amazing string of brilliant military successes, played up even further by court flattery, gave him the conviction that his deeds had eclipsed those of his ancestor Heracles. Notions of godhead were not slow to follow.

With Alexander's death, all that remained was, in effect, a huge pirates' treasure chest and an even larger mass of spear-won territory, stretching from Anatolia to Afghanistan and beyond, that were there for the taking, as Alexander had predicted, by the strongest. Justin (13.1.8) got it right when he wrote that "the officers had their eyes on the empire and positions of authority, the rank and file on Alexander's war chest and its great hoards of gold." There had been no sense of cultural proselytization about the expedition, no concerted effort (despite all the Panhellenic propaganda) to export Hellenism to Asia except as comfort for upper-class Macedonians and Greeks abroad. Even though their aim was largely pragmatic, Alexander's attempts at fusion (for instance, the mass marriages at Susa) were vigorously repudiated the moment he was dead by his culturally and ethnically xenophobic followers.

On the other hand, his latter-day efforts to be treated as a god gave some interesting ideas to the would-be dynasts among his successors. Alexander's own murderous paranoia had reduced the available heirs to his mentally defective half-brother, Arrhidaeus, and (better late than never) a still unborn child by his first wife, the Bactrian princess Roxane. His vast territorial ambitions had shifted the focus from Pella to Babylon: the Macedonian king had become the Lord of Asia. Mainland Greece had lost its primacy. New great cosmopolitan cities such as Alexandria were shaping men's thoughts. Except for a certain social matiness among the elite, Macedonians, the military old guard in particular, had never paid much attention to democracy. What proved an irresistible lure to them in the summer of 323 in Babylon was the dream of empire—and, possibly, a new kind of kingship.

In the event, like so many apparent historical novelties, Hellenistic kingship was most remarkable for its mix of old traditions. Alexander's casual habit of taking over conquered administrative systems and simply putting in Macedonians at the top left its mark in unforeseen ways. His marshals may have resented his Orientalizing gestures—how to be all things to all men always presents problems—but those of them who later assumed the purple soon began to modify their own warrior tradition much as he had done. Seleucid monarchs acquired much

Babylonian ritual; it was not long before the Ptolemies began to look quite strikingly pharaonic. At one level, these Macedonian overlords stressed their foreign otherness as conquerors; at another, their iconography and ideology were framed in terms familiar to the conquered, for whom the king set over them was, by tradition, the source of grants and favors no less than the recipient of tribute and taxes. In this area as in so many, overall generalizations break down. What we find instead is an infinitely varied kaleidoscopic patchwork.

2

HAWKS AND HYENAS: THE STRUGGLE FOR EMPIRE

(323 - 276)

On the afternoon of June 11, 323 BCE, Alexander III of Macedon, Lord of Asia, conqueror of the Achaemenid empire, son—as occasion dictated—of Philip II or Zeus-Ammon, and a self-styled deity in his own right, died in Babylon.[1] In his final months, and particularly since the death of his lifelong intimate Hephaestion, Alexander had been showing increasing symptoms of paranoia and megalomania. There had been a number of alarming purges. Antipater, summoned to Babylon from Greece to be replaced as viceroy by Craterus, at once assumed that this was a thinly disguised death-sentence, and he may well have been right. The king's plans were becoming increasingly unreal. Philip was to get a tomb that matched the Great Pyramid. Lavish temples were to be built at Delos, Delphi, and elsewhere. The Susa weddings had hinted at delusions of grandeur: Alexander's dictatorial scheme for mass relocation of populations between Europe and Asia "to bring the largest continents to common concord and familial amity by intermarriage" (DS 18.4.4) did more than hint. The gigantic overdecorated funeral pyre and monument he ordered for Hephaestion (at a reputed cost of 10,000 talents: the monument was never completed) might be ascribed to hyperbolic grief, but his military plans were on an equally grandiose scale. The Arabian campaign was just a beginning. One thousand warships, larger than triremes, were to be laid down. A road was to be built along the entire North African coast, as far as the Pillars of Heracles, with harbors and shipyards at regular intervals. The expedition was to conquer all non-Greek peoples in the western Mediterranean, from Carthage to Mauretania, from Spain to Sicily.

What is really remarkable and significant is the way in which Alexander's death brought every single one of these projects to an abrupt and unceremonious halt. Most of the Susa marriages were abandoned. Neither Philip's tomb, nor Hephaestion's monument, nor the projected temples, were ever completed. No mass relocations took place between Asia and Europe, and the notion of "common concord" was abandoned to Stoic and Cynic intellectuals. Preparations for the campaign to subdue the western Mediterranean, seemingly in full swing during the summer of 323, vanish overnight and are never heard of again. The rejection of Alexander's insatiable pursuit of glory through conquest was total and unanimous. Yet such was his charismatic power and authority that no one, even during those final hypermanic months, challenged his increasingly grandiose plans. Only when he was safely dead did his chief of staff, Perdiccas, now in possession of the royal signet-ring, persuade the Macedonian assembly to cancel them all on the grounds of excessive expense.

Though extravagance was a legitimate complaint, the underlying truth was that Alexander, in his obsessional and never-ending quest for Homeric renown through conquest and his increasing readiness to eliminate those who got in his way or argued against him, had become a terrifying embarrassment. Officers and men, above all those who had survived the full eleven years of combat-heavy active service, wanted no more military adventures, but a profitable share in the spoils of empire already won and in most cases a return home. Ethnocentric, xenophobic—they had little more time for Greeks than for Persians—and indifferent to their leader's insatiable ambitions (though they were not above copying his dress, hairstyle, and mannerisms), the Macedonians showed no interest whatsoever in Asia except as a prize of war. This, of course, was exactly what Isocrates had held out to them as a Panhellenic inducement. To the propagation of Hellenism that was supposed to accompany such an invasion, they were, for the most part, massively indifferent.

Nor was there any strong continuity of command. Alexander's early indifference to marriage meant that the Argead dynasty's succession depended on a mental defective (Arrhidaeus, Philip's son by Philinna of Larissa and thus Alexander's half-brother) and Roxane's unborn child, who might not even be male. The prospect of a long, and weak, regency offered a classic invitation to at least a dozen veteran marshals with high ambitions and a loyal following. Worse, the vast realms through which Alexander had hewn his path of triumphant militarism were neither fully subjugated nor properly organized: he had brought disruption rather than unity. His eastern frontiers began to crumble even in his lifetime. For most of his career he had no fixed capital: he was continually on the move. He did not live long enough to establish stable government throughout Asia and in any case was far more concerned with pursuing further conquests in the West.

Though some of the Successors, as we shall see, set their sights on acquiring the whole eastern empire, that was the limit of their ambition, and in the end—after over forty years of bitter internecine fighting—the survivors all settled for less. There were no constitutional precedents for the situation in Babylon. Alexander had left Pella as a local Macedonian king but ended up in the heartland of Asia as a fabulously wealthy conquistador. Old rules no longer applied, and attempts to preserve the most obvious—that of dynastic inheritance—were most remarkable for their determined persistence against overwhelming odds. This is often described as a cynical charade. In fact it was the only hierarchy that those involved understood, and it served, however inadequately, as a working formula while the Successors were slowly coming to terms with, and inventing ad hoc rules for, a new world and a new concept of royal power. The events of the half-century after Alexander's death dictated the entire shape and nature of the Hellenistic world. It has been argued that "to pay undue attention to the events of 323–276 would produce an unbalanced picture of the hellenistic period as a whole" (Shipley, 2000, 40). On the contrary: they form the essential key to understanding it.

———

Until it actually happened, the idea of Alexander dying was inconceivable. No one was prepared for it. Like all charismatic and powerful autocrats, he left a void that no one man could fill. The darkness over a silent Babylon as fires were quenched in mourning well symbolized a widespread uncertainty as to what the future would bring. The major figure to emerge in the immediate aftermath is Perdiccas: royal Bodyguard (*somatophylax*)—one of seven only—since Gaugamela, inheritor of Hephaestion's position as commander in chief of the Companion Cavalry, Alexander's second in command or chief of staff, and, most important of all, recipient before witnesses of his master's signet-ring, the one gesture toward an orderly transfer of power that Alexander is recorded as having made.

It might have been thought that this was enough to identify the heir-apparent and that the dying man's alleged identification of his successor as "the strongest" was (as indeed a supporter of Perdiccas afterward argued) a repudiation of the dynastic principle. But this was something that the Macedonians flatly refused to accept. Traditionalists to a man, they insisted on getting an Argead king of the blood royal, and all other propositions foundered in the face of this obstinate and immovable determination. If Perdiccas was in fact offered supreme power (*summam imperii*), as Curtius alleges, he had by now sensed the general mood and prudently offered a temporizing alternative: Roxane's unborn child, if male, would be king, with Perdiccas, Craterus, Leonnatus, and Antipater as "guardians." The proposal was accepted.

At this point, the rank-and-file of the infantry phalanx, under the leadership of Meleager, launched a violent protest against what they saw, understandably, as a power bid by the cavalry elite (who had indeed dominated the original meeting). Roxane was no more a Macedonian, they shouted, than Alexander's mistress (and Memnon's widow), Barsine. Perdiccas was going to use a long regency to snatch the throne, just as Philip had done with Amyntas. The troops wanted a king, and they wanted him now, not at some indeterminate point in the future. Arrhidaeus, weak-minded or not, was the only eligible surviving Argead, and they were determined to have him. Foiled in debate, they stormed the palace, and the senior cavalry officers, with the bulk of their troops, left Babylon.

Perdiccas stayed behind to negotiate, and Meleager revealed his own ambitions by a failed attempt to have him assassinated. The cavalry coolly cut off food supplies to the city. Frantic negotiations followed— in which Eumenes, Alexander's Greek secretary, played a leading role— and civil war was barely avoided. Each side compromised on the other's proposal: the cavalry accepted Arrhidaeus (now retitled Philip III) as joint king, the infantry endorsed Roxane's unborn child. A ceremony of reconciliation followed, in the presence of Alexander's dead body.

Despite this display of *Machtpolitik,* Perdiccas' position remained ambivalent. Throughout he carefully avoided the title of regent (*epitropos*), preferring the vague term "manager" (*epimelêtês*). But given that he was commander in chief and holder of Alexander's signet-ring, his de facto power in Babylon was unrivaled. Unfortunately, not all the great marshals were within his jurisdiction. Antipater, viceroy of Macedonia all through the Persian expedition, had ignored Alexander's summons to Babylon (see p. 21) and was well established on home territory with a strong army. The popular commander Craterus, carrying a commission to replace him, was in Cilicia with over ten thousand veterans earmarked for repatriation and discharge. Last, there was Antigonus One-Eye, at his Asia Minor base of Celaenae, in command of a large and seasoned force that had successfully, against considerable odds, kept Alexander's lines of communication open throughout his campaign. How any of them would react to attempted coercion from Babylon was completely unpredictable.

Perdiccas undoubtedly bore all this in mind when considering the assignment of offices that followed, which he made in the name of Philip III Arrhidaeus. Seleucus was appointed to Perdiccas' own top command, that of the Companion Cavalry. Perdiccas himself thus moved upward by implication. Craterus was to return to Macedonia, where instead of replacing Antipater, he was to share power with him. Antigonus One-Eye was confirmed in the satrapy he already held, that of Greater Phrygia, Lycia, and Pamphylia. Ptolemy was given Egypt, Lysimachus Thrace, and Leonnatus Hellespontine Phrygia. Eumenes—the only Greek in this Macedonian conclave—was allotted Cappadocia, which had not yet even been conquered. These appointments reversed Alexander's policy of assigning less important figures to the satrapies and led directly to the disunity, and ultimate dismemberment, of the empire that followed. Finally, Roxane gave birth to the hoped-for healthy male child, who was enthusiastically acclaimed king as Alexander IV. There were now two heirs in Babylon, and Perdiccas—together, technically, with his fellow "managers," all now elsewhere—had them in his charge.

———

While the Macedonian commanders reacted to Alexander's death by summarily canceling all his future plans, the Greeks saw this move, and the chaotic uncertainty it engendered, as a perfect occasion to revolt against Macedonian domination. Alexander's order to satraps and regional commanders to discharge all their mercenaries had left Asia full of wandering bands of brigands. More dangerous still was a concerted revolt by the southern Greek states, under the leadership of Athens, that erupted—after a period of simmering preparation—in the fall of 323 and came to be known as the Lamian (or, by the rebels, as the Hellenic) War. Hatred of Macedonian overlordship was sharpened by resentment at the enforced repatriation of political exiles that Alexander had ordered. Mercenaries (now available in abundance) were hired: some of the funds came from Harpalus, Alexander's absconding treasurer. A brilliant Athenian general, Leosthenes, occupied Thermopylae and besieged Antipater—whom Alexander's endless demands had left dangerously short of trained troops—in the Thessalian city of Lamia. Demosthenes returned from exile. An Athenian fleet of over two hundred triremes patrolled the Aegean.

But this success proved ephemeral. Leosthenes was killed outside Lamia. Leonnatus—in receipt of an offer of marriage from Alexander's now widowed sister, Cleopatra, and with designs on the kingdom of Macedonia—brought his army across the Hellespont and raised the siege of Lamia. Unfortunately for his plans, he himself died in the battle: the first of the Successors to be eliminated. Cleitus, sent by Craterus to organize the Macedonian fleet in the Aegean, scored a crushing victory over the Athenian fleet off Amorgos (spring 322). Craterus himself now arrived with his Macedonian veterans, and in August they defeated the combined Greek forces at Crannon in Thessaly. Athens thereupon surrendered unconditionally to Antipater.

———

When Leonnatus was about to cross into Europe, he had tried to enlist Eumenes' support. Eumenes, whose activities as Alexander's chief secretary had not endeared him to Antipater, turned down the invitation. Leonnatus, to persuade him, then revealed his own true intentions, promising Eumenes high office under him. Eumenes, uncharacteristically for a Successor (but then he was a Greek and thus ethnically debarred from any top prize in the Macedonian power game), refused to have anything to do with Leonnatus' secret plans. Leonnatus, a far more typical Successor and scared of having his intentions revealed, arranged to have Eumenes assassinated.

Eumenes, anticipating this, slipped away by night with his entourage and went straight to Perdiccas, now in Sardis. Apprised of Leonnatus' intentions, Perdiccas made Eumenes his trusted lieutenant. Eumenes seems to have been a genuine royalist (he conducted staff meetings in the presence of dead Alexander's arms, scepter, and other regalia), and Perdiccas, whatever his own ambitions, was the two kings' official guardian. What was more, in gratitude he at once conducted a successful campaign to subdue Eumenes' satrapy of Cappadocia for him. Eumenes, characteristically, left subordinates in charge of it and remained with Perdiccas and the kings.

Perdiccas himself, like Leonnatus (and indeed most of the Successors at one time or another: the dynastic tradition died hard), had ambitions to marry Alexander's sister Cleopatra, now conveniently widowed by the death of Alexander of Epirus in Italy. Eumenes, for whatever motive, encouraged this, acting as his agent and go-between. The idea also appealed to Olympias, who encouraged Cleopatra—now once more, with Leonnatus out of the way, officially available—to make her way to Sardis. The problem was that Perdiccas had earlier, when angling for Antipater's support, married the viceroy's daughter Nicaea and thus was not anxious to have his new plans publicized.

(Two other daughters of Antipater, Phila and Eurydice, were shortly afterward married, respectively, to Craterus and Ptolemy: Antipater believed in hedging his bets.) The marital scene in Sardis was complicated further by the threatened appearance of Cynane—Amyntas' widow and Alexander's half-sister—with a plan to marry off her ambitious daughter Adea to Philip Arrhidaeus. Perdiccas' deputy Alcetas, sent north to head Cynane off, solved the problem, predictably, by having her murdered. At this his Macedonian troops, always loyal to an Argead, forced him to convey Adea to Perdiccas, who had no option but to let her marry Arrhidaeus after all.[2]

Perdiccas was also determined to rein in that dangerous man Antigonus One-Eye and summoned him from his command in Greater Phrygia to answer the charge of having failed to support Eumenes, as ordered, in Cappadocia. Antigonus instead fled to Craterus and Antipater, then in central Greece, stamping out the last embers of rebellion among the Aetolian mountaineers. His account of Perdiccas' marital intrigues and reported plans to march on Macedonia ("as king," Antigonus asserted), with the intention of removing Antipater from office—not to mention a dramatic retelling of the murder of Cynane—brought quick action. The three marshals, with their troops, promptly made for Asia Minor. Eumenes, sent by Perdiccas to hold the Hellespont against them, was too late to stop the crossing but resisted overtures from Antigonus and Craterus to change sides. He sensibly avoided any confrontation for the moment and spent his time building up his forces in both the west and Cappadocia.

By now (321/0), Perdiccas thus had Antipater, Craterus, and Antigonus (together with Lysimachus, whom they co-opted) against him, but what he found especially alarming were the actions of Ptolemy. The master of Egypt had not only extended his western frontier to include Cyrene (on which he duly imposed a new constitution), but intercepted Alexander's funeral cortege on its way back to Macedonia and appropriated the royal corpse. After a short spell in Memphis, Alexander's embalmed body was put on permanent display in Alexandria, a silent legitimization (like Lenin's in Red Square) of Ptolemy's own authority. Burying one's predecessor was a royal duty and prerogative. Kingship, if not yet openly proclaimed, was very much in the air. The rumors put about that Ptolemy was Philip's bastard clearly date from this period. To Perdiccas, the hijacking came as a clear sign that his rival aspired to supreme power.

So Perdiccas left Eumenes with a command that now included Caria, Lycia, and Phrygia (and facing desertions to the coalition by both Neoptolemus, a personal enemy, and Alcetas) and marched on Egypt. Arrogance and bad intelligence combined to destroy him. A botched attempt to cross the Nile at the wrong point lost him over two thousand men to drowning and crocodiles. This was no successor to Alexander. A cabal of officers including Peithon and Seleucus murdered him in his tent that same night. Ptolemy, who surely had spies in the enemy camp, early next morning approached Perdiccas' troops, offering an armistice and much-needed supplies (Perdiccas' logistics seem not to have been up to much, either). In return, the grateful Perdiccans—many of whom will have served with Ptolemy—offered him the now vacant supreme office of *epimelêtês* to the two kings. (Perdiccas, who could not trust these bargaining counters out of his sight, had brought both of them, and Roxane, to Egypt with him.)

Ptolemy, canny as ever, politely turned the offer down. Instead he recommended that two of Perdiccas' killers, including Peithon, "to whom he owed a debt of gratitude" (which suggests that he was privy to the plot), should share an acting appointment. His proposal was unanimously endorsed. Once again luck had been on his side, since two days later messengers arrived with news of a great victory won by Eumenes in Asia Minor. The despised Greek secretary, scorned by Macedonians as a pen pusher, had not only shown himself a formidable strategist and tactician, but had killed Neoptolemus in a hand-to-hand duel. Craterus, too, had died. As Diodorus says (18.37.1), "Had [the arrival of the news] happened two days before Perdiccas's death, no one would have dared to lift a finger against him, because of the magnitude of his success." Perdiccas had as much bad luck as Ptolemy had good. As it was, the army proclaimed Eumenes and his close associates traitors (primarily for the killing of Craterus), to be hunted down and executed.

Four of the leading Successors—Leonnatus, Neoptolemus, Craterus, and Perdiccas—were now dead, and their commands needed to be reallocated. A general meeting was held (? July 320) at Triparadeisos, a great game-park in northern Syria. The Egyptian contingent arrived unpaid and ripe for trouble, skillfully fomented by Philip Arrhidaeus' firebrand of a wife, Adea-Eurydice, who egged them on to demand an immediate cash settlement. The acting supremos, scenting trouble, resigned, and Antipater (who had not yet arrived) was voted "manager with plenary powers" in their place. He was, of course, the obvious choice, though Eurydice at once stirred up opposition to him—so successfully that when he appeared he was saved from lynching only by Seleucus and Antigonus.

The elderly Antipater could not produce ready cash, but by a nice blend of discipline and conciliation he restored order, made Eurydice behave herself, and worked out an acceptable new settlement. Eumenes' condemnation let Antipater strip the Greek of his Cappadocian command and commission Antigonus One-Eye—still satrap of Greater Phrygia—as commander in chief of the Macedonian army in Asia, with the prime task of bringing Eumenes to justice. At the same time, Antipater was (rightly, as things turned out) suspicious of Antigonus' own imperial ambitions. He therefore assigned his son Cassander to Antigonus' staff as deputy commander, to keep an eye on him. He also arranged a marriage between his own daughter Phila, Craterus' widow, and Antigonus' son Demetrius, the future Poliorcetes ("Besieger"). (Antigonus welcomed the match but had to put some pressure on a protesting Demetrius: Phila was at least a dozen years older than her new teenage husband.) Antipater was in no position to shift Ptolemy, well entrenched in Egypt, so left him where he was. Seleucus, previously commander of the Guards Brigade (hypaspists), got Babylonia, while Peithon was rewarded with Media. Killing Perdiccas had paid off. Antipater himself took over the kings ("to restore them to their homeland," DS 18.39.7) and returned with them to Macedonia, his natural and preferred context. If this was a bid to bring the Argead monarchy back to its local, purely Macedonian, pre-Alexandrian status, it proved singularly unsuccessful.

By now, the fragmentation of Alexander's empire was already well advanced and the Hellenistic triangulation of Macedonia-Egypt-Asia clearly apparent: Ptolemaic Egypt, indeed, had already settled into what was to prove the longest-enduring of the Successors' dynastic ventures. Yet even after Perdiccas' death, the increasingly threadbare fiction of imperial unity was stubbornly maintained. Some, like Eumenes and Polyperchon, genuinely believed in a royal Argead inheritance. Most used the kings as camouflage for personal ambitions they felt it wiser not to express openly. Yet for many years what they all claimed to be upholding, ever more improbably as time went on—though the conquered territory did, for the most part, remain under Macedonian control—was Alexander's undivided legacy of empire. For at least two decades, it seems, they literally could not conceive of power in any other terms. From his gold coffin in Alexandria, embalmed and iconic, Alexander still tyrannized the minds of the ambitious and often thuggish captains whom he had dominated so ruthlessly while he lived.

The sick and septuagenarian Antipater did not long survive Tripa-radeisos. He died in the late summer of 319, bequeathing his office as *epimelêtês* not, as expected, to his son Cassander—perhaps, it has been suggested, to avert the charge of dynastic politicking; more probably because of Cassander's violent hostility to Alexander and his heirs— but to Polyperchon, one of Philip's old-guard officers who had been Craterus' second in command. Cassander, unwilling to serve Polyper-chon, went looking for allies and found them in Antigonus, Lysi-machus, and Ptolemy: not coincidentally, those who had most to gain from a repudiation of the royal succession.

Polyperchon, meanwhile, as though confirming all their worst sus-picions, invited Olympias back to Macedonia as guardian of Alexan-der IV. Though he was correct in his assumption that this vengeful matriarch would stop at nothing to see her grandson on the throne of Macedon, he almost certainly underestimated the lengths to which she would go. He also had his eye on Eumenes, who had been under siege by Antigonus at Nora in the northern Taurus Mountains. Re-leased on swearing allegiance to Antigonus, three months later Eu-menes accepted an invitation from Polyperchon and Olympias to become their general in Asia, with command of the Silver Shields (for-merly Alexander's Guards Brigade, the hypaspists). Neither Antigonus nor Polyperchon, when it suited them, bothered with the army's death-sentence on Eumenes; while Eumenes himself seems to have taken his oath to Antigonus in the spirit of Euripides' Hippolytus: "My tongue swore, but my mind remained unsworn" (Eur. *Hipp.* 612).

Royalist and separatist conquistadors were now at each other's throats. It was not only the empire (never securely unified by Alexander) that was beginning to fragment: Alexander's matchless army of Mace-donian veterans, its ranks already thinned by deaths and discharges, was splitting up into a number of groups barely distinguishable from profes-sional mercenaries, whose allegiance went to the commander who em-ployed them and could—as Eumenes, betrayed by his own Silver Shields for the return of their baggage train, found to his cost—be bought by the enemy if the price was right. In Asia especially, ethnic considerations of loyalty came a poor second to self-advancement, loot, and the lure of spear-won territory. The head-on five-year satrapal struggle between the armies of Eumenes and Antigonus was fueled by ruthless political ambition and foreshadowed the shape of things to come. Eumenes claimed dream instructions by Alexander's ghost. Antigonus, more realistic, made it very clear that he meant to seize Alexander's imperial legacy entire; and once he had finally destroyed Eumenes at Gabiene (316), he lost no time in going after potential rivals—Seleucus, Peithon—however faithfully they might have served him through that long campaign.

In the Aegean, meanwhile, Cassander cut off Polyperchon from Eumenes by the destruction of his fleet near Byzantium (spring 317); reimposed Macedonian control on Athens (after a brief and bloody democratic reversion in 318/7) with the appointment of a conservative philosopher, Demetrius of Phaleron, as governor; and with the support of Philip Arrhidaeus' wife, Eurydice, declared himself regent (317). Olympias, for whom Philip was a mere mindless interloper on her grandson's rights and who had never trusted Cassander anyway, promptly launched an invasion of Macedonia from Epirus. Eurydice, the warrior-queen, led against her in full armor.

But once again, dynastic loyalties trumped ambition. At the sight of Alexander's mother, Eurydice's troops laid down their arms. Olympias promptly executed Philip III and large numbers of his supporters. Eurydice was forced to commit suicide. At this, Cassander, who had been campaigning against Polyperchon in the Peloponnese, came north and besieged Olympias in Pydna, eventually starving her into surrender (316/5). The agreement, made during negotiations, to spare her life was ignored (Cassander packed a meeting with relatives of her victims, who enforced a death-sentence), and she died with dignity. Cassander took over Alexander IV and his mother, Roxane, whom Olympias had had with her in Pydna, and kept them under guard, well out of the way, in Amphipolis. He also gave Philip III and Eurydice a royal burial, ordered the rebuilding of Thebes, and married Thessalonike, Philip II's daughter by a Thessalian. Like Antigonus, he was making no secret of his ambitions.

Antigonus, with most of Alexander's eastern empire under his control, was now in a far more powerful position than Perdiccas had ever been: the Persians were already treating him as the new lord of Asia, and he did nothing to discourage the notion. From Alexander, as his actions reveal, he had learned several useful lessons. Peithon, the ambitious satrap of Media, as well as various other veteran commanders, he arrested and executed for allegedly plotting revolt. Peucestas, who was too popular for such treatment, he kicked upstairs into a decorative but powerless role in what was rapidly becoming his all-but-royal court. From the various Persian treasuries, at Susa, Ecbatana, and Persepolis, he withdrew the massive sum of 25,000 talents, a solid reserve against the hiring of top-level mercenaries. Realizing that the Silver Shields, who had won him the Battle of Gabiene by conveniently betraying Eumenes, could never be trusted again, he had them posted to Arachosia (roughly, the mountainous Afghan border with Pakistan) and sent instructions to the local satrap to use them on dangerous missions till they were all killed off.

Finally, borrowing the device that Perdiccas had earlier tried to play on him, he descended on Babylon and required Seleucus to give an accounting of his office. Seleucus—like Belshazzar seeing the writing on the wall—promptly fled to Ptolemy in Egypt (? 315), where his lurid account of Antigonus' activities caused instant alarm. Once more, as with Perdiccas, the outsize ambitions of one Successor led to the others forming an instant coalition against him. Messengers sped north to Cassander and Lysimachus, who at once, ignoring the counterenvoys hurriedly sent out by Antigonus, allied themselves with Seleucus and Ptolemy.

Antigonus moved fast. He marched from Babylon to Cilicia, where he took a further 10,000 talents from the Cyinda treasury: this was in addition to the 11,000 talents his satrapy yielded in annual tribute. The total—a staggering 46,000 talents in all—meant that he could not only hire mercenaries, but build ships more or less without limit. Strong in all other respects, he lacked a fleet, and his enemies (who all had large navies) knew it. Planning from scratch, and laying out vast emergency advance payments, Antigonus now commissioned vessels from Rhodes and the Cilician shipyards. He then marched down into Syria. Here he was overtaken by envoys from the rival coalition, with a set of demands nicely calculated for rejection: the restoration of Seleucus to Babylon and the allocation of all Syria to Ptolemy, of Hellespontine Phrygia to Lysimachus, and of Cappadocia and Lycia to Cassander. They also insisted on a share-out of the treasure captured from Eumenes. The alternative was war. Of these requests, the only remotely justifiable one was the restoration of Seleucus.

Not surprisingly, Antigonus gave them "a pretty rough answer" (DS

19.57.2). What is interesting here, and in the various proclamations that followed, is the unmistakable appeal to public opinion. With the elimination of so many Successors, of which Antigonus was by far the greatest beneficiary, the survivors were beginning, for the first time, to look for allies outside their own tight Macedonian circle. From now on, propaganda, aimed primarily—but by no means exclusively—at the various Greek states and cities, becomes a notable feature of the dynastic struggle.

From Syria, Antigonus pressed on into Phoenicia—like Perdiccas, he clearly meant to deal with Ptolemy first—and made his base at Old Tyre. From here, he commandeered three more shipyards, those of Byblos, Sidon, and Tripolis. (The entire Phoenician fleet was in Egypt on Ptolemy's payroll.) Antigonus now organized a labor force of eight thousand men to fell and transport timber. Before the season was out, he reassured his men (who had to watch Seleucus' ships sailing to and fro with contemptuous impunity), he would have five hundred warships in action. He also—a further huge expense—purchased over 3 million bushels of wheat, approached the princes of Cyprus (with some success) for alliances, set up a system of beacons and dispatch carriers, and laid siege to Tyre itself, which was strongly held by Ptolemy's troops. No one could fault Antigonus for energy and determination.

But he also instantly grasped the significance of the opposition's well-publicized demands. From Old Tyre, he in his turn (314) issued a manifesto, endorsed by the Macedonian army assembly. Cassander was accused of murdering Olympias, marrying Thessalonike by force, and aiming at the throne. He was to surrender Alexander IV and Roxane "to the Macedonians" (presumably that meant to Antigonus himself, who claimed to have assumed the *epimeleia* of the surviving king). He was to destroy Thebes, which he had rebuilt as a gesture of opposition to Alexander's memory and in a bid for Greek support. Failure to do so would mean war. In his own bid for non-Macedonian support, Antigonus announced, finally, that all Greek cities, those in mainland Greece and Asia alike, were to be free, autonomous, and ungarrisoned (DS 19.61.1–4).

The Greeks might be forgiven for receiving this offer with a certain cynical lack of enthusiasm. The Spartans had used it during the Peloponnesian War but then had bartered away the cities of Asia Minor in return for Persian gold. The Persians had found it a useful way of reinforcing their control over those same cities at the time of the King's

Peace (386). Autonomy's main attraction for the power-brokers was the pretext it gave them to break up dangerous leagues or federations. And freedom was a relative term. The cities were not relieved of the need to pay taxes or tribute. Garrisons could be, and often were, imposed or reimposed on the slightest excuse. Overriding everything else was the bitter fact that those who bestowed this "freedom" had the absolute power to remove it again.

Here we come up against a perennial, and largely insoluble, problem of the era. How could the cities' hunger for self-determination be reconciled with the ultimate absolutism of the great Hellenistic monarchies? The Greeks yearned for liberty; the dynasts needed allies and educated specialists. Inevitably, each side made unwelcome concessions in pursuit of the best deal it could get. That such proclamations did find takers is clear from the fact that Ptolemy—who, like his allies, cheerfully held cities down with oligarchies and garrisons—at once issued a similar decree, "wanting the Greeks to know that he, no less than Antigonus, had their autonomy in mind" (DS 19.62.1–2), and that both he and Antigonus persisted in the claim throughout their subsequent careers. Freedom, like the Argead monarchy (Cassander, of course, made no move to release Alexander IV from his deliberately unregal confinement in Amphipolis), was an increasingly fictional but still extremely useful concept.

For several years, Antigonus skirmished with Ptolemy over Rhodes and Cyprus, exploited the naval support of the League of Islanders in the Aegean, tried to turn the Greek mainland against Cassander, and in 313 finally secured the surrender of Tyre. In 312, Seleucus persuaded Ptolemy to bring Antigonus' son Demetrius to battle in the Gaza Strip, where they inflicted a crushing defeat on him. Quickly cashing in on this victory, Seleucus borrowed troops from Ptolemy and recovered Babylon, defeating a far larger force, which he then took over and used to reconquer Media and Susiana. But when Antigonus himself came down into Palestine, Ptolemy prudently withdrew rather than challenge him. The various rivals now (311) patched up a largely status quo treaty to give themselves time to regroup. Cassander was recognized as "general in Europe" until Alexander IV came of age. Lysimachus kept Thrace, and Ptolemy Egypt (plus his neighboring acquisitions). Antigonus was to "be leader in Asia," a significantly vague term. Seleucus, busy consolidating his control of the eastern satrapies, was left out of the negotiations altogether, a serious error of judgment.

Despite its formal nod to young Alexander, the treaty was a tacit recognition of the empire's breakup, something that at least two of the four signatories, Antigonus and Lysimachus, had not the slightest intention of accepting. All of them, however, were careful to insist that the Greeks, as before, should remain autonomous. We have a letter (Austin, 1981, 57–60) dispatched by Antigonus to Scepsis in the Troad, emphasizing this and explaining the circumstances leading up to the peace. We also have that city's fulsome response to it, setting up a precinct and altar for the honoring of their godlike savior. Here, of course, we see another characteristically Hellenistic phenomenon encouraged by Alexander's example: the quasi-divinization of outstanding mortals during their own lifetime. It was not to be all that long (September 290) before Athens welcomed Antigonus' son Demetrius, "with incense and wreaths and libations," as a present god, "not in wood, not in stone, but for real," and thus the suitable object for civic prayers and adoration (Green, 2003a, 260–262). The Olympians' record of aid during the past century had been less than outstanding: perhaps flesh-and-blood heroes could do better?

The 311 treaty left Antigonus free to pursue Seleucus, but he had less success here than against Eumenes. That same year, his general Nicanor suffered a crushing defeat in the east, and Seleucus took over most of his seventeen thousand troops. Demetrius failed to retake Babylon. When Antigonus renewed the attack on Seleucus, he found a united resistance that included the Babylonian priesthood and was fueled by loyalty to Seleucus and a strong personal distaste for Antigonus himself and his violent methods, now evident in his slash-and-burn plundering of Babylonia, which—as the Babylonian Chronicle reveals—resulted in famine and spiraling food prices. Though early in 309 Antigonus captured part of Babylon, the endless resistance wore him down. In any case, the east was not his main objective. Finally, in 308, he seems to have made a non-aggression pact with Seleucus, after which he returned, permanently, to the west. Seleucus, like Ptolemy (with whom, peace or no peace, he kept in contact), was at last recognized as a major player in the imperial struggle. He himself later (303) made a similar deal in the east with the Mauryan conqueror Chandragupta, ceding him the provinces of Gandhara, Gedrosia, and Arachosia in return for intermarriage rights and no fewer than five hundred war-elephants. Two years later, those elephants were to be instrumental in the final destruction of Antigonus' dream of empire.

Cassander's reaction to the treaty was rather different. Probably in 310, he arranged the secret assassination of Alexander IV and his mother, Roxane, in Amphipolis, thus finally putting paid to the fictional charade of an empire united by the Argead dynasty. Certainly in 309 Polyperchon believed Alexander IV was dead, since with Antigonus' connivance he fetched Heracles, Alexander the Great's seventeen-year-old bastard son by Barsine, from Pergamon and began setting him up as the last possible Argead heir. Cassander, with a mix of alarmist predictions and promises of a rich sinecure, plus a 100-talent bribe, fast-talked Polyperchon into executing the boy. Thus deprived of his one trump card, the old general retired to obscurity in the Peloponnese.

In 308, Antigonus too dropped the charade and completed the elimination of the Argeads by having Alexander's sister Cleopatra murdered—on her way to marry Ptolemy, no less. The paradoxical ambiguity of these contenders, all by implication kings of all the Macedonians, had outlived its usefulness. Yet it was still over two years (306) before the remaining Successors—first Antigonus and Demetrius, then Ptolemy, Lysimachus, Seleucus, and Cassander—at last openly assumed the purple and proclaimed themselves kings, not by inheritance but on the grounds of personal prestige. Though this prestige was normally conferred by conquest, it could persist even after territorial losses, so that (as in the case of Demetrius) a king might, paradoxically, remain a king even when he had no kingdom.

The ambitions of Antigonus—now nearly eighty and hugely corpulent: one reason for using Demetrius so much—remained as powerful as ever. In 307, he sent Demetrius to liberate Athens, which Demetrius did with efficiency and panache, getting divine honors as a reward. Cassander's governor, the philosopher Demetrius of Phaleron, departed under safe conduct to Egypt and became Ptolemy's adviser on setting up the Museum and Library. Demetrius, handsome and charming, took off to Cyprus, where he inflicted a crushing defeat on Ptolemy's fleet (306) and was rewarded with a royal diadem from his father. Antigonus clearly meant to secure firm control of the eastern Mediterranean sea routes, since he at once sent Demetrius to reduce that other great naval bastion, Rhodes, whose citizens had rebuffed his diplomatic advances. For over a year (305/4), Demetrius assaulted the island's capital with a fearsome array of siege engines, fire arrows, rams, and torsion catapults. Ptolemy's ships ran the blockade to supply the defenders, and in the end Demetrius was forced to leave the Rhodians independent. His title of "the Besieger" thus has a decidedly ironic flavor about it. The Rhodians celebrated by erecting a colossal statue of Helios at the harbor entrance, paid for by the sale of Demetrius' abandoned siege-gear. They also bestowed on Ptolemy the title of "Savior."[3]

Demetrius' excuse for giving up the siege of Rhodes was that Antigonus recalled him to deal with Cassander on the Greek mainland (just as he had brought him back west from Babylon). Here he scored some quick and striking successes, including the establishment of a garrison on Acrocorinth (so much for autonomy). He drove Cassander out of Attica and quartered himself and his mistress Lamia in the Parthenon (304). By 302, he had actually revived something very like the old League of Corinth (except that it was directed *against* the current Macedonian regime) and got himself elected its captain-general. He and his father now moved north to finish off Cassander, who at once sued for peace. Fatally, and flush with success, Antigonus insisted on unconditional surrender. Cassander made a desperate appeal to Ptolemy, Seleucus, and Lysimachus. This chance to remove the incubus that Antigonus now represented was irresistible. The new allies abandoned Macedonia altogether and lured Antigonus, now eighty years old, to a showdown in Asia Minor. While Ptolemy attacked Syria from the south, Lysimachus and Seleucus brought Antigonus and Demetrius to battle at Ipsus in Phrygia (301). Demetrius' successful cavalry charge got out of control, leaving a fatal gap behind it. Seleucus' massed elephants created havoc. Antigonus himself died fighting. Demetrius, with about nine thousand men, fled to Ephesus.

The most dangerous of all the Successors had at last been eliminated, and the victors were left to share out his vast domain like vultures stripping a carcass. In the deal they worked out, Lysimachus got most of Asia Minor and thus the control of the Hellespont he had always wanted when restricted to Thrace; Cassander consolidated his position on the Greek mainland; and Seleucus was awarded Syria and Mesopotamia, which at once brought him into contention with Ptolemy. Ptolemy had not fought at Ipsus, Seleucus objected. He himself had, and his elephants had won the day. The problem of the Syrian frontier was to sour Seleucid-Ptolemaic relations for as long as both dynasties lasted. It was to be another twenty-five years, marked by a number of significant deaths and entrances, before the last bids for empire failed and the post-Alexandrian world settled, for better or worse, into the pattern it would keep for the next three centuries.

The final convulsions were ugly and murderous. Cassander's death in 298/7 precipitated a civil war between his sons: his widow, Thessalonike—Philip II's daughter—favored the younger brother, so the elder assassinated her. Demetrius the Besieger, still in possession of a powerful fleet based on Cyprus and a scatter of coastal cities, found a cautious ally in Ptolemy, always anxious to preserve the balance of power. Ptolemy insisted on hostages: Demetrius sent him his protegé Pyrrhus, the young (but already twice-exiled) king of Epirus who had distinguished himself at Ipsus and had the additional cachet of being related to Alexander the Great through Olympias. Ptolemy took to Pyrrhus, gave him arms and men, restored him to his throne, and in effect used him as his lieutenant in mainland Greece. A new, and far from negligible, player had joined the Successors' endgame. When Ptolemy turned against Demetrius, Pyrrhus felt no qualms about doing so too. They had good reason. Demetrius, taking advantage of the chaos in Greece following Cassander's death, and angry at being rebuffed by the Athenians after Ipsus (his second period of residence in Athens, in 304, had been an orgiastic public relations disaster), stood off Ptolemy's fleet and took Athens by siege in 295. From this base he moved north, killed one of Cassander's sons, forced the other into exile with Lysimachus, and finally (294) got himself acclaimed king of Macedonia.

Once again the old coalition—Ptolemy, Lysimachus, and Seleucus, with Pyrrhus as a fourth—formed against an overreacher. Demetrius put his own image on his coins, assumed a double crown symbolizing Europe and Asia, and wore a robe portraying him as a sun among stars. He reconquered most of central Greece and married Pyrrhus' ex-wife, Lanassa, who brought him the strategic island of Corcyra as a dowry (291/0). Together they were welcomed into Athens (a quick switch in return for services rendered and anticipated) as living gods. While he was thus preoccupied, Lysimachus stripped him of the Ionian ports, Seleucus took over Cilicia, and Ptolemy seized Cyprus. The Aegean League of Islanders joined the coalition. Pyrrhus and Lysimachus then (287) invaded Macedonia from west and east, and Demetrius fled, a plain black cloak replacing his flamboyant royal robes. Phila, his elderly (and intensely devoted) Macedonian wife, committed suicide. Lysimachus and Pyrrhus divided Macedonia between them.

Yet Demetrius still commanded the loyalty of his troops. He regained the initiative in the Peloponnese, he made a deal with Athens, he crossed into Asia Minor—leaving his son Antigonus Gonatas, of whom we shall hear more, to hold the line in Greece. He captured Sardis, he even found time to marry Ptolemaïs, a daughter of Ptolemy's ex-wife, Eurydice (previously promised him by Ptolemy during one of their brief alliances). But then he made a fatal error. Instead of sticking to the coast, where he had the support (despite Ptolemy's Mediterranean acquisitions) of his still powerful fleet, he struck inland, hoping, like Eumenes, to win over the great eastern satrapies. Like Eumenes, he failed. Lysimachus cut off his supplies. His troops began to desert him as famine and disease struck. Demetrius gave up and recrossed the Taurus range into Cilicia, where he fell ill. In 285, Seleucus forced his surrender. Lysimachus offered Seleucus 2,000 talents to execute his prisoner. Seleucus, with well-publicized moral outrage, refused. Instead, he set up Demetrius in luxurious captivity at Apamea (the former Celaenae), where the Besieger, bored witless, was encouraged to drink himself to death, and duly did so (283).

The same year saw, at last, the death of Ptolemy, the only one of Alexander's marshals except Antipater to die a natural death in his own bed. In 285, Ptolemy had taken his homonymous son by Berenice I as co-regent. The designated heir now succeeded his father without incident as Ptolemy II Philadelphus. But this move sidelined Ptolemy's eldest son by his prior wife, Eurydice, Berenice's aunt: yet another Ptolemy, as violent as he was ambitious and known (with good reason) as Keraunos ("the Thunderbolt"). Prudently, this superfluous sibling left Egypt. Rebuffed by Lysimachus, he attached himself to Seleucus.

Immediately after Ipsus, the elderly Lysimachus had married Ptolemy's teenage daughter, Arsinoë (II), Philadelphus' sister, a woman at least as ambitious as Ptolemy Keraunos and in her own way perhaps even more dangerous. As a result—second marriages were the curse of the Successors' dynastic ambitions—Lysimachus saw his strong position (he had driven Pyrrhus back to Epirus) undermined by domestic intrigue. Arsinoë was all too conscious of the Thunderbolt's predicament. Now, at thirty-odd, she had three sons of her own to look out for.

She therefore talked Lysimachus into executing his popular and militarily brilliant heir-apparent, Agathocles. Agathocles' widow turned to Seleucus, and many of the wealthy cities in Asia Minor, oppressed by Lysimachus' fiscal extortions, followed suit. Seleucus brought Lysimachus—like Antigonus One-Eye by now an octogenarian—to battle at Corupedion near Sardis (281) and left him dead on the field.

Though Alexander's empire had been fought over by all his senior marshals, it remained, by and large, in Macedonian hands; so when Seleucus crossed into Europe—for the first time since setting out with Alexander over half a century earlier—he must have believed the great prize to be at last within his grasp. But Ptolemy Keraunos, who coveted the throne of Macedon himself, had other ideas. En route to Lysimacheia, he murdered his patron, got himself acclaimed by the army (an emergency distribution of booty helped), and became king (fall 281). He then—against the urgent warnings of her eldest son, who fled the country—lured Lysimachus' widow (and his own half-sister), Arsinoë, into marrying him, upon which he promptly killed her two remaining children. She herself barely got away to Samothrace, just as she had barely escaped from Ephesus (leaving a faithful slave girl in her royal robes as a decoy) after Lysimachus' death at Corupedion. Her extraordinary career, as we shall see, was far from over.

But at this point, the internecine conflicts of the last Successors were rudely interrupted by outsiders. In Egypt and Asia (where Seleucus had wisely named his son Antiochus as co-regent and heir-apparent before setting out for Corupedion), the new dynasties were firmly established. In Macedonia and Greece, it was another matter. To fight Seleucus, Lysimachus had drafted troops away from his northern defenses, and in 280 there was a mass invasion of Celtic tribesmen. The Thunderbolt (disdaining a vital offer of help from Dardanian mountaineers on the frontier) went out to fight them and was defeated and killed. The Celts paraded his head, stuck on a pike, as they swept south into Thrace, Asia Minor, and the Balkans: very satisfying for Arsinoë, a source of panic for everyone else. Chaos ensued. Macedonia had no king. One horde was driven north from Delphi by the Aetolians. And in the south, Antigonus Gonatas, Demetrius the Besieger's unremarkable Stoic-trained son—beaten at sea by the Thunderbolt, threatened by Antiochus and Athens, barely clinging to his bases of Piraeus, Corinth, Chalcis, and Demetrias—set himself, with the last of his father's wealth, to gather a fleet and a strong mercenary army and march north (summer 277).

We do not know his original motive. It is not clear if he intended to confront the Celtic invasion. He may simply have hoped to acquire a little more territory. If his goal was to seize the empty throne of Macedon (also claimed by Antiochus on the basis of Seleucus' victory), he had an odd way of going about it, since he ended up in Thrace. It was here, near Lysimacheia, that he met, outmaneuvered, trapped, and massacred a huge horde of Gauls, some eighteen thousand strong, that was making for the Chersonese.

The kudos that accrued from this victory was enormous. Antigonus Gonatas, self-styled, if kingdomless, king of Macedonia since his father Demetrius' death in 283, finally made good his claim. He set up a non-aggression pact with Antiochus, received honors as the savior of Greece, drove out his rivals, and reconquered Thessaly. He took Pan—to whose images he bore a marked facial resemblance and who had reputedly obliged him by panicking the Celts outside Lysimacheia—as his patron deity. Snub-nosed, knock-kneed, as uncharismatic a figure as could well be imagined, the Besieger's son now embarked on a highly successful reign of over thirty-five years and founded a vigorous dynasty that was terminated only by the Romans in 168.

With the deaths of the last Successors and the establishment of Antigonid Macedonia, a workable balance of power was achieved between Egypt, Asia, and Europe, the three corners of Alexander's empire. The funeral games the conqueror had foreseen on his deathbed were over at last.

3

KINGS, CITIES, AND CULTURE: THE MYTHIC PAST AS THE FUTURE

I t should by now be apparent that the factors combining to produce what today is known as the Hellenistic age—but for which antiquity, significantly, had no collective title—were numerous, highly complex, and to a striking degree unrelated to the direct intentions either of Alexander himself or, a fortiori, of the Successors (*Diadochoi*). Indeed, some fundamental and characteristic changes that took place, particularly in the civic and cultural development of the Greek cities (poleis), would have come about had Alexander's eastern conquests never happened: were, in fact, already well advanced by the time of his birth. It was Choerilus of Samos, we recall, who—before 400 BCE—lamented the fact that all poetic possibilities had been explored, that there was nothing left for the younger generation of creative artists to do.

This tendency to look over one's shoulder, to be overwhelmed by the legacy of the past, crops up everywhere. Tragedies went on being turned out by Athenian playwrights; but now they had to compete with regular official revivals of plays by the canonized fifth-century trinity—Aeschylus, Sophocles, Euripides. These were the summum bonum: no one, the revivals implied, could ever do better. It is not fashionable today to regard this legacy as unmatchable; but to the post-Alexandrian world its superiority was axiomatic, the inspired work of a lost golden age. The prime concern for a modern historian is to understand why that particular kind of creativity lost ground when it did: why (again, in Athens) there was a visible shift from poetry to prose, from drama and lyric to philosophy, science, and rhetoric, from creative innovation to scholarly conservatism, from political and civic involvement to individualistic quietism, from public to private life.

The shattering of Athens' sea empire in 404 had far-reaching political, economic, and psychological implications. That unself-conscious high-riding pride and confidence that shine through so much fifth-century Athenian art, architecture, and literature vanish. Athens' record in the first half of the fourth century is marked by hardscrabble (and often less than honest) politics, fantasy-ridden rhetoric, endless local conflict (both internal and external), and a grim determination, as with the so-called Second Athenian Sea-League of the 370s, to recapture past polis glories in a world where the kind of imperial benefits popularized under Pericles were gone beyond recall. The second half of the century reinforced this sense of disappointed frustration by brutally exposing the fundamental weaknesses of the polis system as such. Philip of Macedon, an autocratic monarch whose chain of command answered to him alone, played havoc with the squabbling representatives of city-state democracy, while their citizen hoplites and commanders were no match for his professional generals and highly trained phalanx.

The practical advantages of one-man rule as opposed to government by democratic committee (pithily emphasized by Homer and now relearned the hard way) were not forgotten, particularly by Athens' oligarchs. Defeat by Macedonia in the Lamian War (322) meant it was they who were called on to negotiate peace with Antipater and found collaboration not only acceptable but advantageous. Among other things, Antipater disenfranchised the lower orders, always a popular move with Athenian conservatives. Theophrastus' Boastful Man, in the *Characters* (c. 320), claims to have had letters from Antipater inviting him to Macedonia, offering him a license to export timber duty-free. It was men such as this who subsequently (317–310) supported the rule of Demetrius of Phaleron and accommodated themselves to the royal overlordship of Alexander's Successors. The urge for independence never died in the major city-states; but it was now offset by a neo-con trend that had success through self-enrichment as its prime goal, shunned radicalism of any sort, and regarded democracy as a privilege best restricted to the upper classes.

———

One little-noticed major change brought about by Alexander's conquests was the elimination, in short order, of the Barbarian Other that for two centuries had not only figured as the natural enemy of the Hellenic world, but provided the main impetus for the whole concept of Panhellenism. Greek propagandists such as Isocrates had drawn a picture of Persian Orientalism in which wealth beyond the dreams of Croesus was matched only by the corruption and effete decadence of its unworthy guardians. Here was a prize for the taking, and Xerxes' invasion of Greece in 480 could always be invoked as a natural excuse for any reprisals. Panhellenism, as we have seen, was the initial banner under which Alexander launched his own crushing assault; ironically enough, his far-reaching success at once rendered the slogan obsolete. As Cavafy asked, at the end of his most famous poem, "Now what's to

become of us without barbarians? These people were some sort of solution."[1] The Persians were never really replaced. The Celts were
transitory and unpredictable (and soon revamped, in Pergamon and
elsewhere, as Noble Savages); the Macedonians were officially pro-
Greek (had not Alexander I been known as "the Philhellene"?); the
Romans were discounted as serious bogeymen until it was far too late.
Yet Panhellenism had left its indelible—and deleterious—mark on the
Greek world: it offered a splendid moral justification for ethnocentric
colonialism. The Achaemenid empire was, to both Alexander and the
Successors, "spear-won territory" (*gê doríktetos*), there for the con-
querors' exploitation, and so, in essence, despite modifications, it al-
ways remained.

———

Among the traditional prestigious prerogatives, and duties, of an ancient king was that of founding cities. During his short life, Alexander
was responsible for creating a good many (though fewer than were once
ascribed to him: Seleucus did better), naming most of them after himself. The most famous, and by far the most successful, was Alexandria-
by-Egypt, built on the one deep-water harbor along the eastern stretch
of the North African coast: that "by" rather than "in" hints eloquently
at the city's non-Egyptian status as the Ptolemies' cosmopolitan capital. Like Alexander, the Successors too established their homonymous
foundations: Lysimacheia, Antioch, Cassandreia, Ptolemaïs, Antigoneia,
Seleucia-on-Tigris, Seleucia-in-Pieria, and—an occasional nod to
the always forceful distaff side here—Apamea, Arsinoë, Berenice, and
Laodicea. The practice was in fact of considerable antiquity in the Near
East, where great cities such as Babylon, Tyre, Nineveh, and Uruk had
sustained flourishing international commerce on a basis of royal and
theocratic centralization. Now, with a resurgence of monarchy in the
Macedonian kingdoms carved out of Alexander's Achaemenid conquests, old patterns of government began to reassert themselves.

Here it helped considerably that, almost to a man, the new rulers
were not city-state Greeks but Macedonians, brought up on a royal system, however superficially egalitarian, in which the king had the last
word. As has often been pointed out, the government of the Hellenistic kingdoms stood far closer to the Persian administration it replaced
than to any version of Athenian-style democracy. Yet the relationship of these Macedonian governments to the independent or quasi-
independent Greek cities throughout their territories, and even (the

case of Alexandria is particularly instructive) to the Greek population of their own capitals, is decidedly ambiguous. The Greeks, after all, had a good deal of experience in the business of colonization and very firm ideas about what to expect from their new cities. At the dawn of the Hellenistic age, moreover, there was more urbanization than ever before: population figures were everywhere on the rise, the migrant drift to the cities—political exiles, unemployed mercenaries, the rootless, the indigent—continued unabated, flourishing commerce swelled traffic by sea and land. Cities grew a great deal larger, and their administration became correspondingly more complex.

The result was a curious civic hybrid. While ultimate power resided with the kings, the Greek cities under their aegis retained all the defining trappings of polis democracy: defensive walls, an agora that served as both market and political forum, a council and assembly, a theater, and a gymnasium. As countless inscriptions reveal, they were excellently run, encouraged civic pride, and cooperated one with another when not, as so often, fighting. More widespread than they ever had been in the classical era, they constituted a powerful, if in ways paradoxical, manifestation of what it meant to be Greek in this new age.

The paradox, of course, lay in their political status. The tension between royal authority and civic independence was, as noted earlier, a permanent problem throughout the Hellenistic age, where compromise operated on a sliding scale dictated by political advantage, and no fixed principles (even as regards what autonomy precisely meant) were ever established. For some there were advantages, not all impalpable, outside the scope of dynastic control. Athens in particular may have been crippled politically by Macedonian overlordship but still contrived to stamp the expanding cultural scene as, in essence, an Athenian creation. The new cities were built according to the well-tried Piraeus-style grid-pattern. Their education and democratic usages were Athenian-based. They imported Attic drama. Above all, the common tongue (*koinê*), the Greek lingua franca that came to be universally employed throughout the huge polyglot expanses of Asia, was a modified version of vernacular Attic Greek.

Though Alexander may have planned Alexandria primarily as a strategic bastion for the eastern Mediterranean (which indeed it remained until World War II), it rapidly emerged as the greatest cosmopolitan center of the ancient world. Its position favored international commerce. Its boulevards were planned to catch the cool breeze off the sea. The immense wealth poured into its creation produced facilities of unparalleled sophistication, luxury, and attractiveness, including the great harbor lighthouse, the Pharos, that became one of the Seven Wonders of the ancient world (all of which reflected a characteristic Hellenistic, and especially Ptolemaic, taste for extravagant gigantism). A liberal immigration policy, coupled with lavish patronage of scholarship and the arts through the royally funded Museum and Library, produced an exceptionally varied and intelligent corps of foreign residents, including the Alexandrian Jews who translated the Pentateuch. Alexandria, in short, had something for everybody. The mime writer Herodas lists a few of its advantages: wealth, power, public spectacles, philosophers, pretty boys, women galore, the Museum, vintage wine. Long before Thorstein Veblen, the Ptolemies were into conspicuous consumption.

None of the other Hellenistic foundations ever quite equaled Alexandria's unique mixture of commercial success and intellectual panache. Perhaps the most interesting was Pergamon, set high on a spur of the mountains in northwest Asia Minor. Its governor under Lysimachus, a reputed eunuch named Philetaerus, first shrewdly transferred his loyalty (and 9,000 talents in the treasury) to Seleucus, but after Seleucus' death moved cautiously toward independence, spending his wealth on cultivating the influential, including the oracular priesthood of Delphi. In 263, he was succeeded by his nephew Eumenes I, who died in 241. Eumenes' successor, Attalus I, his cousin's son, scored a great victory over the Galatian Celts and (like Antigonus Gonatas in similar circumstances) finally claimed royal status as a result.

A new Hellenistic kingdom thus came into being, its influence out of all proportion to its diminutive size. The Attalids, like the Ptolemies, were wealthy. Their Lysimachean treasure was reinforced by a solid list of profitable exports: wine, oil, grain, horses, hogs, sheep, dairy products, and the parchment that took its name from Pergamon. The city's lofty acropolis, with its monumental buildings, was designed in imitation of Periclean Athens, and the Attalid public library sought to challenge Alexandria in the range and amplitude of its holdings (Mark Antony later raided these for the benefit of Cleopatra).

The Attalids were also great patrons of the visual arts. Their ambivalent attitude to the Galatian Celts—seen not only as enemies to be vanquished, but as emblems of primitive nobility—inspired some of the Hellenistic era's greatest sculpture. Pergamenes went as students to the Academy in Athens (rather than to the Aristotelian Lyceum) and in due course supplied more than one of its future directors. Pergamon's public gymnasium ranked among the largest and most luxurious then in existence. Wealth, munificence, and strictly limited ambitions (they acquired a reputation as arbitrators and power-brokers) served the Attalids well: Ptolemy I's lesson had been taken to heart. When the time came, they were among the first of the Asiatic Greeks to cultivate a special relationship with Rome.

———

Among the more notorious of Alexander's actions during the last few months of his life was his demand to be worshipped as a god. In fact the idea was not new and appealed to a wider range of the public at large than educated reactions to it (which of course are all we have) might suggest. Offerings to notable figures as "on a par with the gods" (*isotheoi*) were not uncommon. Philip II, a shrewd political psychologist, had taken the notion to its logical conclusion by having his image borne in procession with those of the Olympian pantheon, while his son's pursuit of Homeric glory, in the opinion of many, went further still by *excelling* the recorded achievements of Heracles and Dionysus.

The age of the Successors was more than ready for human deification. To the new dynasts, divinity offered a powerful extra ingredient—part numinous, part political—to help strengthen their freshly acquired royal status. The one ad hoc monarch who rejected the whole idea of his divinity ("My pisspot-bearer knows better") was Antigonus Gonatas, not so much on account of his Stoic training (as philosophers like to think) as because Macedonia, alone among the post-Alexandrian kingdoms, was no colonial fief, Asiatic or Egyptian, but a traditional European monarchy. Elsewhere Macedonians lorded it over other subject races, but Antigonus was king *of the Macedonians* and so styled himself. His subjects understood the Greek notion of hubris, the long-established separation between gods and mortals.

Yet a strong countertrend also existed. The notion of *isotheotes*, mortal parity with a god, goes back to Homer and Sappho. Heracles had bridged the gap, had been admitted to the Olympian pantheon. Empedocles as shaman drew a huge following when he proclaimed, "I go among you a god immortal, mortal no longer." Eupolis, the Athenian playwright, has a character say of Athenian generals during the Peloponnesian War: "We used to pray to them as gods, *for indeed so they were* [emphasis mine]." There is more than a jokey metaphor here: in early

Greece, kingship had in fact been widespread, and the king was, precisely, not only the warrior-shepherd of his people, but in some sense the divinized mediator between them and the gods.[2]

Nevertheless, in Greece kings were, with some special exceptions, ditched early, and philosophical rationalism (the so-called Greek miracle) took over. The result was a fundamental dichotomy in Hellenic culture. While intellectuals from Protagoras to Euripides either ignored the gods altogether in favor of scientific inquiry or attacked Homer, and the Olympian pantheon generally, for failing to match contemporary standards of social and sexual morality, the majority (including many in public office) responded by instituting a number of trials for impiety (*asebeia*), on charges ranging from atheism and moral relativism to the teaching of astronomy. A sacral element was missing from civic life, and that element had once been closely associated with kingship.

In addition, the traditional gods had shown themselves less than helpful in times of crisis. By contrast, Alexander's royal achievements had been not only superhuman but tangible. There was something here for everybody. The religious would recall the role of the king as sacral mediator between earth and heaven. Rationalists, latching on to the influential contemporary arguments of Cassander's court guru Euhemerus, could comfort themselves with the reflection that the so-called gods were really nothing more than great generals and statesmen of the past who had been "divinized" by popular acclaim for their mortal achievements. And a living god could at least be petitioned in person.

———

Aristotle's teaching had left its mark on his royal pupil. For whatever reason—a growing shortage of responsible Macedonian commanders and administrators seems the most likely—Alexander dropped his tutor's advice "to deal with the barbarians as with beasts or plants" (fr. 658, Rose); but however much he himself came to modify this intransigent attitude, his officers, notoriously, like most Macedonians, remained unabashed racists, and the whole acquisitive thrust of Panhellenism will have reinforced such an attitude. If Alexander, thrifty in his personal habits, merely sought the whole of Asia as spear-won territory to enhance his fame (*kleos*), the troops he led were avid for riches and booty. The expedition was not only an act of colonial exploitation on a hitherto inconceivable scale: it combined Panhellenism and Aristotle's notions of the Barbarian to justify such exploitation as a way of life. For Macedonians, from the lowest individual braggart soldier to successive Ptolemaic and Seleucid monarchs, Egypt and Asia were there, ultimately, to be squeezed of their wealth, de haut en bas, by the victors.

This fact should always be borne in mind when we come to consider the wholly unintended consequences of Alexander's invasion. Perhaps the most difficult to assess is its economic impact. As we have seen, Alexander's own notions in this area were not all that far from those of a Homeric hero or pirate (the two being often barely distinguishable). He financed his expedition (and artificially postponed his troops' ultimate refusal to go farther) by commandeering the accumulated contents of Persia's several treasuries, to the tune of at least 180,000 talents. This vast sum (worth nearly a hundred billion dollars, at a minimum guess, in modern currency) was rapidly dissipated, not only on day-to-day military expenses (in which the funding of increasing numbers of mercenaries bulked large), but as lavish payoffs, retirement donations, and what amounted to plain bribes. The injection of all this specie into the Asiatic and (to a lesser extent) the Mediterranean economy drove the gold-to-silver ratio—not surprisingly—down from 1:13 to 1:10. It has also been estimated that it halved the value of both in relation to the now increasingly popular copper-alloy small-currency issues.

Yet overall the effect seems to have been far less dramatic, and in ways more beneficial, than might at first sight have been expected. Prices, indeed, remained comparatively steady throughout the fourth and third centuries. Here the Persian practice of melting down surplus tribute bullion into ingots and keeping it largely out of circulation, in a Fort Knox policy unrelieved by any sort of recognizable credit system, in fact caused more financial trouble than Alexander's depredations. Progressive draining of the empire's gold and silver reserves had led to chronic inflation and spiraling prices. Comparing the Achaemenids' theoretical annual tribute (14,560 Euboic talents) with the amount that the Macedonians removed from the imperial treasuries makes it clear that by the mid–fourth century, much more of this annual tribute was being returned, one way or another, to circulation. But Alexander's openhanded onetime infusion of ready cash into the market, combined with a vast influx of colonists, merchants, and adventurers of every sort into Egypt and Asia under the early Successors, cannot have failed to stimulate trade. One of the most remarkable symptoms of this is what Davies (in Bugh, 2006, 90) rightly describes as "the vertiginous rise in maritime traffic."

It is also true, and important, that by setting up mints and imposing the Attic 17.2-gram tetradrachm as his currency standard throughout the conquered territories, Alexander in effect created a monetary common market. Yet we should not assume, as has sometimes been done, either that it was he who first monetized Asia or that the new system ousted all others. The Persians had long been coining their own currency (shekels, darics) as well as using Greek issues, while various moneyless systems, by barter or warehousing, remained widespread throughout the empire. Again, we have to remember Macedonian priorities. When they took over a region, they seldom changed the financial or administrative system in place: they simply put in top officials to ensure that the existing tribute and taxes were now channeled primarily to *them*. What went on below that level did not much concern them.

Thus, to what at first may seem a surprising extent, little changed. Local food production, both arable and animal, was (as always) paramount, in the hands of subsistence farmers who seldom moved far from their farms (till very recently, this remained true of the Mediterranean world and to some extent still is). These smallholders used cash only either to buy what they could not produce (for instance, pottery, knives, agricultural tools), as a hedge against bad harvests, or to pay fixed taxes (those calculated on the basis of income could often be avoided by a communal barter system). The result, in the Hellenistic kingdoms, was a bewildering variety (especially in Asia) of local practices, above which we find a middle-level bureaucracy responsible for extracting the maximum possible amount of income for the royal fisc, whether by tax-farming or direct levies.

There is a very good reason for this state of affairs, which has more to do with social prejudice than with economic realities. From Homer to Plato and beyond, farming one's own land was the most acceptable mode of moneymaking for a gentleman, and inheriting wealth or property was even better. Soiling one's hands with commerce was unthinkable: leave that to the *metics* (resident aliens). All manual labor and trade was despised as "banausic," a term originally meaning "to do with handicrafts" but soon equated with anything lower-class, common, or in bad taste. This last was precisely how Aristotle characterized any practical study of methods of acquisition. The notion permeates Greek society: Athenian democracy never killed it, and the Hellenistic reversion to authoritarianism found it highly congenial. It even affected the sciences: Euclid and Archimedes regarded the application of theory to practical or, worse, profitable ends with withering contempt and would have nothing to do with it: it took the Roman siege of Syracuse in 212 to make Archimedes turn his mind to the problem of defense artillery.

We now see why Greek economics so signally fails to match the extraordinary achievements made in other areas, from mathematics to astronomy. By considering themselves above such demeaning matters as getting and spending, the best brains of the age not only remained in profound ignorance of how these processes actually operated, but were happy to explain them, as good philosophers, in purely moral terms. Why, asked Isocrates (8.117–119), do the Megarians, with no good harbors, mines, or fertile lands, own the most splendid houses in Greece? His answer says nothing about their manufacture of cheap woolen goods or their profitable carrying trade. No, their success is due entirely to self-control and prudent moderation (*sôphrosynê*)! Similarly with the generous response from almost every Mediterranean power to the disastrous earthquake in 228/7 that flattened Rhodes and brought down the Colossus. The notion that this generosity might be due to the fact that the superb Rhodian navy prevented Mediterranean piracy, that Rhodes itself acted as a useful free agent and exchange center between the major powers, does not occur to Polybius, who tells the story (5.88.4). For him the huge handouts are a direct reaction to the stoic dignity and restraint of the Rhodian envoys when soliciting aid.

To a quite remarkable extent, then, the leading rulers of the early Hellenistic years were trying to come to terms with new international realities while still thinking—insofar as they consciously considered the problem at all—in terms of what remained, for Macedonians especially, a heroic-age economy. A growing appetite for affluence in the upper social stratum of society did not bring any real sophistication as regards the most effective way of gratifying such tastes. Besides, Alexander's invasion had underlined the advantages to be got from that other traditionally sanctioned mode of self-enrichment: warfare. In other words, rather than produce goods yourself, acquire by main force the products of others. Rulers still relied on the spoils of victory as a regular source of income as well as prestige. The conquest of the Achaemenid empire significantly extended this concept. A late-fourth-century treatise, the *Pseudo-Oeconomica*, ascribed by error to Aristotle, gives various instances of how capital was raised: by raiding temple treasures, by taking bribes from both sides during arbitration, by fraudulent currency deals, by monopolizing the grain-trade, by raising special taxes on defense work that was never carried out.[3] All of these deals are in fact forms of theft. For Macedonian administrators in particular, the notion of spoliation had become endemic.

———

"The Hellenistic states had their origin on the battlefield," Yvon Garlan emphasizes, "and that is where they met their doom."[4] Throughout the three centuries of their existence, warfare was continuous and ubiquitous, the main, and often the exclusive, topic of contemporary historians. Polybius saw the Mediterranean as a single battlefield. We think first of conflicts between the great Hellenistic kingdoms, and these indeed seldom ceased: military rivals for spear-won territory have to keep their spears ready and sharp. But at a lower level, the picture is the same. We find endless local conflicts between cities—most often over disputed territory, though unprovoked sacking and plundering (for instance, by the Aetolians) were far from uncommon. There were also frequent small but vicious civil wars, revolts by subjugated native inhabitants or discharged mercenaries (these last often unwillingly settled in remote regions), and unpredictable incursions by northern barbarian tribes. Armed conflict was not only the primary means of resolving differences, but the source of royal mystique and, more to the point, of royal income, whether through taxation, the ransoming of captives, or the acquisition of profitable new territories, such as forests for shipbuilding.

Ancient, like modern, warfare also tended to boost the economy by creating a greater need for goods and services. The vast numbers of mercenaries, predominantly Greek, that were now employed had to be paid, and spent their pay lavishly wherever they happened to be quartered. Though they became the butts of comic poets for their macho posturing, rowdy conduct, and drunkenness, it was often their settlements, ironically enough, that brought Greek lifestyles, gymnasia, and religious cults to the Asiatic outback. An enormous amount of the Successors' funds was also diverted into researching and creating new and more efficient siege equipment: artillery that included torsion catapults to project arrows, stone balls, or incendiary projectiles; huge wheeled towers with swing bridges; and suspended battering rams. Yet these apart, the era saw singularly little real advance in military effectiveness till the Romans appeared on the scene. A Ptolemaic phase of gigantism in naval architecture—rows of oarsmen rising from four or five to twenty and more as the motive force for increasingly unwieldy vessels—got nowhere, and navies soon reverted to triremes and quadriremes.

———

When we consider the social impact produced on the "inhabited world" (*oikoumenê*) by all these far-reaching changes, the first and most obvious conclusion is that it made an enormous difference who you were and where precisely—that is, under what kind of regime—you lived. Most of the indigenous peoples of Asia, or the Egyptian fellahin, cared very little who, many hundreds of miles away, was their new overlord: they simply wanted to be left alone to get on with their lives. Even the Jews were glad enough to cooperate with any Seleucid government that respected their stringent religious requirements. The Greek merchants, soldiers of fortune, and other adventurers who flocked to Egypt and Asia Minor under the Macedonian umbrella shared their masters' appetite for rich pickings. Most interesting, and not surprisingly best documented, are the reactions of educated Greeks: both those who made careers as writers, scholars, or administrators at the courts of rulers such as Ptolemy II or Antigonus Gonatas and those who chose to remain in one of the old city-states, Athens above all, where lack of ultimate political freedom was offset—for those with the incomes and connections—by numerous new luxuries and civic amenities.

It might be supposed that Athenians nostalgic for the lost glories of fifth-century art and the spoils of empire would differ sharply in their attitudes from those poets and scholars gathered by the early Ptolemies to staff the great new Alexandrian Museum and Library; but at least in one respect their take on their heritage was identical. Both looked to the past as the only viable basis from which to face the future. In this, oddly, they resembled Alexander, whose quest for the world's end, far from being treated as pioneering exploration, always affected to be following in the footsteps of mythical predecessors: first Heracles and then, in India, Dionysus.

The major preparatory task of the Library's academic staff—a task never in fact totally completed and one that continued long after the Renaissance—was the retrieval, classification, and editing of what we now term the archaic and classical literary heritage, from Homer to the great tragedians, a high proportion of which had been generated in Athens. (As a result, for us the social impact of Alexander and his successors is—despite epigraphic, archaeological, and numismatic evidence—inextricably bound up with the literary record.) To this obstinate trend we largely owe the ultimate survival of that small percentage of ancient Greek literature that we possess today.

What gave the obsession such force is harder to explain. One possible answer is the absence, often remarked on, of any body of scripture that could be appealed to for moral precedent. If Homer was treated as the "bible of the Greeks," it was faute de mieux. Hence, too, the extraordinary spread of ethical theories among rival philosophical creeds. Yet it is also hard to escape the impression (unpopular among classicists today) of a widespread ancient belief that with the close of the classical era, a sense of creative direction and purpose was lost that, try as they might, the Greeks never quite succeeded in recovering.

Nor should we forget that the new Greek emigrants—of Alexandria in particular—had, like the Alexandrian Jews who translated the Pentateuch, been cut off from their ethnic roots. The heritage that the Library's savants strove to retrieve was already subtly alien to them, and not merely because of the passage of time. This may hint at the reason for a well-known literary paradox: while they were the first, as critics, to formulate rules for the various genres they analyzed, they were also at the same time the first, as poets, to break those rules wholesale in the pursuit of novelty. Tradition and innovation, past and future, were to fuse in a precarious, but at times brilliant, tension of opposites.[5]

Thinkers like Aristotle and Theophrastus lost no time in adapting their classificatory systems to literary uses. Theophrastus' *Characters,* which applied the technique to supposed generic types of human beings, may even have been a sly parody. Aristotle's *Poetics*—no parody, though at times one wishes it were—already shows its distance from the phenomenon, old Attic tragedy, that he is discussing. Creativity has given way to formalized critical analysis, based on the evidence of a past record that, it becomes all too clear, is not expected to change. The principles of Sophocles' *Oedipus* are being set in stone.

Furthermore, in picking on Attic tragedy for his experiment, Aristotle pointed the way for the Library's researchers, not only as regards drama, but also when dealing with a genre such as lyric (already near the end of its original creative run in the fifth century, except for the vague and hence infinitely adaptable dithyramb). Thus Pindar was classified by "forms" (*eidê*) into odes (victory or other), hymns, dithyrambs, and so on. Sappho, on the other hand, yielded only one formal genre, the wedding hymn, but otherwise baffled the classifiers on form and function and so was organized alphabetically or by metres. The categories established by Hellenistic scholars tell us a lot about their mental world. In many ways, they reveal a widening gap between a genre's original social context and the assumptions of its Alexandrian interpreters. How far the latter were conscious of this gap, and used innovative variations to bridge it, remains debatable.

Equally debatable, though to me highly plausible, is the thesis that sees major discernible changes in the various literary genres as for the most part occasioned indirectly by the sweeping historical events described in my first two chapters. Not all of these were due to Alexander, though his career undoubtedly accelerated them. The most all-pervasive, the shift of emphasis away from public collective involvement in the affairs of the polis to private and individual concerns, had, as we have seen, already got well under way by the start of the fourth century. Aristophanes' last surviving play, the *Plutus* (*Wealth*, 388), with its resourceful slave and attenuated chorus, foreshadows the Hellenistic New Comedy of Menander. In newly subject cities like Athens, Pericles' despised private individual (*idiôtes*, hence our "idiot") has come into his own. He is encouraged to make money rather than fight. His Macedonian overlord is more likely to hire mercenaries to defend the city than to call on its citizen militia. Collaboration is profitable. There is still, and will always be, a nucleus of patriots ready to fight for freedom against heavy odds (one reason the overlord mistrusts citizen levies), but a quiet private life looks increasingly attractive to the well-heeled upper classes. The plays of Menander, with their lost-and-found situations, rich dowries, and comforting platitudinous aphorisms, reflect this world with disconcerting accuracy. Piracy, brigandage, and braggart mercenaries, besides providing plots, hint at the endless warfare and near-anarchy going on in the real world outside. At the same time, escapism is rampant: virginities are miraculously preserved, the lost are found, dowries materialize, everything comes out right in the end.

The *idiôtes* may or may not reflect on the degree to which Euripides, and the new individualism in the visual arts, has fostered his self-conscious concern with his own emotions. But the benefits of international trade will soften him: politically, he will be loath to rock the boat or prejudice his investments. Beneficent oligarchy will begin to look increasingly attractive when it comes to local government. Philosophically, negative ideals attract: *ataraxia,* undisturbedness; *alypia,* avoidance of grief; *akataplêxia,* absence of upset. *Apathia* lurks in the background. Removed from this world, yet in pursuit of the same heritage, are the subsidized intellectual establishments of the Successors, at Pergamon, Pella, and Antioch and, above all, in the Museum and Library of Alexandria.

Prior to Ptolemy II's groundbreaking venture, advised by Demetrius of Phaleron, Cassander's former governor of Athens, the whole idea of a public library had been virtually nonexistent, and even private collections of books were uncommon (in this, as in so much else, Aristotle was a pioneer). But here the times were propitious. The slow shift from oral to written as the basic mode of communication, already incipient by the end of the fifth century, was given a tremendous boost by Alexander's opening up of the East, and Alexandria was perfectly placed as both a mercantile and an intellectual center. It is interesting to speculate on this new relationship between individualism and reading. Which first stimulated the other? Reading, an essentially solitary practice, surely encouraged the *idiôtes;* yet the individual mind, in turn, must have fostered the development of a medium unconnected with public occasion and collective performance. A growing civic bureaucracy had indirect consequences of which its officials never dreamed.

The Library's declared function of cultural retrieval also revealed Ptolemy's ambition. Just as the hijacking of Alexander's embalmed corpse had aimed to legitimize his rule, so the collection and classification of all Greek texts was a bid to make his capital the guardian and controlling center of the Hellenic heritage. Alexandria was to be the new Athens, Pericles' famous "education of Hellas." Athenians had called Macedonians barbarians. Now they must acknowledge the so-called barbarians as not only their military, but also their cultural superiors. In more than one sense, knowledge is power: that appropriation brought control was a lesson most of the Successors had learned the hard way. But what was won must—like Alexander's body—be the real thing. When Ptolemy's grandson Euergetes I refused to return the master copies of the three great Athenian tragedians that he had borrowed and sent copies back to Athens instead, he knew exactly what he was doing. That his act—like the moneymaking devices in the *Pseudo-Oeconomica*—was blatant daylight robbery remained immaterial.

———

Ptolemaic Egypt enjoyed two incomparable advantages: a geographic environment that offered excellent natural protection against attack; and accumulated pharaonic wealth so great that when Octavian finally laid hands on it in 30 BCE, even after three centuries of expensive wars and untrammeled royal self-indulgence, the standard interest rate in Rome at once dropped from 12 to 4 percent. No accident that the Ptolemaic dynasty outlasted all its rivals. If all else failed, a Ptolemaic king—modern parallels suggest themselves—could nearly always buy his way out of trouble. The court in Alexandria was famous for its opulence and generosity. The Museum and Library, like the J. Paul Getty Center (which in many ways they much resemble), never seem to have had payroll problems, and their resident scholars enjoyed permanent appointments. Research in most branches of learning, from history to astronomy, from medicine to mathematics, was amply funded. As a result, the city became a magnet for poets and intellectuals from all over the Mediterranean.

There was, of course, a price to pay. Scientific research tended to be directed into military fields (for instance, the improvement of siege artillery), while the scholar-poets were expected to tailor traditional genres, primarily the encomium, in new ways to proclaim the glories of the regime that underwrote them. Much of the Hellenistic literature that we possess, in part or whole, falls one way or another into this last category; most of it is also Alexandrian. Though we need to exercise caution in drawing general conclusions—what survives is no more than a tiny fragment of the whole—it does look as though Alexandria indeed led the field in the third century, just as Athens had done in the fifth. Conditions were certainly propitious.

What primarily strikes us from a survey of the surviving Alexandrian authors—Theocritus, Herodas, Callimachus, Apollonius Rhodius—is the degree to which, in a very short time, upper-class society has become urbanized. Theocritus, indeed, presents a virtually new genre, the pastoral or bucolic idyll, a sanitized and idealized version of country matters calculated to appeal to city-based intellectuals and others hankering after the simple life but disinclined to face its harsh realities.

In these poems the sun is always shining, and the flocks can seemingly take care of themselves. Mixed in with the rustic piping and elegantly bawdy peasant banter is much enthusiastic flattery of Ptolemy: so kind, so generous, so civilized—but also a powerful general and a reliable paymaster, whose incestuous marriage to his sister Arsinoë is legitimized, and equated, by skillful allusion, to that of Zeus and Hera. In the last resort, he who paid the piper also called the tune.

What we have here is court poetry; and court poetry implies a special, limited, well-read, class-conscious audience, its place in the social and financial sun contingent on its unqualified and active support for the current regime. (Theocritus' Idyll 15, with its vivid snapshots of Alexandrian street life, manages both to flatter Arsinoë for the quality of the concerts she sponsors and to mock the provincials who attend them.) It is essentially city-based. In Alexandria, its art and literature reveal not only an urban hankering after pastoral fantasy, but an equally unreal de haut en bas penchant for Alexandrian low life: dwarfs, drunks, cripples, brothel-keepers, bawds, cobblers with a flourishing trade in under-the-counter dildos for bored housewives (as in the *Mimes* of Herodas). The sculpture is self-referential, the concern with myth dwells on the erotic (Leda and the swan). What remains significant is the *need* for myth, even in an ultracynical upper-class generation brought up on the antitheological logic chopping of the Sophists. At the very top intellectual level of Alexandrian poetry, with Callimachus and Apollonius Rhodius, we are never far from a recurrent obsession with *aitia*—causes, roots, origins, the why and how of lovingly retrieved ancient customs.

Nothing more vividly conveys the paradoxical tensions of Alexandria—this new world still in so many ways inextricably wedded to the old—than Apollonius' *Argonautica.* Here was an epic retelling, in not quite Homeric hexameters, of the myth that took Jason to Colchis, at the farthest eastern reaches of the Black Sea, in quest of the Golden Fleece and brought about the famous, and tragic, love match between him and the Colchian king Aeëtes' daughter Medea. That Apollonius tried epic at all was remarkable. Conventional wisdom agreed that the genre was passé, that Homer had said it all, that huge sprawling poems were out (so Callimachus: "Big book, big mistake") and elegant miniaturism was the ideal. In ways Apollonius surely agreed: his hero is no Achilles, but a nervous Everyman whose one real talent (sex again) is bedding women and who triumphs in the test Aeëtes sets him only after being magically tefloned by his inamorata. The Greek text of the *Argonautica* is loaded with smart neologisms, littered with recondite *aitia*, and reveals a weakness for sly intertextual jokes.

Yet, astonishingly, Apollonius makes no effort whatsoever to rationalize the traditional narrative. Sea-traffic had long been threading the Bosporus, but Jason and his crew still have to deal with the Clashing Rocks. Aeëtes can still muster his fire-breathing brazen oxen, and Medea still knows a magical *pharmakon* that will immunize Jason against them. Dragon's teeth planted still spring up as armed men. Apollonius' Heracles, too big in every sense, is treated as a joke and dumped in mid-narrative, but otherwise this Everyman has to cope with the demands of a mythical world. His incendiary relationship with Medea gives Apollonius a chance to exploit, superbly, the Hellenistic fascination with the psychopathology of erotic passion, as Virgil knew well when he came to draw Dido, but there remains a slightly more than human aura about her, as there does about the Fleece itself. Amid the upheavals of the early Hellenistic world, one constant factor emerges clearly: in Alexandria as in Athens, and under whatever kind of regime, the demand for ancient mythic—and, as we have seen, religious—roots remained paramount.

———

Perhaps no change in knowledge due to Alexander's expedition was so fundamental—or, for Alexander himself, so dearly bought—as the refutation of several fantasies regarding the basic geography of the known world. It was not all that long since the Ionians had held that the earth was a flat disk surrounded by Ocean. Aristotle's generation had, correctly, replaced the disk by a sphere but still retained much of the old thinking. Greeks had—have—an ingrained tendency to think of themselves as occupying the center of the world, whatever its shape. Anything outside the western Mediterranean, or the more central satrapies of Cyrus' Achaemenid empire in the east, was still largely terra incognita, visualized, as always with the unknown, in mythic terms and increasingly fabulous toward its oceanic perimeter. Northern and southern zones were held, despite Herodotus' skepticism, to be symmetrical mirror images of each other: thus the Nile was somehow a septentrional version of the Danube. About northern Europe, China, most of India, and all Africa south of the Sudan (despite a famous Phoenician circumnavigation of that continent, later disbelieved),[6] ignorance remained profound.

When Alexander set out to conquer Asia, he was as much a victim of current geographic theories as anyone. (Some of these he persisted in till his dying day—for instance, the notion that Africa was part of Asia rather than an independent continent.) Imagined symmetries and interconnections, chiefly of mountain ranges and rivers—the Taurus and the Hindu Kush, the Nile and the Indus—led him to grossly underestimate distances in the unexplored world. The bematists, a group of specialists who recorded the ground actually covered by the army on the march, continually had to correct his, and Aristotle's, estimates. Almost all the existing information about major rivers east of Ecbatana proved hopelessly wrong.

Worst of all, the eastern shore of circumambient Ocean—in a very real sense the world's end that Alexander had made up his mind to reach—was, as Herodotus again had suspected, a fiction. Aristotle claimed it was visible from the summit of the Hindu Kush.[7] It was not. Somehow, again and again, Alexander talked his troops into going on. Finally, at the Beas river local informants reported ahead not Ocean, but innumerable war-elephants and an interminable desert plain. The Macedonians, already exhausted by three monsoons and the indescribably bloody battle of the Jhelum river, mutinied. Ironically, what finally stopped Alexander was no living enemy but a geographic legend: one myth defeating another.

4

EASTERN HORIZONS AND THE CLOUD IN THE WEST

(276 - 196)

Though the wars of the Successors were at last over, the regimes that ensued could not be said, by any stretch of the imagination, to have ushered in a new era of peace. The Ptolemies' praise-singers might extol their masters' godlike virtues, but not, as Virgil with Augustus, for having put an end to a half-century of debilitating conflict. What a diplomat might euphemistically term "the adjustment of frontiers" kept these ambitious new dynasts and their (mostly hired) armies very busy indeed. Ptolemy II, sole king after his father's death in 283, cut loose from the policy of limited empire he had inherited and not only pushed north in Syria, but picked up cities and islands (Samos, Miletus, Halicarnassus) in the eastern Aegean and most of what is now the Turkish Riviera (Caria, Lycia, Cilicia) at the expense of the Seleucid Antiochus I. If he was merely establishing (as has been suggested) an outer defensive perimeter for Egypt, together with controllable sources of essential imports, he had a decidedly aggressive way of going about it. How far this was due to his vigorous sister-wife, Arsinoë, still game after disastrous marriages to Lysimachus (p. 39) and her half-brother, Ptolemy Keraunos (p. 40), remains an open question: in any case, by 270, after duly adopting the heir to the throne, she was dead and divinized.

Distracted by uprisings and fresh Celtic incursions, Antiochus was hard-pressed to keep control over his now vast and unwieldy Seleucid domains. In 278, he had made a non-aggression pact with Antigonus Gonatas, based on the traditional dividing-line between Europe and Asia; but a year or two later (275/4), Gonatas ceased to be a problem for a while, since his old nemesis Pyrrhus of Epirus (who had been away in Sicily and south Italy as, in effect, a hired mercenary captain) reappeared in Macedonia and drove him out once more. Thrashed by the Romans at Beneventum in 275, Pyrrhus figured the Antigonid throne would prove an easier mark. At first it looked as though he was right: he claimed the crown and was endorsed by Athens (the Macedonian garrison in Piraeus was not popular). But then he made the mistake of marching on the Peloponnese to liberate it from Antigonid rule. While he was away, Gonatas handily reconquered Macedonia, and during street fighting in Argos (fall 272), Pyrrhus was knocked unconscious by a tile an old woman threw at him from a rooftop and then decapitated.

When presented with his severed head, Gonatas expressed sorrow but must have felt considerable relief. From now on until his death in 239, his Macedonian regime and de facto authority over the rest of Greece remained, if not unchallenged, at least secure. The new Aetolian and Achaean leagues, no less than Athens and Sparta, resented his overlordship. But while he held key sites like the great rock of Acrocorinth, and maintained garrisons there and at other crucial points such as Chalcis and Demetrias (known, with good reason, as "the fetters of Greece"), his position was safe. When, in the early 260s, Athens and Sparta, with Ptolemaic support, launched the revolt known (after Chremonides, its official Athenian advocate) as the Chremonidean War, Gonatas had little trouble in holding and defeating the Spartans near Corinth, putting Athens under siege, and, more surprisingly, scoring a decisive victory over Ptolemy at sea off Cos. With the blockade of Piraeus thus unbroken, the Athenians were starved into surrender (? 261). The city lost the right to elect its own magistrates and passed under the control of Macedonian officials.

Yet despite his record of tough dealing, Gonatas was by no means unpopular among the Greek educated classes. His Stoic training left its mark on him. His court at Pella included the astronomer-poet Aratus of Soli and Hieronymus of Cardia, the soldier, scholar, and diplomat who had served Gonatas' father and grandfather and now in his old age composed a major history of the wars of the Successors that would appear (not surprisingly) to have favored Antigonus One-Eye as much as Ptolemy I's memoirs did their author. It was not long, either (245/4), before the usual propertied moderates—a group whose history made it more than clear that with them indeed nothing succeeded like success—began offering Gonatas honorific sacrifices, undeterred by his sardonic take on deification (p. 50). He was now, at last, the acknowledged master of Greece. What is more, even after his death, Antigonid power was, if anything, consolidated. When Gonatas' son Demetrius II was killed fighting the Dardanians (229), leaving an heir (the future Philip V) only nine years old, the boy's guardian (Demetrius' cousin Antigonus Doson) stepped in as monarch pro tem and handed over power to Philip without any trouble after an eight-year reign.

It is not always appreciated, given the nature of the Hellenistic dynasties, just how remarkable an achievement this was. As Sheila Agar remarks, and the genealogical tables amply confirm, "[By] the time two generations had passed, all the rulers of the Successor kingdoms were related to one another,"[1] in this much resembling the royal families of pre-1914 Europe and, like them, never letting mere consanguinity get in the way of dynastic ambition. When Antiochus I died (261), he left his designated successor, Antiochus II—co-regent since 266, vice an executed elder brother—problems and to spare. The threat of secession was everywhere: Bactria, Sogdiana, Parthia, Pontus, Bithynia, and Cappadocia were all moving toward independence from the eastern empire. Nearer home, Eumenes of Pergamon (a dedicated patron of Athens' philosophy schools) handily defeated a Seleucid force sent to whip him into line. Though he still refused the title of king, Pergamon had been effectively lost to the Seleucid empire long before. Indeed, until the accession of Antiochus III ("the Great") in 223, the frontiers established by Seleucus I had been steadily shrinking almost everywhere.

Yet nothing, it is safe to say, caused Antiochus and his successors more trouble than the festering, never fully resolved conflict with the Ptolemies over disputed territories: primarily in Coele-Syria around the then timber-rich Bekaa Valley (hence the title of "Syrian Wars" given to these confrontations), but also in Cyrene and western Asia Minor. The First Syrian War (274/3–271), a largely successful move by Ptolemy II to expand his position in the Aegean and the eastern Mediterranean, we have already noted (p. 67). The Second (260–253), for which we have a bare minimum of evidence, was Antiochus II's attempt—covertly supported by his uncle Antigonus Gonatas, with whom he had a concordat—to reverse the first. This, up to a point, he did. Cyrene revolted; Antiochus regained Miletus and Ephesus (and was rewarded with the title of "Theos"). Ptolemy meanwhile lost ground in Pamphylia and Cilicia and by 253 was glad enough to make peace. The peace was cemented, characteristically, by a dynastic alliance. Antiochus married Ptolemy's daughter Berenice Syra and got an "enormous dowry" with her: probably the revenues of Coele-Syria, a principal bone of contention between the two monarchs.

Unfortunately, in order to wed Berenice, Antiochus had first to get rid of his existing wife, Laodice, on whom he had already sired at least five children, three of them sons. Remarriage in the circumstances was a sure recipe for dynastic disaster, especially since Berenice promptly bore him a son, too. To complicate matters, in 246 both Ptolemy and Antiochus died (the latter allegedly poisoned by Laodice). In Alexandria, Arsinoë's son succeeded without trouble as Ptolemy III Euergetes. In Antioch, the two queen mothers went at it. Laodice claimed that Antiochus had named their son Seleucus as heir on his deathbed. Berenice argued that Laodice's repudiation disqualified all her offspring from the succession. She also, with good reason, sent an urgent appeal to her brother, the new king in Egypt. Ptolemy marched on Antioch (to a rapturous welcome by the mob, he afterward claimed) and occupied it, but too late: both Berenice and her son had already been assassinated by Laodice's agents.

As a result, the Third Syrian (or "Laodicean") War got under way and dragged on until 241, during which time Ptolemy III and Laodice's son (now enthroned as Seleucus II Kallinikos) campaigned a good deal, but mostly not against each other. Seleucus was busy in Asia Minor. Ptolemy meanwhile secured Antioch's port of Seleucia-in-Pieria (his one undisputed achievement during this war) and put out a barrage of propaganda claiming to have made a kind of triumphal progress through the Seleucid empire without needing to strike a blow.

Whatever the truth behind these inflated claims (he is unlikely to have got farther than Babylon, if so far), the gains were mostly transient and due largely to the fact that Seleucus was, for the moment, otherwise occupied. His teenage brother, Antiochus Hierax, the well-named "Hawk," whose appetite for power was notable even by Hellenistic standards, had set himself up as an independent sovereign north of the Taurus Mountains, and it took Seleucus, aided by Attalus of Pergamon, six years to eliminate him (he was finally murdered by Gauls in Thrace). Ptolemy himself had to get back home. His absence had prompted a native Egyptian uprising and encouraged Antigonus Gonatas both to step up his naval campaign in the Aegean (where he once more defeated a Ptolemaic fleet, off Andros) and to meddle in the dynastic affairs of Cyrene.

The Cyrene affair, like so much to do with the Ptolemies, is pure dynastic soap-opera. Cyrene's governor Magas (Ptolemy II's half-brother) had declared independence. On the other hand, he betrothed his daughter Berenice to Ptolemy III, with the idea of reuniting Cyrene and Egypt after his death. However, when this took place (he allegedly choked to death as the result of gross obesity), his wife, Apame (Antiochus I's daughter), who had come to enjoy being queen of a small kingdom, backed Gonatas' alternative suggestion for Berenice's husband: his Macedonian half-brother, Demetrius, a matinee idol known as "the Fair." The prior engagement was annulled; the new marriage took place (250).

Demetrius styled himself king of Cyrene. He also obligingly bedded his royal mother-in-law, Apame. Berenice—not a lady to trifle with—had her adulterous husband executed while in the act, spared her mother, and in due course married Ptolemy III after all (246), thus returning Cyrene to Egypt's control and acquiring a famous reputation, as Berenice II, for wifely virtue. (She also raced chariot-teams and was a noted equestrienne.) It was while he was actually on honeymoon with her that Ptolemy III received the frantic appeal from his sister—the Syrian Berenice—in Antioch. His bride, again famously, dedicated a lock of her hair for his safe return. The lock mysteriously vanished, Conon the astronomer claimed it had been elevated to the heavens as the Coma Berenices, and Callimachus wrote a famous poem about it, which Catullus in due course translated.[2] This inextricable blend of sex, myth, literature, and power politics offers valuable clues in understanding the nature of court society as it evolved during the third century.

———

In mainland Greece, the uneasy tension between local autonomy and Macedonian overlordship continued, further complicated by the Ptolemies' hostility to Antigonid expansion in the Aegean, which led to their supporting, with cash subventions and, on occasion, naval backup, any state with a record of anti-Macedonian activity. This meant, first and foremost, the new Aetolian and Achaean federations. The Aetolians now controlled most of central Greece; the Achaeans, under their powerful general Aratus of Sicyon, had in 243 captured the great hilltop fortress of Acrocorinth in the northern Peloponnese. (That same year, the Achaeans named Ptolemy III their honorary commander in chief, presumably in acknowledgment of the 175 talents he had earlier given them.) Antigonus Gonatas' control over Greece was substantially weakened as a result. Though Gonatas made peace with Aratus in 241, after his death two years later his son and heir, Demetrius II, spent most of his decade-long reign fighting the Achaeans and Aetolians.

A new and highly disruptive factor in these interstate relationships was the unlooked-for resurgence of Sparta under two ambitious and idealistic kings, Agis IV (244–1) and Cleomenes III (235–222). Faced with the abandonment of the traditional military training program (*agôgê*), a diminished citizen birthrate, widespread debt, and the consequent absorption of estates into ever-fewer hands, Agis set out to restore the old Lycurgan regime. His forceful methods (exiling his fellow-king Leonidas and eliminating the ephors, Sparta's elected civil magistrates) led to a countercoup by Leonidas and the wealthy minority, whom Agis had thoroughly scared with his talk of debt cancellation and the redistribution of land, those two perennial bugbears of landowners throughout antiquity. Agis was tried, condemned, and executed in short order. But the problems remained, and a few years later Cleomenes—who had taken on his predecessor's widow along with his aims—came a good deal nearer to solving them.

There is something deeply ironic about the fact that many at the time (and, less excusably, more than one modern scholar) became convinced that what Agis and Cleomenes were advocating was radical social revolution. Talk of the reallotment of estates and writing off of debts, the emergency freeing—or even the enfranchisement—of helots, was misleading. Their central aim in fact was both elitist and (something that by now should cause no surprise) an attempt to revive and revitalize past glories, the ancient régime at its zenith, before Sparta's humiliating defeat at Leuctra (371) had destroyed Lacedaemonian military and political supremacy forever. Cleomenes' hope was to bring back the old warrior class, the so-called "Equals" (*homoioi*), and with them recover Sparta's dominant role in the Aegean. This meant restoring the *agôgê*, providing proper holdings (*klaroi*) for the support of the *homoioi*, and getting rid of the crippling burden of debt that had disqualified so many from warrior status in the first place. About the birthrate there was little that could be done. Enrolling carefully picked non-Spartans from the frontier towns was possible but carried considerable risks.

It is not hard to imagine how this program could be misinterpreted by outsiders; on the other hand, the few (perhaps not more than a hundred, including a number of powerful women) who had profited by Sparta's agrarian troubles to become wealthy property-owners saw exactly how they would inevitably be weakened, and very possibly expropriated, by its implementation. Hence the ruthless elimination of Agis. Also, since both he and Cleomenes were forced to carry out draconian and frequently illegal measures to get anything done at all, the opposition always could, and did, play on the ubiquitous fear, endemic among the Greek upper classes, of agrarian revolution.

From 229 on, Cleomenes realized their worst fears. Primed by military success against Megalopolis (Messenia's wheat fields looked temptingly within reach again), he did away with the current ephors and abolished their office. Instead of the traditional Council of Elders (*gerousia*), he installed a "paternal legislator" (*patronomos*), whose evocation of Orwell's Big Brother may not be wholly coincidental. Some eighty of the big property-owners were exiled and their estates split up into four thousand *klaroi* (a fair indication of their size). Exiles were recalled, new citizens enrolled. A Stoic philosopher, Sphaerus, was given the job of reactivating the *agôgê*.

Before 227 was out, Cleomenes had made himself sole ruler of Sparta by—as Polybius put it (2.47.3)—turning his legitimate kingship into a tyranny. To Aratus and the Achaean League, Macedonia began to seem a far less threatening enemy than this dangerous autocrat only a few miles to the south of them. Quiet diplomatic discussions were initiated with Antigonus Doson in Pella. These, of course, soon came to the notice of Ptolemy III, with the result that he promptly switched his financial subventions from Aratus to Cleomenes, who was beginning to look a better anti-Macedonian bet all round. With this backing, Cleomenes hired mercenaries (some of whom he put through the *agôgê*, thus providing himself with a trained personal bodyguard), beefed up his military equipment, and launched an alarmingly successful campaign in the northern Peloponnese. The price he had to pay was the surrender to Ptolemy (who clearly trusted him no farther than he could see him) of his own mother and children as hostages, a concession that was to stimulate two of Cavafy's best poems.

Faced with Cleomenes' victories in Achaea and the Argolid, and the immediate threat of the loss of Acrocorinth, Aratus, staunch anti-Macedonian though he was, acknowledged the iron hand of Necessity and called in Antigonus Doson to pit the Macedonian phalanx against Cleomenes' Spartan hoplites. Antigonus drove a hard bargain: the return of Acrocorinth—one of the original "Fetters of Greece"—to Macedonian control. Aratus reluctantly agreed: better Macedonia than the Spartans. When Doson arrived at the Isthmus of Corinth with an army of twenty thousand, Cleomenes' support rapidly crumbled, and Ptolemy III abruptly withdrew his funding. Unable to pay his troops, Cleomenes—like Antigonus One-Eye or Lysimachus—staked everything on a single battle, at Sellasia, in 222. He fought desperately but was finally beaten and fled to Alexandria. Ptolemy was sympathetic but died the following year (221); his son Ptolemy IV Philopator proved less accommodating. Cleomenes was killed (219) in a hopeless attempt to raise the Alexandrian mob in revolt, and his mother and children were executed.

Antigonus Doson made a ceremonial entry into unwalled Sparta: the first foreign conqueror to do so in the city's history. The ephorate was restored, but the kingship, for the time being, remained in abeyance. Antigonus treated the Spartans courteously but lost no time in establishing firm Macedonian control once more over all Greece (with the exception of the Aetolians). He had already (224) reconstituted the old Hellenic league—including the Macedonian, Thessalian, Boeotian, Achaean, and Epirot federations—as a united "League of Leagues" under Macedonian control. He had also imposed garrisons on Acrocorinth and elsewhere. Now he appointed a de facto governor of the Peloponnese: Sparta's Lycurgan dreams were over forever. At this point, news of yet another barbarian incursion brought him and his troops back posthaste to Macedonia. Victorious on the battlefield, Antigonus—a hereditary consumptive—suffered a fatal hemorrhage but survived long enough to arrange a smooth succession for the young Philip V.

Thus within two or three years, young and untried monarchs had taken over in all three major dynasties. Seleucus II had died in 226 after a fall from his horse; he was succeeded by his son Seleucus III Soter. Soter was soon (223) murdered (like Perdiccas) by one of his own officers, while on campaign against Attalus of Pergamon. Seleucus' cousin Achaeus, governor of Asia Minor, promptly drove Attalus back to Pergamon, recovering most of the lost Seleucid territories in the process, and had Seleucus' young brother proclaimed king as Antiochus III.

Ptolemy III, as we have seen, was, like Antigonus Doson, dead by the summer of 221. The young Ptolemy IV Philopator had a reputation as a debauchee and womanizer, in sharp contrast with both Philip and Antiochus, who soon proved themselves men of great energy, vision, and determination. (Yet Ptolemy was far from ineffectual: in 217, at Raphia, he soundly defeated Antiochus in yet another round of the Syrian frontier conflict. To do so, it is true, he enrolled and trained twenty thousand Egyptians, who subsequently decided they would be better employed fighting for independence than for the Ptolemies, so that Raphia ultimately was an ambiguous, if not a Pyrrhic, victory.) In any case, Polybius was surely right (1.3.1) to see this moment as a watershed in the history of the Greek-speaking world. Yet the most far-reaching impact—and this he also acknowledged—was to be made by a power that hitherto the Greek world had largely ignored: Rome.

The direct impact of all these events upon the lives of those not immediately involved in them is hard to estimate. Economically, as we have seen, unending warfare created a steady employment market for mercenaries. Royal dynasts, of course, hired on a far wider scale than local rulers such as Cleomenes, who still depended largely on their loyal citizen militia; but even Cleomenes opted for mercenaries insofar as he could afford them. Outside the cities, near-universal subsistence agriculture and herding suffered more from exigent tax collectors and the urban drift of failed smallholders than from forced conscription or actual warfare—except, that is, for those unlucky enough to occupy territory that was regularly fought over by rival armies. In such cases, the destruction of property (including vines and olives, which took long years to mature), the disruption of planting and harvesting, the commandeering of livestock and enforced billeting, all took a fearful toll on local communities. From the Peloponnesian conflict on, such agricultural chaos had become a staple feature of Greek life.

In some cases, the result was depopulation. This, Polybius claims,[3] was exacerbated by a falling birthrate due to the increasing preference for luxury over the responsibilities of marriage and procreation. Though one catches a whiff here of our old friend moral economics (p. 54), the social phenomenon is not unfamiliar and may well have been encouraged by the ever-increasing use of slaves. Why waste money raising children to run your estate when the job can be done just as well, and far cheaper (they thought), by servile labor? As so often with our evidence, it applies here primarily to the upper classes, the moneyed conservatives who supported oligarchic government in Greek cities and formed the backbone of the colonialist minority busy reaping the fruits of empire abroad.

The wars of the Successors produced a vast number of slaves (one obvious source of quick profits), and thus not only did the gap between rich and poor steadily widen, but the *attitude* of haves to have-nots hardened at the same time. If a slave was no more, in Aristotle's notorious formulation (*EN* 1161b, 4), than a "living tool," then he—or, worse, she—could in theory be handled like a tool: worked to the maximum and trashed when worn out, without those considerations applicable to a normal human being. Relatively humane treatment during the early Hellenistic period worsened considerably after Roman intervention: it is only then that we find those eschatological fantasies foreseeing eternal hellfire (or the equivalent) for oppressors in the afterlife. Many of these new slaves, moreover, were educated and responsible citizens, *including Greeks*, who, while they had nothing against "necessary slavery" per se, violently objected to being treated as slaves themselves.

There were several highly significant results. First, the enormous resentment thus generated created among the governing classes a widespread, almost hysterical, fear of insurrection. This fear started early. In Macedonian treaties executed by both Alexander and Demetrius the Besieger with cities of the Hellenic League, we already find what seems to have been a regular clause requiring members to cooperate in suppressing any movement that involved debt cancellation, the redistribution or confiscation of land and other property, or the freeing of slaves to implement such "revolutionary" policies. Despite urbanization, the attitude remains both stubbornly agrarian and amazingly old-fashioned. Nothing here (except the last point) would have been unfamiliar to the Athenian reformer Solon three centuries before. What *would* have surprised him is the veto placed on precisely those measures he himself had implemented to resolve a not dissimilar confrontation between rich and poor. The hardening of attitude on the part of those in power is symptomatic. By Isocrates' day, Solon's emergency measures had come to be seen as precursors of social anarchy. The public alarm at Cleomenes' activities—above all when he began selling helots their freedom—was predictable.

Slaves were thus regarded as at once essential and a permanent threat. The solution, a simple one, was to keep them fully occupied: the old adage about Satan finding work for idle hands has a long history. In the first instance, this meant physical labor at every level. The consequence—though perhaps no one ever thought of it in quite those terms—was to give slaves and beasts of burden (horses, oxen, donkeys, mules) a monopoly as regards the creation of energy. All power was to be muscle-power. The effect on Hellenistic science was striking. It has often been pointed out that ancient inventors were familiar with steam power (indeed, produced a model) and could make effective pistons yet never combined their knowledge to build a steam-engine. Water-driven mills were known but not used. The same applied to the compound pulley, which enormously reduced the energy needed to shift a given mass. The reason should now be clear. Any device that left the servile labor force with spare energy was seen as a direct stimulus to revolution.

It is hardly surprising, then, that utopias of the period either presuppose the continued existence of slaves to do the physical work or else develop fantasies in which harvests appear unaided, kitchens do their own cooking, dishes wash themselves up, rivers run wine or gravy, fish are self-baked, and ready-roasted birds fly onto one's plate. As Aristotle clearly saw (*Pol.* 1253b, 33 ff.), and as these fantasies so vividly imply, nothing but automation (which itself, of course, meant exploiting new sources of energy) would ever do away with slavery, and the Industrial Revolution was to prove him absolutely right. Slaves remained indispensable. Even the slave revolts in Sicily and Italy (most notably that led by Spartacus in 70 BCE), which—long before America—dreamed of finding somewhere to establish an alternative society, still assumed the existence of slaves to serve the newly emancipated.

We thus need to consider the large and ever-increasing servile population of the Hellenistic world not only (as is usually done) in terms of domestic or agrarian labor, but as virtually the sole source of energy. In this it has obvious parallels with oil today and, indeed, as an essential commodity attracted precisely the same kind of mercantile entrepreneurism and backstairs political collusion. As in the case of oil, there was a great deal of money to be made from the slave-trade by the unscrupulous. Any human being, rich or poor, high- or lowborn, of whatever nation, if seized in war or by pirates could be legitimately deprived of freedom, turned into a mere commodity. Piracy, indeed, with the greater or lesser connivance and cooperation of governments, had a major share in the slave-trade. Like the oil-cartels, that trade, in a very literal sense, kept the wheels turning. There were, of course, other factors that drove men to piracy; but the huge profits to be made from the traffic in human bodies always remained the prime motive. Strabo (14.5.2, C. 668) estimated the daily turnover of the Delos slave-mart to be in the neighborhood of ten thousand souls: energy was a universal and unending need. Even the Rhodians, whose fleets policed the Hellenistic Mediterranean, were in the business of eradicating piracy only when it conflicted with official monopolies.

———

The shift from public collectivism to personal relationships had some unforeseen and paradoxical effects. While the near-worship of Homer never faltered, the heroic ethos of the *Iliad* and *Odyssey* became uncomfortable, if not irrelevant, for those who paid to have their fighting done for them. In Apollonius Rhodius' *Argonautica,* Jason's involvement with Medea is symptomatic of the new emphasis on the inner psychology of erotic relationships. One odd result of the collapse of the polis ethos (and the weakening of the old aristocratic families) was the growing displacement of formalized pederasty among the upper classes by heterosexual passion leading to marriage (as mirrored in the plays of Menander): familial rather than civic masculine bonding was now becoming the norm. Here and there, as inscriptions tell us, the young men of a polis were still put through defensive training, still served in their local militia, but the overall trend is unmistakable.

Women, by and large—another paradox—did well out of these changes. Homeric and Pythagorean recommendations on a husband's proper consideration for his wife's feelings began to be taken seriously. Greater access to wealth and education (previously restricted, along with the inevitable accompanying social stigma, to courtesans) strengthened the status of respectable married women. Perhaps in reaction, some philosophers started preaching the virtues of celibacy. Female statues, hitherto for the most part more or less decorously draped (though clinging see-through techniques were not unknown), began to appear in the nude. The most famous innovative example is the Aphrodite executed by Praxiteles for the city of Cnidos. Whether women at the time regarded this as an advance or not is unknown: it was certainly matched by the disappearance of ultramasculine warrior nudes like the Attic *kouroi* and the great Riace bronzes, symbols of athleticism, military honor, and the homoerotic ideal. The softer, subtly feminized Hermes by—again—Praxiteles, and datable to the mid–fourth century, heralds a basic shift in sensibility.

Pederasty was too ingrained in Hellenic culture to vanish altogether. It simply lost its civic context (along with the philosophers' moral ban on physical consummation) and became one among many potential erotic attractions. This sexual polymorphism is nicely exemplified by the Hellenistic obsession with the hermaphrodite, a being encountered more often in art and literature than in real life. Significantly, its representations reflect the change in social emphasis. Early specimens are clearly boys with breasts, whereas later ones are, equally clearly, girls equipped with a penis. Both types were seen as objects of desire for the adult male.

The one type of passion that earns public and literary censure in the post-Alexandrian period (apart from the adult passive homosexual, penetrated rather than majestically penetrating) is lesbianism, an escape from all-pervasive male domination that—not surprisingly: Eve breaking loose from Adam—aroused considerable patriarchal anxiety. Whether both sexes favored the marked Hellenistic interest in sleazy low life (p. 61) we cannot tell; but modern comparisons suggest strongly that the prime market for such things was among upper-class males with the money to pay for them. In sex as in many other areas, the Hellenistic age, more than any other period of antiquity, tends somewhat disconcertingly to mirror contemporary preoccupations.

———

Greek interest in Italy from the mid–fourth century onward had been marginal. The Spartan King Archidamus III (360–338), Alexander the Great's brother-in-law, Alexander of Epirus (334–330), and Pyrrhus (280–275), were all three invited in as mercenary captains by the Tarentines. Archidamus and Alexander of Epirus died fighting; Pyrrhus, as we have seen (p. 67), was soundly beaten by the Romans and went back home to try his luck in Macedonia. Shortly afterward (273), Ptolemy II sent an investigative embassy to Rome. If his envoys appreciated the long-term threat of what was later described as "the cloud in the west," there is no evidence of it. In general, the Greek world seems to have been content to ignore these "new barbarians" on the far side of the Adriatic. But from 295, when Roman conquest in Italy extended to the east coast, a number of Adriatic colonies, from Ariminum in the north (268) to Brundisium across the straits from Epirus (244), began to appear. Rome—commercially at first, as so often—was moving into the Greek orbit rather than the other way around.

That orbit, as always, remained prone to violent fission. Racked by internal feuding after the assassination of her queen, Epirus fell easy prey to the Illyrians in the north. Since 231, moreover, Gonatas' son Demetrius II had been paying Illyrian troops to fight the Aetolians: one group of natural freebooters battling another. A crushing victory in Acarnania encouraged the Illyrians, under their queen, Teuta, to go for broke. Why should they, too, not become an imperial power? Piratical raids up and down the Greek side of the Adriatic coast were bad enough, but the Illyrians also set about disrupting (and taking as prizes) commercial traffic between the Strait of Otranto and the Corinthian Gulf, both of which they now controlled (229). This brought loud complaints to Rome from the merchants of Brundisium and other ports on the east coast of Italy. A Roman ambassador, sent in to investigate, was killed. Teuta moved in on Epidamnos and captured the key island of Corcyra. She also informed the Romans, saucily, that Illyria—unlike Rome, she implied—was willing to tolerate private as well as governmental piracy.

Enough was enough. Both consuls, each with a major task force, were sent to stamp out this nuisance. They did so with more-than-Macedonian professionalism, crushing numerical superiority, and what today would be characterized as a brief to terminate with extreme prejudice. The Illyrians, better at privateering than fighting a large-scale war, collapsed in short order. A peace treaty was signed early in 228. Both consuls won triumphs. Roman embassies were sent to Athens and Corinth and to both the Achaean and the Aetolian leagues. Rome's intervention was represented as a service to the Greek states. Pro-Roman gratitude (something the Greeks took a while to learn) was assumed as the quid pro quo. The lesson of this so-called First Illyrian War was double: first, that a Roman legion was not something to tangle with lightly; and second, that when Rome helped you out, there was always a price to pay.

Thus the Senate will have duly noted that neither Demetrius II nor his acting successor, Antigonus Doson, made any move to curb the Illyrians. Indeed, it was Demetrius who had financed and encouraged them in the first place. Some excuse might be found for Demetrius, who in 229 had to face a major Dardanian invasion from the north and died fighting it. But Doson, quietly anti-Roman despite his ambivalent position as guardian of the nine-year-old Philip V, was another matter; and Philip, when he came to the throne (222/1), soon showed himself an independent monarch rather than the obligated client of Roman expectations. The stage was set for an uneasy relationship between Rome and Macedonia that would end, little more than half a century later, in the downfall of the Antigonid dynasty and the end of Macedonia as an independent nation.

For the time being, however, with Hannibal in Italy, the Romans' leisure for action in the Adriatic and Greece remained limited. In 219, they did find time to deal with an erstwhile client, Demetrius of Pharos, who, first with Doson's and then with Philip's support, had been resuming piratical activities from the Adriatic to the Aegean. Again, consular intervention (in a brief Second Illyrian War) put paid to the nuisance in short order, and Demetrius of Pharos fled to Philip's court for protection, where he became something of an éminence grise. The Romans requested his extradition. Philip refused. In June 217 came the news of Hannibal's crushing victory at Lake Trasimene. Demetrius is said to have advised Philip to wind up his local campaign, with the Achaean League, against Aetolian aggression and concentrate on the threat from the west. What he really wanted for himself was a return to piratical control of the Adriatic, the removal of a rival Illyrian corsair, Scerdilaïdas, and the unrestricted profits of the slave-trade in and around the Strait of Otranto. Philip, eager to eradicate Roman influence, duly obliged.

Scerdilaïdas, with cool effrontery, appealed to Rome. A ten-ship investigative team promptly appeared. Philip, equally promptly, retreated. A confrontation was not what he wanted at this stage. Nor, it would seem, did the Romans. But when a Roman squadron headed off Philip's efforts to win a port for Macedonia on the Adriatic, the young king—again on Demetrius' advice—sought and signed a treaty with Hannibal (215). This got him little and instantly made him an object of prime suspicion in Rome. The Romans were now in effect at war with Macedonia. A fleet appeared off Orikos. Philip, who had been in action along the coast, once more avoided confrontation, ignominiously burning his own 120-vessel flotilla and retreating over the mountains (214). But a year later, after subjugating the interior, he secured his Adriatic port, at Lissos; and the Romans, casting around for allies by land, picked on the Aetolians, a people as brutal in action as themselves but considerably less well organized.

The Aetolians, still grumbling at the terms of the treaty of Naupactus that Philip and the Achaean League had foisted on them in 217 (the last treaty, incidentally, that was ever to be signed in Greece without Roman participation), were only too happy to throw in their lot with Rome (the new treaty offered ample gains in both territory and plunder). The fighting that followed involved massacres and wholesale enslavement. Philip, known on his accession as "the darling of the

Greeks," soon became notorious for savagery in the field as well as for political unreliability. When Aratus died in 213 (probably of consumption), Philip was rumored to have had him poisoned.

With Sparta and Attalus I of Pergamon, as well as the Aetolians, now supporting Rome, there was talk of alliance with barbarians, a resurgence of Panhellenic propaganda, and general revulsion at the bloody ruthlessness of this new internecine conflict. The Achaean League even began to edge tentatively toward a rapprochement with Macedonia. Anti-Roman feeling grew: Rome was coming to be seen as the new Barbarian Other, and her allies became prime targets. Philip drove the Aetolians out of Thessaly, sacked their capital of Thermon, and made short work of Attalus I's one incursion into mainland Greece. The Achaean League's general Philopoemen thrashed a Spartan army at Mantinea (207).

It was at this point that the Romans, encouraged by their great victory over Carthage at the Metaurus river (207), decided to concentrate all their attention on finishing off Hannibal and left the Aetolians to carry on by themselves. Robbed of support, the Aetolians promptly (206) made a separate peace with Philip, returning him all his lost territories. This got the Romans' attention. They landed a large force at Epidamnos in 205, with the idea of forcing the Aetolians back into the war, but when the Aetolians took no notice, the Romans ignored Philip's offer of battle, maneuvered him to the conference table, and negotiated their own peace at Phoenice in Epirus (205).

The First Macedonian War was over and the status quo ante largely restored. Any idea the Romans might have had that Philip had been planning an active partnership with Hannibal was a chimera; but equally, if Philip imagined (as he well may have done) that this brush with Rome was his last, he was very much mistaken. For the Romans, this peace was a temporary measure only, handy until they were finally through with Carthage. It also made very clear that there were now two sharply opposed sides in Greece: on the one hand, Philip V of Macedon and his allies (among them the Boeotians and the Achaean League); on the other, the Romans, supported by a mixed bag of opportunists that included the Athenians, Attalus I of Pergamon, and Nabis, the new tyrant of Sparta. The lines were being drawn for a showdown, though whether at the time anyone realized this is more than doubtful.

Neither in Egypt nor in Seleucid Asia, for different reasons, were the Romans at this point actively involved. Alexandria presented no threat. From Raphia in 217 for the remainder of his reign, Ptolemy IV had to deal with a debased currency (owing largely to a shortage of silver) and increasingly dangerous native armed rebellions (Upper Egypt was in fact lost to his regime from 205 to c. 186). When he died in 204, his heir, Ptolemy V Epiphanes, was only six years old, and there were competitors for the regency. The only danger about a weakened Egypt was the temptation it presented to rivals. Of these the most dangerous, Antiochus III, had been otherwise engaged for most of the time since his accession in a remarkably successful effort to recover the territories won by his great-great-grandfather Seleucus I, the dynasty's founder, including the eastern satrapies: no problems for Rome there. But about the time of Ptolemy IV's death, Antiochus was back in the west and aggressively visible. In 202/1, he came down through Coele-Syria; shortly afterward he seized the port of Sidon and thrashed a Ptolemaic army at Panion (200/199).

The Romans, freed at last by Scipio Africanus' final victory over Hannibal at Zama (202) of their long and costly Carthaginian War, began now to assert their authority in Greek affairs. They warned Antiochus not to invade Egypt, which at the time he had no intention of doing (for his subsequent activities, see pp. 89–90). They were more concerned, and with reason, to curb the aggressive conduct of Philip V of Macedon. Ever since the peace of Phoenice (205), Philip had been exerting himself to build up a powerful fleet. To fund this venture, he hired an Aetolian pirate, Dicaearchus, to raid, plunder, and shake down for protection money all the islands of the Aegean. The loot came in, and the fleet was built. Philip captured Thasos and raised more cash by selling the island's population into slavery. He raided the Black Sea grain route. He invaded Ionia and ravaged the territory of Pergamon. He took over the Ptolemaic naval base at Samos (thus swelling his fleet to more than two hundred vessels) and beat a Rhodian fleet off Lade. His atrocities became notorious. The combined navies of Rhodes, Chios, Byzantium, and Pergamon inflicted a crushing defeat on him, but this proved no more than a temporary setback. Rhodes and Pergamon took their case to Rome.

A Roman mission met them in Athens (then at war with Philip) and proceeded to issue an ultimatum to Philip in the form of an order: the first time such peremptory methods had been used in Greece and setting a pattern for the future. He was to desist from attacking Greek states and also must pay compensation to Attalus of Pergamon for the damage he had done. Failure to comply would mean war with Rome. This was an impossible request, and Philip's aggressive response to it was a raid on Attica that penetrated as far as the Academy while the Roman envoys were still in Athens. He then launched an all-out attack on the Hellespontine cities, presumably with the intention of cutting off Athens' grain-supply. At Abydos (summer 200), Rome's final ultimatum reached him. He was now also required to pay compensation to Rhodes and to refrain from attacking Egypt. On the basis of Philip's earlier record (he had carefully avoided tangling with Rome, either at sea or on land), he was obviously expected to behave like a proper client-prince and submit gracefully. Instead, he stood firm. The envoy, Marcus Aemilius Lepidus, broke off negotiations. Rome and Macedonia were once more at war.

Why Rome should have intervened at this point remains a puzzle. Philip represented no serious threat to Roman interests, and indeed the vote for war was reached only with some difficulty. It was, after all, no more than a year or two since Zama. Scholars who see the Romans of this period as hell-bent on military expansion and the kudos that went with it[4] have no difficulty in attributing the decision to simple aggression. Yet Rome's dealings with the Greek world hitherto had been casual and reluctant, at worst a case (as was said about T. E. Lawrence) of backing into the limelight, and of accepting the role of adult arbiter between a number of childlike squabbling city-states. (There were loud complaints about Philip's Aegean depredations.) Face-saving, too, may have been involved; once that ultimatum had been delivered, neither side was ready to stand down. Besides, in the last resort Philip was undoubtedly a potential menace. His atrocities were notorious, and he had, after all, earlier signed that treaty with Hannibal.

Whatever their motives, the Romans at least showed themselves to be deft propagandists. Acutely conscious of having been seen earlier as mere barbarians, hand in glove with Aetolian freebooters—a view that produced a powerful recrudescence of Panhellenism—they now presented themselves as protectors of the Greeks against Philip, the Macedonian (that is, non-Greek) Barbarian Other. States that had suffered from Philip's attacks hastened to offer their services to Rome. The Achaean League defected from him. The Aetolians also threw in their lot with Rome, as the likely winner, and got small thanks for it (they afterward grumbled that "the Fetters of Greece" were merely changing hands). The consul of 198, Titus Quinctius Flamininus, after a series of diplomatic maneuvers designed to enhance the image of Rome as Greece's savior, finally brought Philip to battle at Cynoscephalae ("the Dogs' Heads") in Thessaly (June 197). Despite an early successful charge by the Macedonian phalanx, the legions prevailed. It was the first victory over Greek forces by a Roman army, and it left Rome completely in control.

Philip was forced to evacuate Greece and pay a 1,000-talent indemnity. Against considerable senatorial opposition, Flamininus—the man who "completed the redefinition of Rome for the Greeks"[5]—proclaimed the "freedom of the Greeks," to delirious applause, at the Isthmian Games of 196, listing all the cities that were henceforth to be independent, ungarrisoned, exempt from tribute, governed by their ancient laws. They included the cities of Asia Minor, a move that was clearly aimed at Antiochus—as was the fact that despite all the heady talk of freedom, Rome decided, like Philip, to keep garrisons in Demetrias, Chalcis, and Acrocorinth, "the Fetters of Greece."

One nuisance, from Rome's viewpoint, had thus been eliminated, but another still remained to be dealt with. Antiochus' activities in Coele-Syria and Asia Minor threatened what, from across the Tiber, was seen as the proper balance of power among the Hellenistic kingdoms. Once again, and with even greater confidence, Rome began issuing orders to an independent Greek ruler. Once again, the orders were rejected out of hand. The ideological conflict between Hellenistic monarchy and Roman imperium now entered upon its final phase.

5

DYNASTIC TROUBLES, ARTISTIC AND SCIENTIFIC ACHIEVEMENTS

(196 - 116)

The Romans' adroit new mixture, in dealing with the Greek states, of libertarian propaganda and unbeatable military power was proving singularly effective. In no time at all, Rome had become the de facto appellate court for Greek interstate quarrels and civic complaints. There were predictable side-effects. It soon became clear that Rome did not tolerate ambivalence in her yes-men, and as a result, ambitious toadies sensed profit in turning informers. The Aetolians were not the only ones whose main aim from now on was to be on the winning side and to paint their enemies as anti-Roman. The Achaean statesman and historian Polybius was later (168/7) deported to Italy on the word of a fellow-Achaean, Callicrates, ostensibly for his over-independent attitude, though in fact Callicrates' prime motive was to get rid of a political rival. Among the monarchies, both the Ptolemies and the Attalids were quick to recognize force majeure and to trim their diplomatic sails accordingly.

On the other hand, Antiochus III, the king who was bent, and hitherto with striking success, on restoring past Seleucid glories, seems to have been confident that, in the last resort, despite Cynoscephalae, he could hold his own against Rome's legions. After consolidating his position in Coele-Syria, he began raiding the Ptolemaic coastal cities from Caria to Cilicia. He also invaded, and laid waste, part of the territory of Pergamon. None of this seriously bothered Rome. But Antiochus was determined to regain all the old Seleucid holdings, and one of these was the abandoned city of Lysimacheia in Thrace, which he coolly set about rebuilding as a European outpost (196), in direct contravention of Flamininus' proclamation at the Isthmian Games.

If Antiochus had meant to test the limits of Roman indifference, he certainly succeeded. He was told to get, and stay, out of Europe. He was reprimanded for attacking "free" Greek cities. Figuring, correctly, that at this point the Senate was saber-rattling, he took no notice. He hung on to Lysimacheia at least until 191. In 195, he made a treaty with young Ptolemy V (now fifteen) that officially ceded him Coele-Syria. He also arranged the boy-king's betrothal to his own daughter Cleopatra (I): they were married a year later. When another Roman inquisitor came calling, Antiochus challenged Rome's right to dictate policy in

Asia Minor, used Seleucus I's defeat of Lysimachus in 281 to justify his own foothold in Thrace, and produced both treaty and betrothal as proof of his nonbelligerent attitude to Egypt. This smart propaganda victory ensured that Rome never trusted him again and, having lost face, would eliminate him at the earliest convenient opportunity.

Against strong opposition (including that of Scipio Africanus), in the fall of 194 Flamininus was recalled and the Roman occupation force withdrawn from Greece. The opposition is understandable: Hannibal had found asylum with Antiochus at Ephesus, and the Seleucid monarch was rumored to be considering an invasion of Greece. Even so, in 193 the Senate, through Flamininus, offered Antiochus a free hand in Asia Minor in return for abandoning his claim in Thrace. It was Europe that mattered. Antiochus refused. He then, fatally, accepted an invitation by the Aetolians (who had acquired Demetrias as a base) to come over and support them. In four years, the Greeks had become decidedly disenchanted with the realities of Roman patronage.

Antiochus arrived with few ships and men and only half a dozen elephants (192). The Aetolians' disorganized bloody-mindedness was making them increasingly unpopular. Potential supporters backed off. Though Antiochus took Chalcis, he was routed by the Romans at Thermopylae and ignominiously driven back to Asia Minor. In an unprecedented move, the legions followed him: the first time a Roman army had set foot in Asia. Rhodes, Pergamon, and even Philip of Macedon (who thus worked off his war indemnity) hastened to support Rome and eliminate their rival, at sea as well as on land.

At Magnesia-by-Sipylos, early in 189, Antiochus, like so many of his predecessors, staked everything on a major engagement and lost it. Once again, a successful cavalry charge overreached itself, this time with stampeding elephants adding to the chaos. The Roman slaughter of fugitives was horrendous and their campaign highly profitable: Antiochus was slapped with an indemnity of 15,000 talents, the highest ever yet recorded (3,000 to be paid at once), a sum that revolutionized Rome's public economy. At the Peace of Apamea (188), he lost his holdings in Thrace and Asia Minor. A year later, while raiding a temple in Elam for desperately needed cash to meet his obligations, he was killed. In effect, the Romans had executed him. Rhodes and Pergamon were rewarded (Eumenes II had knocked out Antiochus' left wing at

Magnesia) but remained in favor only as long as their support for Rome was total and unquestioning.

The removal of Antiochus altered very little in the uncomfortable equation between Rome and the Greek states. The Achaean League got away with destroying traditional Sparta (188), but only because Peloponnesian politics did not essentially affect Roman notions of the balance of power in the Greek east. During the next twenty years, any Greek illusions of dealing between equals (*isologia*)—as Philip or Eumenes might still conceive such an exchange—were to be proved just that: illusions and nothing more. Persistent anti-Roman feeling in the Greek world had one paradoxical result. Any Greek leader, *even if pro-Roman,* who attracted interstate support or became notably popular and successful was automatically regarded with suspicion at Rome, where any signs of the *clientela* courting the limelight, let alone political power, were seen as a clear prelude to rebellion. Potential alternatives to Roman authority were not looked on kindly.

The Ptolemies at this point presented no problem. For most of his short reign, Ptolemy V had been fully occupied with the major rebellion in Upper Egypt. By 185, his troops had recaptured Thebes and begun to restore order. Another two years saw the suppression of the last insurgents in the Delta. But in 181/0, the young king died: he was only twenty-eight, and there were the usual rumors of poisoning. His wife, Cleopatra—Antiochus' daughter—became regent for their son, the future Ptolemy VI Philometor. The regime was weak, but for the moment reasonably stable: exactly what Rome preferred.

Macedonia was another matter. Philip, who had occupied Antiochus' Thracian strongholds and refused to turn them over to Eumenes, sent his younger son Demetrius—formerly a hostage in Rome and very popular there—to negotiate on his behalf (184). Though Demetrius' diplomatic mission failed (Flamininus forced Philip to withdraw: the shaky treaty of friendship, *amicitia,* between Rome and Macedon remained in place), Demetrius himself came home in high favor all round (183). This seems to have thoroughly alarmed the heir to the throne, his elder half-brother, Perseus, who accused him of being a would-be usurper backed by Rome and produced documents (almost certainly forged) to back up his charges. Philip hesitated, then executed Demetrius for treason (180) and died himself the following year—of remorse, Livy speculated (40.51.9–10).

Perseus was thus an object of suspicion in Rome from the start, and not only as his brother's putative murderer. The Senate reluctantly confirmed him and renewed the treaty of friendship, probably calculating that this was a hothead who could safely be left to hang himself. His subsequent actions may well have convinced them they were right. Perseus married Laodice, daughter of Antiochus III's son and heir, Seleucus IV. His own half-sister married Prusias II, king of Bithynia. Rumors began to circulate of a "royal coalition." He got the support of Rhodes. He won quick popularity at home by strengthening Macedonia's northern frontiers against tribal incursions, by amnestying exiles, and by writing off fiscal and other debts. This at once got him a reputation as a dangerous radical. He also went out of his way to cultivate Delphi. His influence and popularity among the Greeks grew fast. A Roman commission sent to investigate his activities (173) was refused a hearing and concluded, wrongly, that he was ready to go to war.

In 172, Eumenes, faced with the threat of a Macedonian-Seleucid entente, went to Rome with a lurid list of charges against Perseus. He had made approaches to Carthage. He was stirring up populist revolution. He had imperialist designs. He had tried to have Eumenes assassinated by means of an opportune rockfall near Delphi. He had plans to poison the Roman Senate (or, alternatively, the Roman envoys and commanders on their way to Greece). The Romans, far from dismissing this farrago out of hand, not only accepted it but had the charges publicly displayed at Delphi. In fact, Perseus had done nothing but work to establish himself: it was not his fault that he was now regarded as by far the most attractive leader in Greece, for Rome perhaps his most dangerous quality. A preemptive strike—or at least the threat of one—was clearly felt to be desirable.

When the Romans made a conditional declaration of war against him in 171, it was very probably in the belief that he would back down and accede to their demands. Like Antiochus, he did nothing of the sort; and like Antiochus, he may well have made this decision because the Roman ultimatum left him with only two alternatives: complete and humiliating public surrender of authority or a fight to the finish. Not surprisingly, he chose to fight. Yet for the first three years of this Third Macedonian War, nothing much happened except minor skirmishes, and Perseus kept putting out diplomatic feelers for peace, which must have encouraged Rome in the belief that he would, ultimately, give in.

In fact, at the time it looked as though more real trouble could be expected from another quarter altogether. In 175, Seleucus IV had been assassinated by one of his ministers and succeeded by his younger brother, who took the throne as Antiochus IV. (Eumenes was widely suspected of being the broker behind this dynastic change.) While Rome was dealing with Perseus, young Antiochus descended on Egypt by way of Coele-Syria (169), scattered the Ptolemaic defense forces, and threatened Alexandria. Ptolemy VI wanted to negotiate. The Alexandrian mob had other ideas and acclaimed his young brother (the future, famously potbellied Ptolemy VIII) and sister-wife, Cleopatra, as joint rulers. Antiochus left them to fight it out over the winter (all three reconciled) but was back in 168. His fleet had meanwhile captured Cyprus, where his troops were going on a rampage of looting and destruction. How much he was betting on his early popularity in Rome (where he had spent time as a youthful and much-courted hostage) is uncertain. If he expected special treatment, he was in for a rude awakening.

Whether it was these events that stirred the Romans into faster action against Macedonia or not is uncertain. The fact remains that the consul of 168, Aemilius Paullus, marched north in Greece with the immediate aim of confronting Perseus. Their armies met at Pydna in Pieria on the Thermaic Gulf. Paullus, a seasoned battle commander, said afterward that the massed advance of the Macedonian phalanx was the most terrifying sight he had ever witnessed. But its advance was bogged down by difficult terrain, legionary maniples infiltrated its ranks from the flank, Roman cavalry and elephants added to the confusion, and once again, as at Cynoscephalae, the battle ended in a Roman bloodbath: 20,000 Macedonians were killed.

Pydna marked the end of Macedonia as an independent kingdom: the first of the Hellenistic monarchies to be abolished. The country was split into four minor republican cantons. In Epirus, Paullus turned his legionaries loose to rape and pillage and collected no fewer than 150,000 prisoners to be sold off as slaves. Perseus, the last Antigonid king, adorned Paullus' triumph in Rome and starved himself to death several years later while in captivity at Alba Fucens. The triumph itself was loaded with fabulous treasures from the royal palace at Pella and elsewhere. The loot in cash terms was so vast that it replaced all extraordinary taxes in the public treasury for over a century. Senatorial leaders, equestrian businessmen, tax-farmers, and potential army recruits all now began to scent the possibilities of large-scale exploitation.

The legion, as Polybius admitted,[1] had finally proved its superiority over the phalanx, and the repercussions were enormous. Rhodes, which had veered toward Macedonia during the war, lost Caria and Lycia and was economically crippled by the establishment of Delos as an Athenian free port (Athenians, anti-Macedonian to the end, had fought for Rome at Pydna). Polybius and many other Achaeans were deported to Rome. More unexpectedly, Eumenes of Pergamon, en route to Rome to offer congratulations on Pydna, was told to leave Italy. His increasing wealth and international prestige alone were enough to damn him in Rome's eyes. Wild rumors of the kind that he himself had spread against Perseus—that he was plotting with Antiochus IV, that he had even secretly planned to join Perseus—ensured his fall from favor.

Having thus dealt with Perseus, the Romans immediately (July 168) turned their attention to Antiochus IV, who was beginning to look a good deal more dangerous. He had worked hard to court the favor and support of the Greek states, and his overtures had met with considerable success. The Seleucid economy, to judge from his excellent and abundant coinage, had taken an upswing. Now he had occupied Cyprus, penetrated Egypt, and was poised to replace the weak regime in Alexandria. A Seleucid empire that included the kingdom of the Ptolemies—thus destroying any balance of power in the Greek east and setting up a dangerously powerful rival—was not something Rome had any intention of tolerating. Drastic measures were called for.

The Roman ambassador Popilius Laenas met Antiochus in Eleusis, a suburb of Alexandria, with the Senate's ultimatum: evacuate Egypt and Cyprus or face war. Antiochus asked for time to debate the issue. Popilius' response was to draw a circle in the dust with his stick around the Seleucid king and to demand an answer before Antiochus stepped out of the circle. Antiochus—no fool, for all his bravado, and with both Cynoscephalae and Pydna fresh in mind to temper any show of proud independence he might be tempted to put on for public consumption—bowed to the inevitable and withdrew. Peace with Rome, he informed the Senate, was preferable to any victory in Egypt. To temper his humiliation, and to send a signal of strength to his Greek allies, on his return home he held games that for sheer lavishness outdid even Aemilius Paullus' triumph. As Ptolemy II had proved long before, expensive displays made good propaganda.

———

One remarkable phenomenon associated with Rome's penetration of Greece and the Greek cities of Asia Minor was the wholesale removal, by generals and others, of high-quality Greek works of art. There had been sporadic looting earlier (for instance, from Syracuse in 212), but the large-scale trend seems to have been started by Flamininus in 194. In 187, Marcus Fulvius Nobilior brought back 285 bronze and 230 marble statues from Ambracia. After Pydna, Aemilius Paullus collected enough artwork to fill 250 carts in his triumph. The scale of these depredations dwarfs even the Nazis' similar activities in Europe during World War II. They were still proceeding unchecked in 146, when after the fall of Corinth Polybius saw soldiers playing checkers on stacks of famous canvases.[2] Eventually—after the organization of the province of Asia for the most part shut the door on unregulated wars of conquest—the wholesale theft of artistic works was brought under control and something like a modern art-market emerged; but until then, Romans continued to "liberate" Greek artifacts with the same thoroughgoing zest that Alexander had displayed in ransacking the Achaemenid treasuries.

The influx into Italy of this material had an immediate and lasting impact. In no other area did Horace's claim (*Epist.* 2.1.156) that "captive Greece took her savage conqueror captive" (*Graecia capta ferum uictorem cepit*) apply more strongly. From the start, Romans (as the old saw goes) may not have known much about art, but most certainly knew what they liked; and what they liked was the painting and sculpture of the fifth-century classical apogee and the neo-classical tradition that had followed it. After the first bout of artistic piracy had run its course and shown what was available, collectors in Italy made it very clear—competitive social fashion quickly kicked in here—that they were prepared to pay the earth for certified Old Masters and good prices for well-executed copies or neo-classical imitations. Portraiture, in the form of busts or statues, proved especially popular. A huge and profitable new field of patronage had opened up, and Greek artists—as soon as it looked as though they might actually be paid for their work—quickly set about exploiting it.

It might be thought that neo-classicism was the natural visual component of that energetic general drive to retrieve the cultural treasures of the fifth century that we noted earlier when looking at the Museum and Library in Alexandria. To a great extent, of course, this was true. In painting especially, the trend was reinforced by the fundamental, and universally accepted, criterion of realistic naturalism: painted grapes so real that birds pecked at them, the painted horse the sight of which made real horses neigh. This, too, was what Romans wanted from art, even if the realism was based on illusive tricks such as the use of perspective, trompe-l'oeil in a very literal sense. But the vast social and political changes that we have seen at work in the Aegean and eastern Mediterranean—in particular the seismic shift of emphasis from the polis to the family, from public and civic collectivism to private individualism, from radical democracy to oligarchic conservatism—inevitably left its mark on the visual arts as elsewhere, and with some of its manifestations Romans were not entirely comfortable. When the Elder Pliny said of the period between 295/2 and 156/3 that "art stopped then" (*cessauit deinde ars*), what he meant was art of the kind that he and his peers were prepared to accept.

The establishment of royal, or quasi-royal, courts from Syracuse to Alexandria and beyond encouraged honorific portraits as well as encomiastic literature. The incipient cult of personality, so shunned in the classical era, led not only to heroic honors and ultimately deification, but to gargantuan private tombs that almost (as with the Mausoleum) came to challenge public shrines. Public buildings themselves tended to emphasize the practical and the secular: Athens under Antipater built an arsenal and the Panathenaic Stadium. Architectural gigantism—huge theaters, stoas, and, in Asia, temples—became increasingly popular, feeding on the determined self-promotion of Hellenistic monarchs. Male statues lost their macho militarism, female ones their clothes. Portraiture shifted from idealism toward realistic (and often unflattering) likenesses. Urban courtiers dabbled in literary and artistic pastoralism. Political impotence bred sexual fantasy (see pp. 61 and 78–79). The decoration of private houses became increasingly elaborate, mainly with murals and mosaics: the latter in particular required an extremely expensive technique, and their abundance in houses excavated at Pella, the Macedonian capital, datable to the late fourth century, hints eloquently at the vast wealth brought back from the East by Alexander's conquistadors.

It seems likely—and the scattered evidence tends to confirm this—

that Macedonian art patrons, both before and after Alexander, had rather different requirements from those of their Greek contemporaries. As early as the fifth century, King Archelaus of Macedon hired the Greek painter Zeuxis to decorate his palace, at a time when elsewhere in Greece figured art was restricted to temples and other public buildings. In fact, our only surviving examples of figured art from this period come from Macedonian private tombs. Most of the Macedonian artifacts—from the lavishly decorated dining rooms in Pella (staghunts, lion-hunts) to that stunningly vulgar item, the gilded Derveni krater showing Dionysus and Ariadne in high relief—are remarkable for their luxurious ostentation and self-promotion. Impressing guests with one's wealth and power became the name of the game. There is a clear line running from Macedonian moneyed taste to the splendid display (Dionysus and mosaics again) of the millionaire slave dealers on Delos and beyond them to the pretensions of the ex-slave Trimalchio in Petronius' *Satyricon*.

Greeks elsewhere, while slowly (as we have seen) shifting from public polis-based collectivism to the same kind of individualistic self-regard that had always marked the Macedonian aristocracy, had had very different problems to cope with, defeat and apparent marginalization uppermost among them. On the other hand, for those with originality and resilience, the future was inviting. Colonialism brought freedom of another sort. The old rules no longer applied; experimentalism (in the arts as in other areas) beckoned temptingly. The result was an upsurge, in sculpture above all, of quasi-baroque emotionalism and expressionistic, sometimes pathological, trivia. This was the phenomenon that Pliny refused to recognize as· art at all and which (combined with Rome's large-scale penetration of the art-market) provoked a nervous but financially profitable retreat into academic neo-classicism.

Some of the private manifestations of this breakout from tradition—the obsession with sex and violence, the peculiar interest in the geriatric flotsam of a ruthlessly laissez-faire society—we have already glanced at (see p. 61). Those with the money to pay for such art, in a world lacking any kind of insurance or social safety net beyond haphazard charity, doubtless found their collections a half-comforting, half-admonitory reminder of the fate they themselves had, by fair means or foul, somehow contrived to avoid. This was escape rather than escapism, though escapism too flourished: the fantasized world of

New Comedy (p. 58), the ubiquitous theatrical masks (persona merging with personality), the literary utopias of Euhemerus or Iamblichus, the sanitized pastoralism of Theocritus, the charming Tanagra figurines.

Public sculpture and architecture, however much it might profess to emulate the classical tradition in technique and subject matter, embodied some profoundly unclassical features. It was marked, as we have seen, by gigantism: bigger was better, a fundamental belief of the Ptolemies, who had to measure themselves against the Pyramids and the great temples of Karnak. Rulers who toyed with the idea of being worshipped as gods were not slow to commission grandiose buildings to demonstrate their own grandiose opinions of themselves. Things had indeed changed since 479, when scandalized Spartan authorities erased the name of the Greek commander in chief, Pausanias, from the memorial of victory over Xerxes, replacing it with a simple laconic statement—"These fought the war"—followed by a list of the states involved. The cult of personality, long shunned as anathema to the polis ideal, staged a remarkable Hellenistic comeback. The Colossus of Rhodes was reckoned one of the Seven Wonders of the ancient world. The Parthenon was not.

Escapism of a more rarefied sort can also be seen in the remarkable—yet intriguingly limited—scientific achievements of the Hellenistic era. The limitations sprang, most obviously, from a crippling absence of methods for accurate measurement, experimentation, or timekeeping. Since disciplines such as mathematics and astronomy were essentially elitist pursuits, followed by highly educated, often aristocratic individuals with secure private incomes, the preferences of Hellenistic monarchs as patrons of research had less influence on the directions that this research took than is sometimes supposed. Furthermore, the kings' interests tended to be pragmatic and frequently restricted to their favorite occupation, the pursuit of technically efficient aggressive warfare. Here they ran up against the virulently antibanausic class-prejudice that permeated Greek society of all periods. Pure mathematicians from Euclid to Archimedes had nothing but the most withering contempt for applied science (a prejudice they shared with the great twentieth-century luminaries of the Cavendish Laboratory in Cambridge), and this social attitude was linked with, and may in part have shaped, their cosmological theories.

From Plato and Aristotle to the Stoics, there was a firm belief—

transmitted largely intact to Christianity and the Middle Ages—in a divinely ordered, mathematically logical cosmos, revolving around an unmoving Earth as its central point. Further, this cosmos was regarded as consisting of living, and in some sense sentient, entities (sun, moon, planets, stars), which through a system of correspondences, macrocosm to microcosm, could affect every aspect of human life and society. Hence the popular pseudoscience of astrology. The regular movement of most of these heavenly bodies encouraged the pursuit of hierarchical, authoritarian systems on earth. However, the perfect regularity of this system faced a challenge from the evident irregularity of the planets (*planetai* = "wanderers"). The anomaly led to increasingly sophisticated astronomical calculations in a frantic effort to preserve overall regularity (and circularity) in the revolutions of the macrocosm: this effort was what first evoked the famous phrase "saving the appearances."[3]

Obviously there were exceptions, but they tended to be few and far between and (a crucial point) were never really accepted socially. The most important were the heliocentric cosmology adumbrated by Aristarchos of Samos (full acceptance of which had to wait for almost two millennia) and the atomic theories of Democritus that were taken up by the Epicureans. The Epicurean rejection of a comfortingly teleological universe (Intelligent Design, in one form or another, has a long history) in favor of bleak atomic materialism, not to mention their indifferent sidelining of the gods, ensured that their ideas never ousted those of the Stoics. Fixed hierarchical principles, in the heavens as on earth, suited Hellenistic Greek oligarchs very well and, later, Roman proconsuls even better. The antibanausic prejudice also militated against development in areas such as chemistry. These, already hobbled by lack of precise mensuration and associated in the minds of intellectuals with artisans' pursuits such as dyeing and mining, were therefore regarded as beyond the pale.

The largest general casualty due to this virulent class-prejudice was technology. The developments attributed to Hellenistic scientists—ranging from cogged gears and the compound pulley system to the torsion catapult, the water organ, and illusionist devices designed to impress the gullible in temples—look wide-ranging at first sight but in fact are restricted to the requirements of a few wealthy patrons, primarily the rulers who wanted the ability to raise ever more impressive buildings, outshoot their enemies' artillery, and enjoy sophisticated toys at court. The kind of hierarchical conservatism that preferred the status quo to increased production, coupled with an ingrained fear of servile revolt (see pp. 76–77), ensured that no efficient source of industrial energy other than human and animal musclepower ever got beyond the drawing board. In any case, primitive notions of economics (and, more important, the traditions of royalty) also dictated that a ruler's surplus did not go into long-term investment but was either squandered on munificent public display or hoarded against emergencies.

Thus the most impressive scientific achievements tended to be made in the pure rather than the applied sciences and in areas that, on the face of it, were least likely to be affected by political, social, or religious considerations. It took the personal intervention of Ptolemy II, against strong religious opposition, to enable the medical researchers Herophilus and Erasistratus to dissect human cadavers; with his death, the taboo was promptly restored. Perhaps the most extraordinary intellectual monument from the period is that of Apollonius of Perge (fl. c. 200 BCE), whose work on conic sections still dazzles mathematicians today. But while conic sections may charm the knowledgeable with their exquisite mathematical logic, they offer no disturbing challenge to what Kipling once nicely termed "the Gods of the Copybook Headings." Displacing this world from the center of the universe was another matter entirely.

———

The Day of Eleusis and the dismemberment of Macedonia (168/7) made brutally public what had long been clear to every Hellenistic ruler: when it came to a showdown, Rome now called the shots. Antigonid Macedonia had already gone under. The Attalids of Pergamon, deprived of Roman support—when in 166 Eumenes II scored a victory over the Celts of Galatia, the Senate promptly proclaimed Galatian autonomy—were not slow to follow. In 133, Attalus III, perhaps taking a hint from Ptolemy VIII (see p. 104), bequeathed his kingdom to Rome. At this, his illegitimate half-brother, Aristonicus, proclaimed himself king as Eumenes III, recruited the landless and, ultimately, the slaves, and launched a revolt that it took the Romans—already dealing with a major slave uprising in Sicily—almost three years to stamp out. When they did so (130), Pergamon was treated as a protectorate and formed the nucleus of what, less than a decade later, was to become the province of Asia: one of the richest sources of systematic exploitation in all Roman history.

Senatorial policy still, fueled by diehards like Cato, contained a moral and isolationist component. Cato might, with his dying breath, have successfully urged the destruction of Carthage (146), but he and his senatorial fellow-conservatives had very little time for the idea of turning provinces into cash-cows for avaricious proconsuls. It was the business community—followed gradually by officials in situ who saw how rich the pickings were—that spearheaded change. Sulla's later reform of the Senate, which he flooded with new entrants indifferent to the old code of the landed *optimates,* was to complete the process. In 169, the Senate was investigating the tax-farmers; by the end of the century, it was hand in glove with them.

The relationship between the Romans and the (titularly independent) Greek or Macedonian rulers of Greece and Asia had come to resemble that of an authoritarian paterfamilias with his feckless and quarrelsome adolescent children. But the dimensions of this game were strictly limited, and when a weaker player overstepped the mark—as the Achaean League did in 147/6, planning an attack on Sparta in defiance of Roman warnings—retribution was swift and ferocious. In the same year as the destruction of Carthage (146), the league and its allies were routed at Corinth; Lucius Mummius, the Roman commander, similarly turned the city over to his legionaries to sack and destroy. Corinth was still a ruined site when Cicero visited it nearly a century later. Like Alexander at Thebes, the Romans meant their treatment of Corinth as a deterrent; but just as in Alexander's case, what it primarily engendered, as Greek participation in the Mithradatic revolt of 88 (see pp. 115–16) made all too clear, was simmering hatred and resentment. Small wonder that eschatological cults now began to tout lurid sufferings in the afterlife for this world's oppressors of the chosen.

This is not to say that life, and political business, did not continue in the two surviving Hellenistic kingdoms much as usual. Treaties, alliances, local wars, dynastic marriages, bureaucratic *papyrasserie,* public shows and benefactions, honorific decrees—all went on unabated. Ordinary people, absorbed in their day-to-day activities, have scant time for, and even less interest in, the eruptions of history, which they tend to regard as, at best, an unmitigated nuisance and more often as sheerly calamitous. The Roman Senate had simply become a new player in Greek interstate relations—albeit a powerful and unpredictable player that could, if so minded, change the rules of the game whenever it wanted to. But with increasing power, the Roman penchant for requisitions, confiscations, and, where deemed necessary, the destruction of cities and the mass sale of their inhabitants as slaves—mainly to ensure that campaign finances stayed in the black—became increasingly noticeable.

Such concerns were for the most part limited to their own immediate sphere of interest. Ironically, the Romans' lack of concern regarding the Seleucid eastern provinces led them to ignore, or certainly to underrate, the steady rise of an increasingly powerful nation that would not only prove the Seleucid dynasty's nemesis, but also in the long run present a serious challenge to Rome itself: Parthia. It was partly to deal with the Parthian threat that Antiochus IV (after stamping out, Roman style, a Jewish insurrection) left for the East. He got no farther than Media, where he fell sick and died, though not before rescinding his tough-line policy on the Jews and restoring their freedom of worship. He left an under-age son, Antiochus V, and a regency: exactly the kind of weak regime that Rome favored. This is probably why, when Seleucus IV's son Demetrius, then a hostage in Rome— handsome, vigorous, intelligent, and arguably the legitimate heir to the Syrian throne—pleaded his case before the Senate, he was turned down flat.

His return, it was objected, would mean civil war. Nothing daunted, Demetrius organized his escape (with the connivance of Polybius[4] and, very probably, his powerful Scipionic patrons) and made straight for Antioch. He received a rapturous welcome, support for young Antiochus and his regent, Lysias, evaporated, and Demetrius became king. Lysias, Antiochus, and their supporters were executed. The Senate sent Tiberius Gracchus out to investigate. Demetrius charmed him, behaved like the ideal client-prince. Tiberius reported favorably. The Senate recognized Demetrius—conditionally, with the usual Roman caveat about satisfactory conduct. He was also warned not to mess with the Jews (Rome in 161 had made a treaty with Judas Maccabaeus). This warning (having sized up Roman foreign policy well during his years as a hostage) he ignored. He crushed the rebellion, in which Judas himself died. Rome, as he had foreseen, took no retributive action.

But the Romans never trusted Demetrius and, when he showed signs of restoring Seleucid power, gave support to a supposed bastard son of Antiochus IV—one Alexander Balas, almost certainly an impostor— promoted, to make trouble, by Pergamon and Egypt. Balas went to Syria, in 151/0 defeated and killed Demetrius (whose solitary habits and autocratic rule had destroyed his initial popularity), and became king. His usurpation ushered in a period of chronic and spiraling dynastic instability: the second major factor (after Parthia) responsible for the ultimate collapse of the Seleucid regime. The rest of the century saw a succession of transient rulers (including one, Demetrius II, the two halves of whose reign were divided by a decade of Parthian captivity, and a second impostor, Alexander Zabinas). When not fighting would-be usurpers, family claimants attacked one another. As their territories shrank, their titles grew more grandiloquent and their royal consorts more ruthlessly ambitious (most notably Cleopatra Thea, daughter of Ptolemy VI and wife in turn to Balas, Demetrius II, and Antiochus VII). "Decadence" is not a popular term these days when discussing Hellenistic history, but if ever dynasties showed symptoms of decadence, the Seleucids and Ptolemies from about 150 onward have to be prime candidates.

It might seem, at first sight, that the Ptolemies were in an even more parlous state than their rivals. Antiochus IV had made it all too clear that Egypt's much-touted natural defenses could be breached in short order by a well-planned attack from Syria. The odd ruling triad of Ptolemy VI Philometor, his sister-wife, Cleopatra II, and his young brother, the future Ptolemy VIII, was hardly an advertisement for family harmony or unity of purpose. Their father might temporarily have quelled the major nationalist insurgency in Upper Egypt, but the native priests, the fellahin, and above all the trained Egyptian infantry, the *machimoi*, had tasted blood and achieved a marked degree of success: they would not be quiet for long.

However, against these factors other even more powerful considerations militated. Popilius Laenas' treatment of Antiochus had shown that Rome would not tolerate an Egyptian takeover by the Seleucids. More vital still was the fabulous wealth that the Ptolemies controlled. The Seleucids had never been able to match it, and their resources were now being gutted, in addition, by the reparations they were compelled to pay to Rome. Even a lack of native silver and a consequently debased currency made no difference to the Ptolemies' ability to hire all the mercenaries they needed at preferential rates. As a result, they could afford to wear out by persistence any rebellion they failed to eradicate in short order with overwhelming strength. The one essential requirement for the dynasty was to keep control of the army, the treasury, and the bureaucracy firmly within the family. Hence the policy of sibling incest. However, just which members of the family held the levers of power was sometimes hotly contested.

After the Day of Eleusis, the Ptolemaic brothers, Physcon ("Potbelly") and Philometor, were temporarily reconciled. But in 164, Physcon, a consummate intriguer, managed to expel Philometor from Alexandria. He went to Rome, played poor, and expected sympathy. The Romans, unimpressed, merely opted for reconciliation (163). Their commissioners agreed on a plan for partition: Philometor returned as king; Physcon as heir-apparent got Cyrenaica. Physcon, complaining that partition had been forced on him, persuaded the Senate to endorse—though of course not to implement—his claim to Cyprus. When his attempt to conquer the island failed, the Senate simply canceled its alliance with Philometor and sent his ambassadors home (161).

After several years of Physcon's machinations, Philometor tried to have him assassinated (156/5). The attempt failed. Physcon then (155) proclaimed that if he died childless, he was bequeathing Cyrenaica to Rome: a realistic, if defeatist, acceptance of the Western barbarians as heirs to the Hellenistic world. Perhaps as a result, he now got token support (five ships, advisers, the right to levy Greek troops at his own expense) from the Senate. Physcon's second attempt at capturing Cyprus was an even bigger fiasco than the first, and he himself was captured by Philometor. Wisely unvindictive, Philometor simply sent him back to Cyrene and offered him his daughter Cleopatra Thea in marriage. This offer, Physcon—who had nothing against incest as such but was unwilling at this point to risk nullifying the condition of his bequest to Rome—refused in short order. Philometor then put in his own son as governor of Cyprus.

Till Philometor's death in 145—predictably, on campaign in Coele-Syria—Physcon was effectively stalemated, and Philometor himself, partly by bestowing lavish gifts on those whose goodwill he sought (he built Athens a library) and partly by regaining Rome's support through maintaining partition, consolidated his authority. But on his death, Physcon made up for lost time. Cleopatra proclaimed her adolescent son by Philometor king, as Ptolemy VII. Physcon paid the mob to riot for his return. Cleopatra's support shrank. An amnesty was declared. Physcon came back, married his brother's sister-wife, and (taking a hint from his ancestor Keraunos, p. 40) had the new heir assassinated during the wedding celebrations. There was now no viable claimant to the throne but Physcon himself. He duly became king as Ptolemy VIII Euergetes II and had himself consecrated as pharaoh in Memphis (144), mainly to get the support of the powerful priesthood.

Alexandrian wits lost no time in revising Euergetes ("Benefactor") as Kakergetes ("Malefactor"), and with good reason. Like Hitler, Physcon revealed a powerful distaste for Jews and untrustworthy intellectuals: his purges of the Jewish community, and of Alexandrian scholars and artists generally, by executions and exiling were so thorough that the city's rich cultural heritage was virtually wiped out for a full century. Philosophers, mathematicians, doctors, philologists, the refugees—again, like those from Hitler's Germany—created what one witness[5] termed a "cultural renaissance" in the Greek cities outside Egypt. Physcon's prime motive may have been security (Cleopatra's palace guard had Jewish officers, and her main support came from the intellectual community), but the overkill was disastrous. This Ptolemy had huge appetites for power and every kind of sensual gratification, no moral restraints of any kind, an alarming mixture of political shrewdness and megalomaniac fantasy, and enough wealth to satisfy his every whim. He was the ultimate parody of what all Alexander's Successors had dreamed of becoming.

Having sired a son on Cleopatra (144), he then, a year later, seduced and married her daughter by Philometor: another Cleopatra and (to confuse matters even further) Cleopatra Thea's sister. Perhaps to clarify this incestuous tangle, Philometor's widow, Cleopatra (II), is now referred to in inscriptions as "Cleopatra the Sister," and Physcon's niece Cleopatra (III) as "Cleopatra the Wife." What Scipio Aemilianus made of the regime—or at least of its titular head—when he arrived at the head of a Roman commission in 140/39 can be guessed from his behavior. Welcomed by Physcon at the quayside, Scipio insisted on the obese king accompanying him on foot, sweating and waddling in his ample linen robes, through the streets of Alexandria to the palace. The members of the commission took note of Egypt's wealth, fertility, and abundant cheap labor. With worthy rulers, they reported, a very great power could be created there. A century later, both Antony and Octavian came to the same conclusion.

After eight years of Physcon's high-handedness, the volatile Alexandrian mob (probably with Cleopatra the Sister's connivance) set fire to the palace, and Physcon fled to Cyprus with Cleopatra the Wife and their children. Cleopatra II—rashly, considering the fate of her son by Philometor—got the mob to proclaim her now twelve-year-old son by Physcon king. Physcon, whose paternal sense seems to have matched his moral instincts, abducted the boy, dismembered him, and sent the pieces back to his mother, reportedly on her birthday. The mob raged but could do nothing. By 130, Physcon was back, based on Memphis: cultivating the priests had paid off. Civil war broke out, and Physcon, like Antiochus before him, besieged Alexandria.

Cleopatra II, whose daughter Cleopatra Thea had meanwhile married the Seleucid Demetrius II, appealed to her son-in-law for help. Demetrius tried but was trounced at the frontier by Physcon's mercenaries and retreated to Syria, soon to be followed by Cleopatra II with the royal treasure (127). In Syria, he faced rebellion from a pretender, Zabinas, thoughtfully provided to the rebels by Physcon (129/8). Defeated, he sought refuge with his on-again, off-again wife, Cleopatra Thea, who not only shut the door in his face, but seems to have been responsible for his subsequent murder in Tyre (126/5). By now it should come as no surprise that by 124 (and probably much sooner), Cleopatra the Sister had taken the treasure of Egypt back to Alexandria and—parricide and incest notwithstanding—was officially reconciled not only with her potbellied and murderous brother-husband, but also with Cleopatra the Wife.

Cleopatra Thea, meanwhile, took her sixteen-year-old son, Antiochus Grypos ("Hooknose"), as her co-regent (125) and successor, with the title of Antiochus VIII Philometor. Physcon promptly provided him with a bride: Cleopatra III's daughter Cleopatra Tryphaena. Antiochus got rid of Physcon's pretender, Zabinas (who had outlived his usefulness but showed signs of popularity), and remained properly wary of his own mother, who had earlier promoted his elder brother, Seleucus V, to the kingship (126/5), only to kill him when he showed signs of independence. In 121/0, Cleopatra Thea decided it was time to get rid of Antiochus VIII the same way. Instead (like Darius III with the eunuch Bagoas), the son forced the mother to drink the poisoned wine she had prepared for him. This left Grypos ruler—at least till

114—over the now sadly diminished Syrian remnants of the once enormous Seleucid empire.

The new monarch amused himself by writing poems about poisonous snakes, of which the most lethal, it might be thought, was his appalling father-in-law in Alexandria, where domestic life remained anything but peaceful. In 118, however, Physcon, now in his sixties and eager for a little peace, promulgated a detailed amnesty decree, writing off arrears of taxes, making solid concessions to the temple priests, abolishing various overpunitive penalties, and condemning the more flagrant official abuses. How much of this was ever implemented is highly doubtful, though it made good propaganda at the time. In any case, less than two years later, in June 116, Physcon—more properly Ptolemy VIII Euergetes II—died, "after thirteen years' unbroken possession of the desirable things for which he had intrigued and murdered."⁶ The treasures of Egypt were now underpinning a scandalous, and ongoing, dynastic soap opera.

6

SWORD OVER PEN: ROME'S FINAL SOLUTION

(116 - 30)

As colonial rulers, the Romans neither bothered much with bene-factions nor showed any real interest in democracy. The citizens they were most comfortable dealing with were those who, as they saw it, most resembled their own *optimates,* the wealthy senatorial class, the upholders of order and class privilege. It followed that many cities, such as Athens, that had long supported Rome as an ally against the detested Macedonians now began to look around hopefully for a more congenial patron. The grim lesson of Pydna, that nothing brought out Roman fury like a direct military challenge to Roman imperium, had either escaped their notice or was overridden by the courage of despair and hatred. As we shall see, the evidence for hatred is startling; the pa-tron, when found, scored some impressive successes; but the final up-shot was, inevitably, to bring about Rome's complete absorption of the region that, to begin with, she had dealt with so carefully at arm's length.

Cities that broke away from dynastic control (and an increasing number did) simply wanted to be left alone to maintain some kind of social stability and have their inhabitants lead reasonably undisturbed lives. If that meant becoming Rome's enthusiastic clients, so be it. Meanwhile, Seleucids and Ptolemies continued their internal feuding, their endless wrangling and intrigue, which seemed to get more vi-cious and intensive the smaller the imperial prize at stake became. In Egypt above all, the illusive sense of absolute power bred an atmo-sphere of unreality largely insulated from the outside world. This sense was compounded by the Romans' seeming indifference, though the truth was that for some Rome had far more pressing problems to face than the squabbles of two fading Macedonian monarchies: invasion by Germanic tribes (Cimbri, Teutones), servile risings in Greece and Sicily, rebellion in Spain, riots in Rome, increasing piracy, and, from 91 onward, the outbreak of the Social War, heralding—with the conflict between Sulla and Marius—the first fatal cracks in the fabric of the Republic.

———

Ptolemy VIII (Physcon) had maliciously willed the succession to Cleopatra III (the Wife) and whichever of her sons she preferred, well aware that her favorite was not the eldest and heir-presumptive, Ptolemy IX, known as Lathyros ("Chickpea"), but the younger, Ptolemy X Alexander I. The potbellied one had also sired on his complacent niece at least three daughters—Cleopatra IV, Cleopatra Tryphaena, and Cleopatra Selene—to be available as wives for their brothers. The Wife's attempt, on Physcon's death (116), to promote young Alexander caused a riot, encouraged by her mother, Cleopatra II, the Sister. Lathyros was brought back from the governorship of Cyprus, and Alexander was sent out to replace him. The Wife—freed from the interference of her mother, who died before the year was out—forced Lathyros to exchange his much-loved sister-wife, Cleopatra IV, for her sister Selene, who was regarded, wrongly, as being more pliable. Cleopatra IV then, after failing to marry Alexander in Cyprus, raised an army and took it to Syria, where she duly snagged as a husband Antiochus IX Cyzicenus, son of Antiochus VII and Cleopatra Thea, who at the time was challenging his cousin and half-brother, Antiochus VIII Grypos ("Hooknose"), for the Seleucid throne.

Grypos was, of course (see p. 106), married to Cleopatra IV's sister Tryphaena, and this gave an extra twist of nastiness to the conflict. When Grypos captured Cleopatra IV (112), Tryphaena had the wretched woman's hands hacked off as she clung to an altar in sanctuary. This did not stop her mother, the Wife, from backing Grypos. When Antiochus IX retaliated by seizing Tryphaena (111), he burned her alive as an offering to her deceased sister. This did not stop her brother Lathyros, who had loved his ex-wife, from backing Cyzicenus. By 108 Grypos held most of Syria, with Cyzicenus restricted to some coastal cities. In 107 the Wife drove out Lathyros with accusations of attempted matricide. Alexander returned and assumed the crown. Lathyros took over Cyprus. Cyrenaica was held by a bastard son of Physcon's, Ptolemy Apion. By 103/2 the Wife decided she had had enough of Alexander, too, and he fled from Alexandria. However, he soon (101) returned—allegedly in pursuit of a reconciliation with his mother—and did what she had feared Lathyros would do: that is, he murdered her.

This, combined with his marriage to Cleopatra Berenice, daughter of his brother Lathyros and Lathyros' sister-wife, Cleopatra IV, left Ptolemy X Alexander I as titular monarch of Egypt until 88, with Lathyros on Cyprus and Ptolemy Apion in Cyrene. (In 100, a Roman law on piracy appealed to all three as legitimate monarchs in good standing.)

When Apion died in 96, he did what his father, Physcon, had once threatened to do: he bequeathed Cyrenaica to Rome. In 90, yet another revolt broke out in Upper Egypt, which led to unrest in the capital. Alexander, expelled from the palace (88), sold his famous namesake's gold coffin to hire mercenaries and, like Apion, willed his kingdom (of which he was no longer in control) to Rome, which accepted both legacies but was in no hurry to cash the checks.

Alexander (now almost as obese as his father) died at sea in a hopeless attempt to recover Cyprus, from where the Alexandrians then recalled Lathyros to resume the reign so rudely interrupted two decades earlier and bestowed on him the nickname (how far with tongue in cheek we cannot tell) of Pothinus, or "the Much-Missed One." He suppressed the Theban revolt, took his daughter Cleopatra Berenice as his co-regent, brought Cyprus back into the Alexandrian orbit, celebrated a thirty-year Egyptian jubilee (dated from his original accession), and ruled unchallenged until his death in 80. He also maintained a highly diplomatic neutrality in dealing with that dangerous Roman proconsul Lucius Cornelius Sulla (see p. 116): a proscribed rebel in Rome, his dictatorship still in the unpredictable future.

In the same year that Cyrenaica was bequeathed to Rome (96), Antiochus Grypos was assassinated by one of his own generals. He left no fewer than five legitimate sons, a guarantee of dynastic mayhem. They had to compete not only with one another, but with a still very active rival, Antiochus IX Cyzicenus. Heads rolled fast. Grypos' eldest son, Seleucus VI, defeated and killed Cyzicenus (95). Cyzicenus' son Antiochus X Eusebes ("the Pious") drove Seleucus VI out of Syria to Cilicia, where he was burned alive in his palace by an angry mob. Eusebes still had to compete with four of Grypos' sons, including a pair of twins. One twin was drowned in the Orontes. Another brother was captured by the Parthians. This left Philip Epiphanes in Antioch and Antiochus XII Dionysus holding Damascus. Antiochus XII was defeated and killed by the Arabs. Antiochus X Eusebes finished off Philip but got little benefit from his victory: between 90 and 88 the Arabs claimed his life, too. In 83 the citizens of Antioch, weary of this fratricidal killing spree and the anarchy it bred, offered the throne to Tigranes of Armenia, who accepted it. One modern work[1] makes a spirited counterattack against well-established notions of Seleucid decadence. Sensibly, its authors avoid carrying the story—and their argument—beyond the death of Antiochus VII.

While the Ptolemies and Seleucids, amid widespread secessions and revolts, pursued their self-destructive internal rivalries, the Greek cities of Asia Minor were getting a taste of the laissez-faire methods of Roman private enterprise. This appalling and largely uncontrolled regime of graft and exploitation—the ne plus ultra of the Successors' attitude to "spear-won territory"—had engendered a violent, if seemingly helpless, groundswell of furious resentment, already responsible for two major Sicilian slave revolts. No one (including the rebellious slaves) was against slavery as such, but a dangerously large number of educated victims of warfare and piracy felt they had been wrongly consigned to the servile category. The time was ripe for a savior (a local miracle worker had surfaced briefly in the slave revolt of 132), and in due course one appeared whose formidable talents were matched only by his sheer improbability.

Mithradates VI Eupator Dionysus (to give him his full eventual title), a semihellenized, Achaemenid-related monarch, was king of Pontus in Anatolia, on the southern shores of the Black Sea, and had the distinction of being the first ruler since Perseus of Macedon to offer a direct challenge to Rome. He modeled his appearance on that of Alexander and was an equally dashing cavalry commander, though, fatally, he lacked Alexander's strategic flair. In many ways, he imitated Hellenistic dynastic habits. But unlike other Hellenistic dynasts, he was abstemious, an indomitable fighter, and had the charismatic knack of getting men to follow him. Like Alexander, too, Mithradates was in the business of empire building: first via Colchis to the Crimea, then westward into Bithynia.

Here he first became apprised of the extortionate havoc being wreaked throughout Asia Minor by Roman entrepreneurs and at once (having a remarkable flair for creative propaganda) saw how he could cash in on the resentment thus aroused. From 103 onward, using the well-tried Hellenistic blend of diplomacy, aggression, intermarriage, and murder, he extended his power into Bithynia, Cappadocia, Paphlagonia, and Galatia. Rome, once freed from the threat of a Teutonic invasion, took notice. In 99/8, Gaius Marius, on a mission to the East, bluntly warned Mithradates either to be stronger than the Romans or to obey their orders. The Pontic king followed the second alternative while methodically preparing for the first. In 89, Rome's puppet monarchs of Cappadocia and Bithynia, whom he had ousted, came complaining of their treatment by Mithradates. The Senate ordered them reinstated, slapped Mithradates with an indemnity, and sent out a commissioner, Manius Aquillius—son of the brutal suppressor of the revolt of Aristonicus (p. 100), something that had not been forgotten—to enforce their orders. The client-kings were restored; but Mithradates refused to pay, ignored Aquillius' ultimatum, and then expelled the wretched king of Cappadocia for the third time. This meant war with Rome.

Mithradates in fact had a lot going for him: a large fleet and army, protective terrain, useful allies, Roman preoccupation with the Social War, the advantage of surprise—no one expected another Hellenistic princeling to try conclusions with the legions—and, above all, the hatred of Rome fomented throughout Asia Minor by the uncontrolled depredations of the tax-farmers and business tycoons. By painting the Romans as the new Barbarian Other, Mithradates could appeal both to the Greeks, for whom he portrayed himself as the Hellenist with a mission to rid Asia of materialist invaders, and to the Asiatics, who saw him as the descendant of Achaemenid kings such as Cyrus the Great and Darius. Portents circulated about his birth, as did inflammatory oracles predicting dire retribution against Rome for all her fiscal and commercial exploitation. When his armies swept across Anatolia to the Aegean (89/88), to begin with they carried all before them. Aquillius, captured in Mytilene, was reportedly executed by having molten gold poured down his throat.

The message was unmistakable and reinforced by an event that sent shock-waves across the Mediterranean. At some point in the summer of 88, Mithradates sent out secret orders to every town in the province of Asia, calling for the coordinated slaughter, on the same night, of every Roman and Italian—man, woman, and child—there resident. No fewer than eighty thousand tax-farmers, moneylenders, and other entrepreneurs, together with their families, are said to have perished. The effectiveness and secrecy of this pogrom were matched only by the unanimous enthusiasm—and frequent savagery—with which it was carried out. If, as has often been suggested, Mithradates was trying to bind the Asiatic Greeks to him in a kind of collective blood guilt, he found more than willing collaborators. This is all the more remarkable in that it committed those involved to a war to the death with the greatest Western military power then existing and the prospect of deadly punitive reprisals in the more than likely event of defeat. For these desperate rebels, such risks clearly paled beside the sufferings already inflicted on them.

It is the enormous support for Mithradates during the first two (very successful) years of his campaign that is really significant. Nothing more underlines this than the fact that when he moved across into mainland Greece, Athens joined him. For long now the city had been ruled by a mixed group of oligarchs, culled from both the aristocracy and the business world. The original driving motive of rooted hostility to Macedon had been lost after Pydna; what remained was commercial ambition and social elitism, based on unswerving subservience to Rome. When frustrated Athenian democrats showed sympathy for Mithradates, their leaders closed the gymnasia, banned public assemblies, and suspended university lectures. The result was a coup that threw out the oligarchs, restored some kind of democracy, and made a direct approach to Mithradates, who was more than glad to have the use of Piraeus for his fleet. Something like a reign of terror against the old regime (now denounced as "anarchy") began. The wealthy fled to Roman protection; some were hunted down and killed. Athens went into one of its recurrent fits of political hysteria.

Expectations that Rome would be too preoccupied with the Social War to deal with Mithradates received a rude shock in the spring of 87 with the arrival in Greece of no fewer than five legions under the command of that formidable general Lucius Cornelius Sulla. He made straight for Athens. Already notorious because of his march on Rome, and there regarded as a rebel, Sulla knew well that his future depended entirely on his military successes, and he was not disposed to be conciliatory. Attica's remaining woods (including the trees of the Academy and the Lyceum) were felled wholesale for siege engines. Convoys were intercepted. Starving Athenians boiled leather and ate it. Roman catapult balls hit targets in the Agora. In March 86, Sulla's troops scaled Athens's walls and sacked the city. The Kerameikos, famously, ran red with blood. The great port of Piraeus, including its arsenal, was burned to the ground. Democratic leaders were executed, their supporters disenfranchised. The oligarchs were returned to power, but in a city that had lost all its political privileges. Valuable works of art were dispatched wholesale to Rome. Sulla raided the treasury for what little remained there. Athens' resultant insolvency became so acute that the government was forced to sell off the island of Salamis. Nothing could obliterate the city's ancient prestige; but little else of Athenian greatness survived. It was, indeed, the end of an era.

———

Yet Athens, after all, remained for centuries, despite all vicissitudes, the acknowledged center of Greco-Roman intellectual life and, above all, the base for every philosophical school. What impact did all the seismic shifts of power, the cultural and ethnic disruptions, and the notions of colonial exploitation as an established way of life have on an intellectual elite divided between covert resistance and—to an increasing degree as time went on—profitable collaboration with the regime in power? How far, as their ideals faded through increasing unfamiliarity with power-based polis democracy in action, did these thinkers and writers, Athenian and other, acclimatize themselves to having the last word only in philosophical debate, mathematical problems, and historical glorification of a lost past? What led them, variously, to deify rulers (or, by extension, to see gods as rulers once deified), to dream up utopias in the Indian Ocean, to believe in astrology and a world-soul, to aim for purely negative ideals—*absence* of pain, grief, suffering—to sideline the divine pantheon in favor of a random dance of atoms, to aspire to be *cosmopolitae,* citizens of a large and radically changing world?

Paradoxically, it was the polis in its external manifestations—theaters, gymnasia, civic officialdom, the religious year cycle, traditional cults, honorific decrees, endless litigation and public debate—that survived through all the Sturm und Drang of Hellenistic power politics to give the Greeks of this new world a nostalgic sense, despite the loss of real independence and control, that things had not really changed, that the fundamental structure of their lives remained the same. In a sense, of course, this was true. The polis had always been, in essence, a local—not to say parochial—phenomenon, and so it remained; what it had lost was the strictly limited world over which it ruled. One of the unlooked-for novelties that Alexander and the Successors had introduced was true internationalism: the proportions of political life had simply been upscaled to a hitherto inconceivable degree, and the communication systems—physical, verbal, mental—necessary for these wider horizons soon followed. The spread of Attic Greek as a lingua franca, the development of the monsoon-based seatraffic between India and the West, even the concept of the *cosmopolites:* all sprang naturally from Alexander's conquests.

The shift of emphasis from public to private life that we have seen manifesting itself in various ways throughout this study was, looked at politically, a formal resignation of public ambition in the old Periclean sense, an abandonment of pretensions to empire. It did not come easily, and the philosophical panaceas produced during the Hellenistic era tend to confirm what Hesiod had learned the hard way in the eighth century: that those lacking superior force need to convince themselves—and they may be right just often enough to keep the belief going—that the pen is indeed mightier than the sword. Even so, to a remarkable degree all Hellenistic creeds, from Stoicism to the counterculture of the Cynics, were agreed that, as Xenocrates (head of the Academy 339–314) put it, in the immediate aftermath of Chaeronea and the collapse of the Achaemenid empire, "[the] reason for discovering philosophy is to allay that which causes disturbance in life."[2] The full implications of this attitude are not always appreciated. What such statements—and they came to be a commonplace—imply is a kind of intellectual tsunami, a universal disaster from which philosophy must attempt to salvage what it can, and for the survivors of which it sets out to provide some kind of makeshift comfort.

As always, the articulate witnesses to this phenomenon are the educated, and for the most part moneyed, elite, and it is their reactions that survive. Even the Cynics, with their ostentatious poverty, their rejection of the polis with all its social restraints and civic conventions (including property, capital, and the class system), were largely upper-class intellectuals masquerading as itinerant beggars, still parasitically dependent on the society they spent their time abusing. The invisible masses, both rural and urban, toiled unseen and unheard, except when (as happened with increasing frequency, especially in the overpopulated cities) they revolted. The record we have, though limited to an intellectual minority, still speaks with some eloquence to the dilemmas that faced a thinking man in a world where, no longer master of his fate, he had to content himself with being, in one way or another, captain of his soul.

It should thus come as no surprise that by far the most popular branch of philosophy throughout the Hellenistic era was that of ethics. Moral guidelines became essential, and they could very easily be dressed up as advice to rulers (an increasingly popular literary form): if one could no longer control an autocrat by force majeure, one at least had a chance of reasoning him into agreement. And the rulers themselves were by no means averse to acquiring cultural prestige through the presence at their courts of distinguished poets and philosophers. Those whose prime goal was *ataraxia*, absence of upset, were unlikely to upset their patrons. Indeed, even before Aristotle, a treatise such as the *Rhetorica ad Alexandrum* (generally attributed to Anaximander of Lampsacus) is already enthusiastically promoting free enterprise oligarchy and attacking any kind of democratic radicalism.

When the Successors declared themselves kings, there was thus no shortage of intellectuals eager to provide them with a theoretical basis for their rule. Indeed, during the centuries that followed, the class hierarchy hardened, the gap between haves and have-nots widened, the indifference to slaves and poverty increased. To a considerable extent, this attitude was backed and encouraged by the tenets of Stoicism, which promoted a geocentric universe, a perfect cosmological harmony of movement (*sympatheia*) between the heavenly bodies and this world, a belief in teleological Intelligent Design with Zeus as prime mover, and the ability of any man to plan his life in accordance with both divine will and nature. Anything that happened was fated to happen. Nature was providentially well-disposed toward mankind: thus, whatever happened had to be right. Astrology was justified. This fixed order of things might have been designed to reinforce the eternal ratification of a ruling class. Posidonius equated Rome with the cosmic microcosm. Stoicism became the intellectual bulwark of the empire.

It was perhaps inevitable, then, that Stoicism should, before the end of the Republic, have worked out a flexible moral creed that allowed businessmen and provincial governors to maintain high-minded principles and still have extremely profitable careers. A classic instance is Marcus Brutus, the assassin of Julius Caesar, whose well-known moral purity did not stop him charging 48 percent annual interest on loans. That persistent upper-class contempt in the ancient world for all things banausic (pp. 53–54) must have encouraged such double-standard thinking. For those, on the other hand, without political ambitions, the urge to remove oneself entirely from public life must have been strong, and stronger still as Rome's control over the Greek world became absolute. Hence the popularity of Epicureanism, the nearest thing to a modern commune, even to a kind of secular monasticism, that the period has to offer. It also possessed many of the features of a sectarian cult, including leader worship, ideological dogma, and regular financial support by the faithful.

Embraced by progressive individuals, it was—for all the same reasons—anathema to public-minded traditionalists. Epicureanism sidelined the gods into a blissful Elysium irrelevant to this world. It declared pleasure to be the central principle of life; and though—characteristically for a Hellenistic creed—it equated pleasure with the removal of pain, nothing could have been better calculated to elicit the shrill diatribes of puritan moralists. Worst of all, from their point of view, it challenged the comfortingly teleological view of the universe embraced by the Stoics, declaring creation a random dance of atoms and denying any kind of afterlife. Thus a good deal of Epicurean discourse (to judge from Lucretius) was devoted to reconciling the faithful to this life as a one-shot, with death as its terminus. There are interesting parallels here with modern existentialism.

It all sounds a trifle bleak. Yet the communal life first worked out in Athens by Epicurus himself (341–270 BCE), and widely practiced thereafter, found a constant stream of devoted adherents. It was egalitarian, in that it admitted all classes, women and slaves included, without distinction: the poor were supported by the subscriptions of the wealthy. This came nearer than anything else to the alternative society sought by slave leaders like Spartacus, and partially explains its powerful attraction. Epicureanism's intellectual objective was to achieve true peace of mind, but here (like so many creeds) it fell short by simply arguing away or dogmatically denying anything, from religious myths to Fate (*Tyche*), that got in the way. It was antisocial, antiprovidential, anti-eschatological, and, in the last resort (despite its atomism), anti-intellectual. If it offered, in a limited way, the perennial upper-class Greek ideal of endowed leisure (slaves did all the commune's work), it was still—in this like Cynicism—ultimately dependent for its security and civic well-being on the society from which it had removed itself. Thus in essence Hellenistic philosophizing tended to be either politically collaborative or economically unreal. As a comment on the Alexandrian legacy of justified exploitation, this has a sour logic all its own.

———

After Sulla's victories, Mithradates retreated to Pontus. His prestige had been shaken, but he was far from finished. His Greek allies, Athens above all, were not so lucky. Quite apart from the systematic destruction carried out by the legions, the Greek cities of Asia were largely insolvent. They had to borrow to pay Sulla's indemnity of 20,000 talents, but the rates of interest on the loans were so extortionate that ten years later, though the debt had been paid twice over, the total still outstanding was six times that of the original sums advanced. The pogrom in 88 had clearly not changed the habits of Roman moneylenders. On top of other reprisals, legions were billeted in the cities (85/4). The bulk of the population in Macedonia, mainland Greece, and Asia Minor was now made tributary. Roman imperium in a uniquely profitable region had been seriously challenged by Mithradates. Commercial and official interests now combined to ensure that such a challenge never happened again. In the process, Rome became firmly committed to the permanent absorption of the Greek east.

The fifty years (80–30 BCE) that saw Rome's final political takeover of the Hellenistic world also witnessed the convulsive death throes of the Roman Republic and its replacement by a professedly benevolent imperial autocrat, Caesar's adopted heir, Octavian, who took the title of Augustus. In this, as in so much else, the new ruler echoed the political lessons of the post-Alexandrian world that now formed part of his empire. Augustus had also learned from his predecessors' omissions. Alexander's indifference to organizing the empire he had won astonished him: that was not a mistake he ever made himself. What emerged, paradoxically, from the protracted civil wars in which Octavian won the final victory was a larger, better-run, and ultimately less exploitative Hellenistic-style kingdom. Its center was on the Tiber rather than the Nile, and that kept Rome's traditionalists happy; but otherwise there was little about the *pax Augusta*—least of all the bread and circuses—that would have surprised Ptolemy Philadelphus or Antiochus the Great.

The internal upheavals and overseas involvements of Rome during this fraught half-century inevitably affected the Greek world. Dictator from 81 (after a bloody civil war and even bloodier proscriptions), and in possession of Ptolemy X's will bequeathing his kingdom to Rome, Sulla added to the confusion in Alexandria by playing the kingmaker. On Lathyros' death in 81/0, he sent out Ptolemy X's son as the successor. The youth (Ptolemy XI) was required to marry Lathyros' daughter Cleopatra Berenice, his stepmother or, possibly, his mother. After the honeymoon, he murdered her and was duly lynched by the Alexandrian mob. Sulla (in this typically Roman) took no further steps to implement the will but washed his hands of the whole business. The succession went to an illegitimate son of Lathyros, a debauchee and playboy known variously as the Bastard or the Piper (only modern historians label him Ptolemy XII), whose chief claim to fame was begetting, in 69, on his sister-wife, Cleopatra V Tryphaena, a daughter who grew up to be the most famous of all the Cleopatras.

In 76, Quintus Sertorius—rebel and traitor or legitimate anti-Sullan proconsul, depending which side you were on—while campaigning successfully in Spain against Pompey, ratified a treaty with Mithradates. (The irony of this Republican diehard being forced into exactly the same position his bête noire Sulla had faced in Asia Minor was lost on no one.) Two years later, Nicomedes IV, king of Bithynia, died and, following a by now fashionable tradition, left his kingdom to Rome. Mithradates, with Sertorius' encouragement and still hell-bent on acquiring Bithynia for himself, declared war on Rome for the second time, still not having learned the lesson that no army he could put in the field was a match for the legions. Despite some naval successes, the old lion of Pontus was beaten, first by Lucullus, strategist and epicure, in a sporadic five-year-long campaign and then (after Lucullus was undermined by political enemies in Rome) from 66 to 63 by Pompey. Pompey called Lucullus a Xerxes in a toga. Lucullus responded that Pompey was a vulture, feasting on carrion that others had killed. Mithradates, faced with the prospect of extradition to Rome, and immune to poison, had a Galatian officer run him through.

Pompey came to this particular task with a high reputation, having in 67 carried out a remarkably fast and successful campaign against the pirates of the Mediterranean. Ever since the mid–second century, and in particular since the opening up of the province of Asia, piracy had steadily spiraled out of control. The secret of the corsairs' huge and ever-mounting success was, of course, the slave-trade. This had resulted in the pirates being given open support by businessmen and entrepreneurs everywhere and covert encouragement by a number of governments, including that of Rome (cf. p. 77). But sheer unchecked accumulation of wealth turned the milch cow into a monster. The pirates crippled legitimate trade throughout the Mediterranean. They disrupted the grain-supply. They raided coastal areas and kidnapped well-to-do individuals (including the young Julius Caesar) for ransom. More alarming still, they began to show signs of political ambition, convinced that "if they united, they would be invincible."[3] They had over a thousand warships. They were viciously hostile to Roman authority. Small wonder that in 74 an *imperium infinitum*, a command without limits, was set up to deal with them. A year later, the great slave revolt led by Spartacus broke out. The notion of an alternative society was very much in the air. Needless to say, the pirates and Mithradates supported each other wholeheartedly.

This dangerously subversive crisis called for special action and got it. By the *Lex Gabinia* of 67, Pompey obtained a three-year special command to clear up the mess. Despite violent senatorial opposition, he finally had at his disposal twenty-four legates, five hundred ships, and 125,000 troops. Dividing the Mediterranean into thirteen separate subcommands, he cleaned out the pirate strongholds from west to east, starting with Sicily, Sardinia, and North Africa, since securing Rome's grain-supply had high priority. The job was done in three months rather than three years. Efficient it undoubtedly was, but the suspicion of a deal remains inescapable. Pirates were normally executed out of hand, and these pirates had kidnapped high Roman officials, sheltered runaway slaves, and fought alongside Mithradates. Yet they got a mass amnesty and were indeed rehabilitated, being resettled in abandoned Cilician cities and encouraged to take up farming.

This leniency was unpopular with the well-to-do, and Pompey's methods make an interesting contrast to those of Crassus, who on finally (71) defeating Spartacus—after several years of hard-fought battles—crucified six thousand rebel slaves along the Via Appia between Capua and Rome as an object-lesson and deterrent. There were no more major slave revolts, but piracy (although never entirely eradicated) ceased to be a major problem, too. The conclusion—that iron hand or velvet glove made little difference to the ultimate outcome—is depressing but probably inevitable.

Under the mandate that had given him the command against Mithradates and Tigranes of Armenia (both already weakened beyond real recovery by Lucullus), Pompey was also empowered, upon victory, to conduct a general settlement of the East. This meant, in effect, disposing of the old Seleucid empire. On arrival in Syria (64), he was met by a ghost from the past. In 69, when Lucullus drove out Tigranes, the Antiochenes—royalists to the end—had acclaimed Antiochus XIII Asiaticus, Antiochus X's son, as their legitimate monarch. Lucullus approved, and Asiaticus was crowned king. Pompey contemptuously insisted on his abdication, and Asiaticus went back to his Arab patron, who (with equal contempt) murdered him. So died the last obscure claimant to Seleucus Nicator's once-great empire. Pompey created three new provinces: Syria, Cilicia, and Bithynia/Pontus. Beyond them lay an outer ring of client-kingdoms, including Galatia, Cappadocia, Commagene, and Judaea. Of the original Hellenistic dynasties, only Ptolemaic Egypt now remained.

———

The machinations of the last Ptolemies to maintain a precarious sovereignty in the face of Roman encroachment never lost sight of the fact that a legitimate ruler, Ptolemy X, had formally bequeathed his kingdom to Rome. It was thus essential to convince the Senate that Rome would be better off with a weak but independent Ptolemaic regime than with a new province. Their best psychological argument (as subsequent events made clear) was that Egypt, with its wealth and natural defenses, offered an all-too-tempting springboard for any Roman proconsul seeking supreme power. Thus when in 65 the ambitious millionaire Crassus proposed implementing the will and taking over Egypt, the suggestion was at once vetoed.

But the existence of that will also dictated the speed with which the Alexandrians had propelled the Piper, Lathyros' son by a concubine, to the throne and had him crowned pharaoh by the Egyptian priesthood in Memphis. It also explains why, at the same time, they created a new precedent by declaring his brother king of an independent Cyprus: Rome, it was felt, would find this division of authority reassuring. The endless bribing of Roman officials (for which the officials themselves raised the stakes to dizzy heights) was a natural consequence of such a policy. What the Piper wanted was Rome's official recognition, and that came expensive. The will could always be used as a way of extorting extra protection money from the Alexandrian treasury. Surprisingly, this dubious arrangement kept the situation relatively stable for some years, until, with Crassus' intervention, the rich prize of Egypt became a bone of contention among Rome's rival would-be leaders.

While the Piper dug into his exchequer for massive handouts to Pompey (who did nothing in return, knowing better than to ruin his reputation in Rome by intervening in Egypt at this point), politicians fought it out in the courts and the Senate. A bill to facilitate the sale of public land in the provinces was fueled by the hope of including Egypt under Ptolemy X's bequest. Cicero and his backers saw, as the Alexandrians had seen, the looming risk of some ambitious aristocrat securing Egypt as a power base from which to attack, and perhaps destroy, the Republic. Their scare tactics worked, and the bill was withdrawn. But Caesar, Crassus, and the *populares* were determined to lay hands on Egypt, and in 60 the formation of the first triumvirate spurred the Piper to frantic activity. He offered Caesar and Pompey no less than 6,000 talents in return for his recognition as the legitimate Ptolemaic dynast. This did the trick. In 59, Caesar, as consul, secured Ptolemy's confirmation by the Senate and his appointment as Friend and Ally of the Roman People (*amicus et socius populi Romani*).

The Piper's expensive investment (it ate up his revenues for an entire year) did him little immediate good. No mention had been made of Cyprus in the deal, and the Romans made a perfunctory nod to Ptolemy X's will by sending Cato to annex the island as part of the province of Cilicia. The Piper's brother committed suicide. Ptolemy's Alexandrian advisers, furious both at this and at his profligate and useless expenditure on bribes, forced him out (58). Since Rome had recognized him, to Rome he went. He was not to return for three years. During his absence, the Piper's neglected wife, Cleopatra V Tryphaena, and his eldest daughter, Berenice (IV), took firm control. Tryphaena died in 57; Berenice, with ambitions of her own and aware that Rome disliked petticoat governments, looked around desperately for a passable husband. A soi-disant Seleucid nicknamed, from his oafish manners, Kybiosaktes ("the Salt-Fish Hawker") proved so revolting that after a few days of marital intimacy, she had him strangled. She then, having reached the bottom of the barrel, fell back on one Archelaus, son of Mithradates' general of that name.

Meanwhile her detested father, as she well knew, was making trouble for her in Rome. One potential Seleucid spouse had already been blocked from Egypt by the triumvirate's man in Syria, Aulus Gabinius. She and her advisers now sent a large delegation to argue their case before the Senate. The Piper had most of them murdered by hired thugs and the survivors intimidated into silence. Opponents of Egyptian intervention were reduced to manufacturing an oracle. This, surprisingly, did the trick. The Piper withdrew to Ephesus, but neither he nor Pompey had given up. Nor had the bankers, above all Rabirius Postumus, who had shelled out vast sums in loans to the Piper and needed to recoup his investment to avoid bankruptcy. Forged letters circulated. The Piper promised more cash. During his consulship (55), Pompey called on Aulus Gabinius to restore the legitimate king to the throne of the Ptolemies, and for the first time ever, Roman legions entered Egypt. Archelaus died in battle. The Piper's first act on restoration was to execute his overambitious daughter Berenice.

All this was watched with intense interest by Berenice's younger sister, the brilliant and even more ambitious fourteen-year-old Cleopatra (VII). Tradition, inevitably, has it that she too was noticed—by Gabinius' cavalry commander, Marcus Antonius, better known to history as Mark Antony—but if so, nothing came of it at the time: both had higher immediate goals in view. Meanwhile, the Piper had been forced to take on Rabirius Postumus as his finance minister. The resultant campaign of extortion produced so violent a reaction from the populace that Rabirius had to be smuggled out of the country. Back in Rome, both he and Gabinius were prosecuted by the opposition for illegal profiteering. The Piper, protected by German and Gallic troops, put a clause in his will making Rome responsible for the maintenance of his dynasty. In 52, he made the now seventeen-year-old Cleopatra (who clearly had steered her adolescent way through this minefield with some finesse) his co-regent and successor, though also, obligatorily, marrying her off to her barely pubescent younger brother, Ptolemy XIII. Early in 51, he died.

Cleopatra lost no time in asserting her independence. By August, she had challenged titular male priorities by dropping her brother's name from public documents and putting her own portrait and name—without his—on Ptolemaic coinage. For over a year, she ruled alone. But then (in the fall of 50, a month or two before Caesar crossed the Rubicon) a court cabal, led by the inevitable scheming eunuch, one Pothinus, succeeded in restoring Ptolemy XIII as leading dynast, with Cleopatra relegated to second place. By the summer of 49 (when Caesar and Pompey were already on collision course in Greece), Pothinus, aided by Ptolemy's tutor, Theodotus, and a half-Greek general named Achillas, had forced Cleopatra and her sister Arsinoë to flee from Alexandria, first to the Thebaïd, then (48) to Syria. The Ptolemaic court supplied Pompey with ships (he had, after all, been the Piper's guest-friend); Pompey in return, ignoring the Piper's will, recognized Ptolemy XIII.

Then came Caesar's victory at Pharsalus (June 48). Pompey retreated to Egypt, confident of a guest-friend's welcome. The cabal gave him due assurances and murdered him on arrival, while the boy-king, in full regalia, watched. Pompey's pickled head was sent to Caesar, who shed tears but must have felt relief.[4] Two days later, he arrived in Alexandria with a small force and preceded by his lictors. The court officials, whose one aim was to preserve Egypt's independence and keep out of Rome's civil war, were not amused. Riots followed. Cleopatra, who had raised troops in Syria and was confronting her brother's defense force at the frontier city of Pelusium, had herself delivered through the lines to Caesar, hidden in her famous carpet, and ended up in his bed. Young Ptolemy screamed he had been betrayed. Caesar made conciliatory speeches. Brother and sister were proclaimed joint rulers again. The opéra bouffe of the so-called Alexandrian War was about to begin.

Whether it was the attractions of Egypt or the person of Egypt's queen that most affected his judgment, there can be no doubt that Caesar had badly misjudged the situation. Pothinus brought the troops back from Pelusium, and Caesar, outnumbered, found himself under siege in the port and palace area. Once he had to swim for it to escape capture, abandoning his purple general's cloak. Part of the great Library's holdings went up in flames. Arsinoë fled from the palace and was proclaimed queen by the mob. Eventually (March 47), Caesar was rescued by an army under Mithradates of Pergamon. Ptolemy XIII's forces were defeated, the boy-king himself was drowned in the Nile, Pothinus executed, and Arsinoë put under house arrest. Cleopatra, now six months pregnant, was taken on a sightseeing cruise up the Nile. To placate public opinion, she married her younger brother, Ptolemy XIV. Her son by Caesar, Caesarion, was born on June 23, 47.

Before that date, Caesar had already left on a whirlwind campaign. He crushed Mithradates' son Pharnaces at Zela (the occasion of his "*Veni, vidi, vici*" mot), reorganized the eastern provinces, put down an army mutiny in Italy (September 47), beat the Republican forces at Thapsus in North Africa two months later, and celebrated four triumphs in the fall of 46, at which time he brought Cleopatra, Caesarion, and their entourage to Rome and domiciled them in his town house across the Tiber. The luxury of this minicourt aroused public disapproval. The queen called herself the New Isis, and Caesar put up a gold statue of her in the temple of Venus Genetrix. Cicero found her both odious and arrogant. Rumors of deification and the establishment of Alexandria as a second capital were in the air: Mark Antony afterward had precedent to work on. When Caesar fell to the daggers of the assassins on the Ides of March 44, there can be little doubt that his relationship with Cleopatra had done much to accelerate his death.

When Caesar's will was read and Caesarion did not figure in it, Cleopatra and her entourage left at once for Alexandria: Shakespeare's "serpent of old Nile" was now at high risk in Rome. She found Egypt ravaged by plague, famine, and social unrest, the result of several years' low inundations and poor crops. The Alexandrian mob was appeased with a grain distribution from the royal warehouses: the queen had other things on her mind. A Hellenistic dynast to the core, she had her adolescent brother and co-ruler, Ptolemy XIV, killed and replaced him with Caesarion, now three years old. At least she would secure the Egyptian succession. In the new civil war at Rome between Caesarians and Republicans, she had no option but to support the former. This was not always a success. She sent the four legions Caesar had left her to Caesar's faithful lieutenant Dolabella: they promptly deserted en masse to the Republican Cassius. But after Philippi (42) had eliminated both Cassius and Brutus and led to the Caesarian triumvirate of Caesar's adopted heir, Octavian, Lepidus, and Mark Antony—who obtained a commission to settle the East—she saw all too clearly where her royal future lay.

The story of Cleopatra's ambitious, and ultimately tragic, liaison with Mark Antony has become justly famous. Yet as should by now be clear, it was not a case of the world well lost for love. The Roman general needed a power base and financing for his Parthian campaign and, beyond that, his imperial aspirations. The Macedonian queen dreamed of restoring the lost glories of her dynasty. What they shared, over and above these hopes, was the vision of a greater united empire than any earlier Hellenistic ruler had imagined. Antiochus IV, before the Day of Eleusis, had seen a chance of combining the Seleucid and Ptolemaic realms. Seleucus I had briefly confirmed all Alexander's eastern conquests. What Antony and Cleopatra glimpsed was an empire that added to all these Rome itself and Rome's new conquests in the western Mediterranean. When Cleopatra made her preferred oath, "As surely as I shall yet dispense justice on the Roman Capitol" (Dio Cass. 50.5.4), it was this vast Mediterranean dominion over which she saw herself enthroned. Not even Alexander had dreamed on a grander scale.

She had charmed the abstemious Caesar by intellect; summoned to Tarsus by Antony the bon vivant in 41, she hooked him, equally fast, with a staggering (and rather vulgar) display of luxury, subsequently immortalized by Shakespeare. No one could beat her at adapting style to audience. She also lost no time in getting herself pregnant by her new lover and bore him twins about the same time as his politically necessary marriage to Octavian's sister Octavia. Octavia remained loyal to her raffish husband; her brother turned against him. Unfortunately for Octavia, she bore the by now dynastically minded Antony nothing but daughters. Cleopatra provided male heirs. In 37/6, Antony began to sever his ties with Rome and develop his and Cleopatra's dream of a biracial new order, a Romano-Hellenistic empire.

In 34, these aspirations were publicized by an extraordinary ceremony in Alexandria, at which their children, in full royal regalia, were proclaimed rulers of territories as yet mostly outside their control: the old Seleucid empire (including Parthia), Cyrenaica, Crete, Syria, and Asia Minor. Caesar's son, Caesarion, was to be King of Kings and joint ruler of Egypt with his mother. Where, exactly, this left Antony remains an open question. Like Perdiccas, like Antigonus One-Eye, like Seleucus, like Lysimachus, he had been seduced by the dream of world empire. In 32/1, he divorced Octavia and put Cleopatra's head, with his, on his official Roman coinage. Octavian declared war on Cleopatra—no mention of Antony—and the propaganda mills got to work: the moviemakers' femme fatale is, in essence, Cleopatra as Horace and Propertius painted her. At Actium on September 2, 31, Octavian's admiral Agrippa, with a crushing naval victory, put paid to her, and Antony's, grandiose ambitions. Less than a year later, both, famously, committed suicide. (One court cynic, parodying Homer [*Il.* 2.204], remarked: "Lots of Caesars are no good thing: let there be one Caesar only.") Caesarion was executed. On August 29, 30 BCE, Caesar's adopted heir, Octavian, in Alexandria, proclaimed the end of the Ptolemaic dynasty. News that the treasures of Egypt were in Roman hands dropped interest rates at Rome from 12 to 4 percent.

The Hellenistic kingdoms were the legacy of Alexander's conquests. Dying, he correctly predicted that his spoils would go "to the strongest." The three centuries we have studied reveal an unswerving policy of competitive exploitation, enabled and justified by military power. In the end, these Greek and Macedonian rulers succumbed to a stronger power: the phalanx was no match for the legions. Octavian's final victory brought an end not only to Greco-Macedonian independence, but also to the internecine struggles of the Roman civil wars. His imposition of the *pax Augusta* led grateful survivors to regard him, in true Hellenistic style, as a god. He curbed private extortion, regularized relations between cities and proconsular authorities, and built on the huge expansion of horizons, the internationalizing of trade and culture that Alexander, all unintentionally, had created.

Perhaps most notably, Attic Greek, as a lingua franca, facilitated the spread of ideas, literatures, and beliefs to an unprecedented degree. Again, this had not been planned. Yet in the end—and if there is a moral to be drawn from the Hellenistic age, this surely is it—the essential condition of the common people, from mountain tribesmen to fellahin and, a fortiori, slaves, had changed little between the coming of Alexander and the death of Cleopatra; nor would it, until the advent of the Industrial Revolution meant that they were no longer the near-exclusive and stringently controlled source of the world's energy and could break free, at last, from that imprisoning and repetitive cycle.

SELECTIVE CHRONOLOGICAL TABLE

359 Philip II of Macedon succeeds to the throne, defeats the Illyrians.

356 Philip's son by Olympias, Alexander, born in Pella (June).

346 Peace of Philocrates ratified between Athens and Macedonia.

343/2 Aristotle invited to Macedonia as Alexander's tutor.

342/1 Olympias' brother Alexander, with Philip's help, succeeds to throne of Epirus.

340 Alexander as regent at sixteen: foundation of Alexandropolis.

338 Macedonian defeat of allied Greek states at Chaeronea (August).
     Alexander ambassador to Athens.
     Repudiation of Olympias; Philip marries Attalus' niece Cleopatra.
     Olympias and Alexander in exile.

337 Alexander recalled to Pella.
     Hellenic League endorses anti-Persian crusade.

336 Advance expedition under Parmenio and Attalus crosses to Asia Minor.
     Accession of Darius III to Achaemenid throne (June).
     Birth of son to Philip's wife Cleopatra.
     Alexander of Epirus marries Philip's daughter; murder of Philip.
     Philip's son Alexander accedes as Alexander III, confirmed as leader of anti-Persian crusade.

335 Alexander's campaigns in Thrace and Illyria.
     Revolt and destruction of Thebes.

334 Alexander and his army cross into Asia Minor (March–April).
     Battle of the Granicus (May).

333 Episode of the Gordian Knot.
     Battle of Issus (fall).

332 Siege of Tyre, capture of Gaza.
     Alexander enters Egypt, is enthroned (?) as pharaoh at Memphis.

331 Alexander visits oracle of Zeus Ammon at Siwah.
Foundation of Alexandria (spring).
Battle of Gaugamela (fall).
Revolt of Spartan king Agis III defeated at Megalopolis by Antipater.

330 Sacking of Persepolis (? January).
Burning of Persepolis temples (spring).
Greek allies dismissed at Ecbatana.
Darius III murdered by Bessus, who proclaims himself "Great King."
Alleged conspiracy of Philotas: execution of Parmenio.

329 Alexander crosses the Hindu Kush, reaches the Oxus river.
Veterans and Thessalians dismissed.
Surrender of Bessus, revolt of Spitamenes.

328 Murder of Cleitus the Black by Alexander.
Defeat of Spitamenes.

327 Alexander marries Roxane.
Recruitment of Persian "Successors."
Pages' conspiracy, execution of Callisthenes.
Alexander recrosses Hindu Kush into India.

326 Battle of the Hydaspes/Jhelum against Indian rajah Porus.
Death of Alexander's horse, Bucephalus.
Mutiny by Alexander's troops at the Hyphasis (Beas) river.

325 Alexander seriously wounded while attacking Indian city.
Revolt of mercenaries in Bactria.
March through Gedrosian desert.
Satrapal purge begins.

324 Alexander moves to Persepolis, then to Susa: the Susa mass marriages.
The Exiles' and Deification decrees.
Alexander moves to Ecbatana: the death of Hephaestion.

323 Alexander returns to Babylon (spring), falls ill after a party, and dies
     on June 11.
Perdiccas assumes control; partition of satrapies (Ptolemy gets
     Egypt).
Outbreak of Lamian War; Antipater besieged in Lamia.
Roxane gives birth to Alexander IV.

322 Antipater wins Lamian War; death of Leonnatus.
Athenian fleet defeated off Amorgos.
Battle of Crannon (August); Macedonian garrison imposed on Athens.
Deaths of Aristotle, Demosthenes, and Hypereides.

321 Ptolemy hijacks Alexander's funeral cortege: his body taken to
     Memphis.
Adea-Eurydice marries Philip Arrhidaeus.
Antigonus One-Eye and Antipater in coalition against Perdiccas.

320 Eumenes defeats Craterus and Neoptolemus (May).
Perdiccas invades Egypt, is murdered by his own officers (June).
Conference at Triparadeisos (? July).
Seleucus enters Babylon (? November).
319 Antigonus defeats Eumenes, besieges him in Nora (spring).
Ptolemy annexes Syria and Palestine.
Death of Antipater; Polyperchon regent.
Birth of Pyrrhus.
318 Democratic revolution in Athens; Polyperchon's "Freedom Decree."
Eumenes released by Antigonus, joins Polyperchon.
317 Athenian revolution collapses; Cassander appoints Demetrius of
Phaleron governor of Athens.
Eurydice supports Cassander, who invades Macedonia, secures
Roxane and Alexander IV.
Philip Arrhidaeus murdered by Olympias; Eurydice commits
suicide.
316 Battle of Paraetacene (fall); Pydna under siege.
315 Eumenes defeated at Gabiene, executed; Antigonus reorganizes
upper satrapies.
Fall of Pydna; execution of Olympias.
Cassander marries Thessalonike, refounds Thebes.
Seleucus flees Babylon, joins Ptolemy in Egypt.
315/4 Coalition of satraps against Antigonus: Antigonus marches on Syria,
rejects coalition's demands, begins siege of Tyre.
Antigonus' "Old Tyre manifesto" (fall).
314 Antigonus organizes League of Islanders.
Ptolemy proclaims Greek "freedom."
313 Tyre falls to Antigonus.
Ptolemy moves capital (and Alexander's body) from Memphis to
Alexandria.
312 Seleucus regains Babylonia, Susiana, Media: first regnal year of
Seleucids.
Ptolemy defeats Demetrius Poliorcetes at Gaza, takes over Coele-
Syria.
311 Seleucia-on-Tigris capital of Seleucid empire.
Antigonus recaptures Coele-Syria; Ptolemy withdraws.
Coalition makes peace with Antigonus: all Greek cities granted
"freedom and autonomy."
310 Cassander executes Alexander IV and Roxane: end of Argead
dynasty.
309 Birth of Ptolemy II Philadelphus.
Execution of Alexander's illegitimate son Heracles.

308 Execution of Alexander's sister Cleopatra in Sardis.
Seleucus in eastern satrapies, clash with Chandragupta.
Ptolemy "frees" Corinth and Sicyon, secures Cyrene.

307 Demetrius Poliorcetes "frees" Athens, Demetrius of Phaleron exiled, becomes Ptolemy's adviser on Museum and Library (June).
Foundation of Antigoneia.
Restrictive law in Athens on schools of philosophy; Theophrastus and others leave.

306 Demetrius Poliorcetes' naval victory over Ptolemy, capture of Cyprus.
Antigonus and Demetrius assume kingship (new dynasty).
Athens: philosophy law rescinded; Theophrastus returns; Epicurus establishes his Garden; Athenian *ephebeia* now voluntary.

305 Lysimachus, Seleucus, Ptolemy, and Cassander all proclaim themselves kings.
Demetrius Poliorcetes begins siege of Rhodes.

304 Demetrius raises siege of Rhodes, scores victories over Cassander in Greece, returns to Athens (quartered in Parthenon).

303 Renewal of coalition against Antigonus One-Eye.
Seleucus makes pact with Chandragupta, cedes eastern satrapies for war-elephants.

302 Antigonus and Demetrius revive League of Corinth; League appoints Demetrius commander in chief. Truce with Cassander.
Antigonus recalls Demetrius to Asia.

301 Battle of Ipsus, death of Antigonus; Ptolemy occupies Coele-Syria.
Demetrius retreats to Ephesus.
League of Corinth dissolved; neutralist government in Athens.

300 Demetrius fighting Lysimachus.
Lysimachus marries Ptolemy's daughter Arsinoë (II).
Foundation of Seleucia-in-Pieria and Antioch.
Magas governor of Cyrene.

299 Pyrrhus in Alexandria as envoy/hostage.
Alliances of Ptolemy and Lysimachus, Seleucus and Demetrius Poliorcetes.

298 ? Lachares now seizes Athens.

298/7 Death of Cassander; Pyrrhus returns to Epirus.
Kingdom of Pontus established.
? Foundation of Museum and Library in Alexandria.

296 Demetrius Poliorcetes besieges Athens.

295 Athens starved into surrender; Macedonian garrison in Piraeus.
Demetrius loses Cyprus (to Ptolemy), Cilicia (to Seleucus), Ionia (to Lysimachus).

294 Demetrius seizes Macedonia, becomes king.
Oligarchic regime in Athens.
Seleucus I makes Antiochus I his co-regent.
Pliny claims that "art stopped at this point."
293 Demetrius reconquers Thessaly, founds Demetrias (modern
Volos).
292 Death of Menander; Philetas of Cos tutor to future Ptolemy II.
Aetolian and Boeotian rebellion against Demetrius.
291 Demetrius recaptures Thebes.
290 Demetrius, returning to Athens with his new bride Lanassa, is
acclaimed a god.
Aetolians seize Phocis, debar Demetrius from Pythian Games at
Delphi.
289 Demetrius invades Epirus; Pyrrhus abrogates treaty with him.
288 Pyrrhus and Lysimachus invade and partition Macedonia (spring).
Demetrius flees to Cassandrea; suicide of his wife, Phila.
287 Athenians rebel against Demetrius, who besieges Athens, lifts siege
in return for control of Piraeus.
Demetrius crosses into Asia Minor, campaigns there.
Ptolemy I repudiates Eurydice I and her son Ptolemy Keraunos.
286 Demetrius' son Antigonus Gonatas assumes kingship.
285 Demetrius Poliorcetes captured by Seleucus.
Ptolemy II made co-regent.
Pyrrhus makes secret treaty with Antigonus Gonatas.
Alexandrian Pharos lighthouse built.
283 Deaths of Demetrius Poliorcetes and Ptolemy I; Antigonus Gonatas
succeeds to Macedonian throne.
282 Lysimachus executes his son Agathocles: Ptolemy Keraunos flees.
Philetaerus of Pergamon defects to Seleucus.
281 Death of Lysimachus at battle of Corupedion (February): Arsinoë
escapes to Macedonia.
Ptolemy Keraunos murders Seleucus I (September), assumes
Macedonian crown; Antiochus I succeeds Seleucus.
280 Celts invade Thrace and Illyria; refounding of Achaean League.
Pyrrhus campaigning in Italy.
Ptolemy Keraunos marries his half-sister Arsinoë II.
279 War between Antiochus I and Ptolemy II.
Celts invade Macedonia, kill Ptolemy Keraunos, driven back from
Greece by Aetolians.
278 Celts invade Asia Minor; Arsinoë II returns to Egypt.
Pyrrhus campaigning in Sicily.
Delimitation treaty between Antiochus I and Antigonus Gonatas.

277 Anarchy in Macedonia; Celts occupy Galatia (East Phrygia).
    Antigonus Gonatas defeats Gauls at Lysimacheia, wins back
        Thessaly.
    Ptolemy II now marries Arsinoë II (?), who becomes co-regent.
276 Antigonus Gonatas reestablished as king of Macedonia, marries
        Phila, daughter of Seleucus I; Aratus and Zeno at his court.
    Ptolemy II defeated by Antiochus I in Syria; Pyrrhus returns to Italy.
275 Pyrrhus defeated by Romans at Beneventum, returns to Epirus.
274 Pyrrhus invades Macedonia and Thessaly: Gonatas flees.
    Beginning of First Syrian War (–271) between Ptolemy II and
        Antiochus I.
273 Brief restoration of Pyrrhus as king of Macedonia.
    Ptolemy II makes treaty of friendship with Rome.
272 Pyrrhus invades Peloponnese; Gonatas reconquers Macedonia.
    Pyrrhus killed in Argos.
271 Gonatas permanently reinstalled as king of Macedonia.
    Ptolemy II wins back coastal Syria, end of First Syrian War; he and
        Arsinoë receive divine honors; his "Great Procession."
270 Antiochus I defeats Gauls in Asia Minor.
    Death and deification of Arsinoë II (July).
    Coalition of Athens, Sparta, and Ptolemy II against Gonatas:
        beginning of the Chremonidean War (–263/2?).
266/5 Gonatas defeats Spartans at Corinth, besieges Athens (–262).
264 Beginning of First Punic War.
263 Accession of Eumenes I of Pergamon; he declares independence.
262 Eumenes I defeats Antiochus I at Sardis.
    Athens capitulates to Gonatas.
261 Peace between Ptolemy II and Antiochus I.
    Death of Antiochus I (June): Antiochus II succeeds him.
259 Second Syrian War (–253) between Ptolemy II and Antiochus II.
    Revenue laws in Egypt; Macedonian-Seleucid alliance.
257 Demetrius II co-regent with Gonatas.
255 Cappadocia secedes from Seleucid empire.
253 End of Second Syrian War.
252 Antiochus II repudiates Laodice, marries Ptolemy II's daughter
        Berenice.
251 Aratus frees Sicyon from Macedonian control, joins Achaean League.
    Ptolemy II subsidizes Achaean League.
250 Death of Magas of Cyrene; Gonatas sends Demetrius the Fair as his
        successor; translation of Septuagint begun in Alexandria.
    ? Bactria and Sogdiana break away now from Seleucid empire.

249 Gonatas' nephew Alexander rebels, bases himself on Corinth.
246 Gonatas recovers Corinth; death of Antiochus II, accession of
    Seleucus II.
    Death of Ptolemy II, accession of Ptolemy III Euergetes.
    Third Syrian/Laodicean War between Ptolemy III and Seleucus II
    (–241).
245 Aratus made general of Achaean League.
    Ptolemy III retakes Antioch and Seleucia-in-Pieria.
244/3 Agis IV king of Sparta (–241).
243 Aratus's second generalship (*strategia*); he retakes Acrocorinth.
    Agis IV's social reforms in Sparta.
242 Antiochus Hierax co-ruler with Seleucus II.
    Ptolemy III honorary admiral of Achaean League.
241 End of Third Syrian War: Ptolemy keeps Seleucia-in-Pieria.
    Execution of Agis IV of Sparta.
    Death of Eumenes I of Pergamon; accession of Attalus I.
    Antigonus Gonatas makes peace with Achaean League.
    End of First Punic War.
239 Death of Aratus (?); death of Antigonus Gonatas; accession of
    Demetrius II (–229); war between Seleucus II and Antiochus
    Hierax (–236).
238 Achaean and Aetolian leagues fighting Macedonia (–229).
    Canopus Decree; birth of Philip V of Macedon.
237 Attalus I defeats Gauls, takes royal title.
236 Seleucus II makes peace with Antiochus Hierax, cedes him area
    north of Taurus range.
235 Cleomenes III king of Sparta (–222); Aratus attacks Argos.
    Megalopolis joins Achaean League.
233 Aratus attacks Athens, reaches the Academy.
231 Attalus I's campaign against Antiochus Hierax (–228).
    Seleucus II launches campaign against Parthia (–227).
230 Illyrian piratical raids in Adriatic under Queen Teuta.
229 First Illyrian War (Rome against Illyrians).
    Death of Demetrius II, accession of Antigonus Doson (–221).
    Argos and Aegina join Achaean League.
    Macedonian garrison removed from Athens.
228 Cleomenes III at war with Achaean League.
    Attalus I expanding frontiers in Asia Minor.
227 Antiochus Hierax murdered by Gauls in Thrace.
    Earthquake on Rhodes shakes down the Colossus.
    Cleomenes III's reforms in Sparta.

226   Spartan victories over Achaean League: Ptolemy III switches
          support from the League to Cleomenes.
          Death of Seleucus II, accession of Seleucus III (−223).
225   Aratus general of Achaean League, forms alliance with Antigonus
          Doson against Cleomenes.
223   Antigonus and Aratus campaigning against Cleomenes in
          Peloponnese.
          Seleucus III murdered; accession of Antiochus III (The Great)
          (−187).
222   Cleomenes III defeated by Antigonus Doson at Sellasia (July).
          Doson enters Sparta, Cleomenes flees to Egypt.
221   Death of Ptolemy III (February), accession of Ptolemy IV
          Philopator.
          Death of Antigonus Doson (July), accession of Philip V (−179).
          Philip fighting Aetolia (−217).
220   Revolt against Antiochus III by Achaeus (−213).
          Antiochus suppresses revolts in Persia, Media, and Babylon.
          Starting date of Polybius' *History.*
219   Second Illyrian War, against Demetrius of Pharos (−217).
          Philip V invades Epirus and Acarnania.
          Fourth Syrian War, between Antiochus III and Ptolemy IV (−217).
          Antiochus takes Seleucia-in-Pieria and Tyre.
          Dardanian invasion of Macedonia; Cleomenes III dies in Egypt.
218   Philip V invades Aetolia and Laconia, sacks Thermon.
          Antiochus in Coele-Syria; Hannibal crosses the Alps into Italy.
          Beginning of Second Punic War (−202).
217   Hannibal wins Battle of Lake Trasimene (spring).
          Ptolemy IV wins Battle of Raphia against Antiochus III (June),
          marries his sister Arsinoë (III) (October); peace of Naupactus
          (August).
216   Antiochus III campaigning against Achaeus (−213).
          Hannibal wins Battle of Cannae; rebellion in Upper Egypt.
215   Philip V makes treaty with Hannibal; First Macedonian War (−205).
214   Philip retreats overland from Adriatic.
213   Philip ravages Messenia, captures Lissos; death of Aratus of Sicyon.
          Achaeus captured and executed by Antiochus III.
          Roman siege of Syracuse begins.
212   Roman/Aetolian alliance (−211); fall of Syracuse, death of
          Archimedes.
          Beginning of Antiochus III's eastern campaign to recover lost
          satrapies (−205).
211   Hannibal's march on Rome; Aetolians attack Thessaly, Acarnania.

207 Nabis in power at Sparta; Philip invades Aetolia.
Spread of rebellion in Upper Egypt.

206 Aetolians make independent peace with Philip.

205 Peace agreement made at Phoenice between Rome and Philip.
Antiochus III returns to Seleucia-on-Tigris, assumes title "Great
King."
Upper Egypt under independent kings (–185).

204 Death of Ptolemy IV, regency for under-age Ptolemy V.

202 Philip V's naval campaign in the Aegean (–201).
Antiochus III invades Coele-Syria, beginning of Fifth Syrian War.
Scipio Africanus defeats Hannibal at Zama.

201 Carthage becomes Roman client-state; Philip defeats Rhodians.
Rhodes and Attalus I appeal to Rome; Antiochus captures Gaza.

200 Antiochus defeats Ptolemy V's forces at Panion.
Athens (backed by Attalus I and Rome) declares war on Philip.
Philip ravages Attica, attacks Athens.
Roman envoys warn both Philip and Antiochus.
Rome declares war on Philip (Second Macedonian War) (–197).

198 T. Quinctius Flamininus takes command of Roman forces in Greece.
Antiochus III consolidates position in Coele-Syria.

197 Flamininus defeats Philip V at Cynoscephalae (June).
Death of Attalus I, accession of Eumenes II (–160/59).

196 Philip evacuates "Fetters of Greece"; Flamininus proclaims
"Freedom of Greeks" at Isthmian Games; "Rosetta Stone" decree
in Memphis.
Antiochus crosses Hellespont, rebuilds Lysimacheia, warned by
Rome.
Ptolemy V consecrated as pharaoh in Memphis (November).

195 Nabis of Sparta submits to Flamininus.
Ptolemy V and Antiochus III ratify peace treaty.
Exiled Hannibal joins Antiochus in Ephesus.

194 Roman forces evacuated from Greece, taking quantities of artwork
as loot.
Antiochus III negotiating with Rome.
Ptolemy V marries Cleopatra I at Raphia (? with Coele-Syria as
dowry?).

192 Nabis murdered by Aetolians; Sparta defeated by Philopoemen,
joins Achaean League; at the Aetolians' invitation, Antiochus III
lands in Greece; Rome declares war on him (–188).

191 Antiochus defeated at Thermopylae, driven out of Greece to Ephesus.

189 Antiochus finally defeated at Magnesia-by-Sipylos (? January); his
son Antiochus IV held as hostage in Rome.

188 Treaty of Apamea; Eumenes II and Rhodians share Seleucid spoils.
Achaean League defeats Sparta, abolishes its ancient constitution.
187 Death of Antiochus III; accession of Seleucus IV.
186 Thebes recaptured, (?) end of secession in Upper Egypt.
184 Philip V's son Demetrius sent to Rome (–183).
183 Deaths of Scipio Africanus, Hannibal, and Philopoemen.
180 Ptolemy V assassinated. Cleopatra I regent for Ptolemy VI
Philometor.
Callicrates leads Achaean embassy to Rome.
Philip V, on forged evidence, executes his son Demetrius.
179 Death of Philip V; accession of Perseus.
178 Antiochus (IV) released from Rome in exchange for Seleucus IV's son
Demetrius (I); Perseus marries Seleucus IV's daughter Laodice.
176 Death of Cleopatra I (spring); accession of Ptolemy VI as minor.
175 Seleucus IV assassinated (September); Antiochus IV regent (–170)
for Seleucus's son Antiochus.
173 Perseus refuses audience to Roman embassy.
Antiochus IV renews Seleucid alliance with Rome.
172 Eumenes denounces Perseus in Rome.
Rome declares war on Perseus (Third Macedonian War, –168/7).
170 Ptolemy VI marries Cleopatra II, takes future Ptolemy VIII
Euergetes II (Physcon) as co-regent; Polybius cavalry
commander in Achaean League.
Seleucus IV's son Antiochus murdered; Antiochus IV becomes king
(–164).
169 Antiochus IV attacks Egypt (Sixth Syrian War), withdraws from
Alexandria.
168 Perseus defeated at Pydna by Aemilius Paullus, later surrenders
(June).
Antiochus IV's invasion of Egypt halted by Day of Eleusis (July).
167 Macedonia divided into four republics; Aemilius Paullus' lavish
triumph.
1,000 Achaean hostages (including Polybius) deported to Rome.
150,000 enslaved in Epirus; Eumenes banned from Rome.
Delos made free port under Athenian control.
Macedonian mines closed (–158).
166 Eumenes defeats Gauls; Rome declares Galatia "free" and Rome off-
limits for kings.
165 Antiochus IV sets out on eastern campaign; Lysias left as guardian of
Antiochus V, is defeated by Judas Maccabaeus in Jewish revolt.
Perseus' death in captivity (or ? in 162).

164 Antiochus IV offers Jews amnesty, dies in Media.
Demetrius I (son of Seleucus IV) rejected by Senate as successor.

163 Ptolemy VI (Philometor) returns to Alexandria; Ptolemy VIII
(Physcon) allotted Cyrene.
Accession of Antiochus V Eupator as minor (Lysias regent).

162 Demetrius I escapes from Rome, reaches Antioch, acclaimed king.

161 Demetrius I Soter executes Lysias and Antiochus V.
Rome repudiates treaty with Ptolemy VI.

160 Rome recognizes Demetrius I Soter.

158 Death of Eumenes II, accession of Attalus II; Macedonian mines
reopened.

156 Pliny's date for art's initial "recovery."
Conflict between Philometor and Physcon in Egypt.

155 Physcon's supposed bequest of Cyrene to Rome.

152 Rome backs Alexander Balas as legitimate claimant against
Demetrius I.

150 Demetrius I defeated and killed by Balas, who becomes king.
Return to Greece of surviving Achaean exiles, Polybius among
them.
Alexander Balas marries Cleopatra Thea.
Beginning of Parthian encroachment on Media.

149 Revolt of Andriscus (Fourth Macedonian War, −148).
Rome begins siege of Carthage (Third Punic War, −146).
Death of Cato the Censor.

148 Defeat of Andriscus at Pydna; Macedonia becomes Roman province.
Parthians occupy Media.

146 Achaean revolt; Mummius sacks and destroys Corinth.
Sack and destruction of Carthage; Africa becomes Roman province.
Polybius in North Africa with Scipio Aemilianus.

145 Ptolemy VI intervenes in Syria, joins Demetrius II against Balas.
Balas defeated and killed, Ptolemy also dies.
Accession of Demetrius II (−140/39, 129−125).
Ptolemy's daughter Cleopatra Thea marries Demetrius II.
Return of Physcon to Alexandria, joint rule with Cleopatra II.
Balas' son proclaimed king in Antioch as Antiochus VI by Diodotus
Tryphon. Demetrius II flees to Seleuceia.

144 Ptolemy VIII (Physcon) murders Ptolemy VII, enthroned as pharaoh.
Purge of Alexandrian intellectuals.

142 Diodotus Tryphon murders Antiochus VI, proclaims himself king.

141 Parthians annex Babylonia; Rome recognizes independence of
Judaea.

140/39 Scipio Aemilianus heads mission to Alexandria.
Defeat and capture of Demetrius II by Parthians.

138 Antiochus Sidetes (second son of Demetrius I) proclaimed king as Antiochus VII, defeats Diodotus Tryphon, who commits suicide.
Death of Attalus II of Pergamon, accession of Attalus III.

136 Outbreak of First Sicilian Slave War (−132).

134 Slave revolts on Delos and in Laurium mines.
Antiochus VII restores Seleucid power in Judaea.

133 Death of Attalus III, who bequeaths kingdom of Pergamon to Rome.

132 Revolt of Aristonicus (? Eumenes III) in Pergamon (−130).
Suppression of Sicilian slave revolt.
Dynastic conflict between Cleopatra II and Ptolemy VIII (Physcon), who murders Ptolemy Memphitis.

131 Ptolemy VIII retreats to Cyprus. Cleopatra II sole ruler in Egypt.
Demetrius II released by Parthians, returns to Syria.
Antiochus VII begins eastern campaign, recovers Babylonia, Media.

130 Defeat of Aristonicus.
Ptolemy VIII returns to Memphis; civil war with Cleopatra II.
Antiochus VII's campaign against Parthians.

129 Marcus Perperna and Manius Aquillius organizing Asia Minor (−126).
Antiochus VII defeated and killed by Parthians.

128 Ptolemy VIII provides Alexander Zabinas as Seleucid pretender.
Cleopatra II flees Alexandria for Syria.

127 Ptolemy VIII reestablished as sole ruler in Egypt.
Zabinas drives Demetrius II out of Antioch.

126 Demetrius II captured, executed in Tyre.

125 Cleopatra Thea executes her son Seleucus V, takes son Antiochus Grypos as co-regent.

124 Dynastic reconciliation and amnesty in Egypt.
Antiochus VIII Grypos marries Cleopatra Tryphaena.

123 Antiochus VIII defeats and executes Zabinas.

121 Antiochus VIII forces Cleopatra Thea to commit suicide.

118 Second reconciliation and amnesty decree in Egypt (April).

117 Antiochus VIII driven out of Antioch by Antiochus IX Cyzicenus.

116 Death of Ptolemy VIII (Physcon) (June); joint reign of Cleopatra III and Ptolemy IX (Lathyros) (−107); Ptolemy X to Cyprus, Ptolemy Apion to Cyrene.

115/4 Ptolemy IX repudiates his wife, Cleopatra IV, marries Cleopatra Selene.

113 Cleopatra IV marries Antiochus IX Cyzicenus.
Mithradates VI of Pontus established in Sinope.

112 Antiochus VIII defeats Antiochus IX; Cleopatra Tryphaena has
     Cleopatra IV killed; Rome declares war on Jugurtha.

111 Antiochus IX captures and executes Cleopatra Tryphaena.

110 Ptolemy X made "king" of Cyprus.

108 Antiochus VIII holds most of Syria; Mithradates VI divides
     Paphlagonia with Nicomedes of Bithynia.

107 Cleopatra III forces Ptolemy IX Lathyros out to Cyprus, brings
     Ptolemy X back to Alexandria as king.

105/4 Surrender of Jugurtha; Roman legions defeated in Gaul by Cimbri
       and Teutoni; outbreak of Second Sicilian Slave War (−100).

103/2 Cleopatra III forces Ptolemy X out of Alexandria.
       Antiochus VIII marries Cleopatra Selene.
       Rome at war with pirates (−100); Marius defeats Teutoni.

101 Ptolemy X returns to Alexandria, murders Cleopatra III, marries his
     niece Cleopatra Berenice.
     Marius and Catulus defeat the Cimbri.

 98 Marius in Asia Minor; meets Mithradates VI.

 96 Ptolemy Apion dies, wills Cyrene to Rome (taken up in 75).
     Antiochus VIII Grypos assassinated.
     Antiochus IX Cyzicenus marries Cleopatra Selene.
     Sulla propraetor of Cilicia, forces Mithradates to cede acquired
     territories.

 95 Antiochus IX killed by Seleucus VI.
     Cleopatra Selene marries Antiochus X Eusebes.

 92/1 Sulla restores Ariobarzanes to Cappadocia and Nicomedes IV to
       Bithynia (both driven out by Mithradates and Tigranes of
       Armenia).
       Rutilius Rufus condemned for extortion.
       Oligarchic government in Athens.
       Outbreak of War of the Allies (Social War) in Italy.

 89 Rome at war with Mithradates VI (First Mithradatic War).
     Antiochus X Eusebes killed fighting Parthians.

 88 Restored democracy in Athens joins Mithradates against Rome.
     Massacre of eighty thousand Romans and Italians in Asia Minor
     organized by Mithradates.
     Sulla's march on Rome; flight of Marius.

 87 Sulla lands in Greece, blockades Athens and Piraeus.
     Ptolemy X expelled from Alexandria, bequeaths kingdom to Rome,
     killed in naval battle off Cyprus.
     Cleopatra Berenice returns from exile, joins Ptolemy IX (Lathyros)
     as co-regent in Egypt; revolt breaks out in Upper Egypt (−86).

 86 Athens falls to Sulla, Piraeus gutted by fire; death of Marius.

85 Treaty of Dardanus between Sulla and Mithradates (not ratified in Rome).

83 Second Roman campaign against Mithradates (–82).
    Tigranes of Armenia accepts offer of Seleucid throne.
    Sulla removes works of Aristotle and Theophrastus from Athens.

82 Sulla wins civil war in Italy; Sertorius makes independent base in Spain.

81 Sulla dictator; death of Ptolemy IX (Lathyros); Cleopatra Berenice left as sole ruler in Alexandria; Sulla nominates Ptolemy XI (X's son) as king.

80 Ptolemy XI marries Cleopatra Berenice, kills her, is lynched by mob.
    Ptolemy IX's bastard son Ptolemy XII, known as the Piper (Auletes), seizes throne, marries his sister Cleopatra V Tryphaena.

78 Death of Sulla.

76 Sertorius in Spain makes treaty with Mithradates VI.

75 Cyrene made a Roman province.
    Death of Nicomedes IV of Bithynia; he wills his kingdom to Rome.
    Mithradates VI declares war on Rome (Third Mithradatic War).

74 Lucius Lucullus sent against Mithradates; special command established to deal with pirates.

73 Spartacus slave revolt breaks out at Capua (–71).

72 Death of Sertorius in Spain.
    Lucullus winning victories over Mithradates.

71 Lucullus defeats Mithradates.
    Crassus defeats Spartacus, crucifies twenty thousand slaves along Appian Way.

69 Tigranes surrenders to Lucullus; Antiochus XIII Asiaticus ascends Seleucid throne in Antioch; pirate squadrons sack Delos.

68 Lucullus' political destruction in Rome.

67 Pompey's special command to stamp out piracy.
    Mithradates' victory over Romans at Zela.

66 Lucullus superseded by Pompey in Asia command.
    Pompey defeats Mithradates.

65/4 Pompey reorganizing the East: Syria becomes Roman province.
    Deposition and death of Antiochus XIII.

63 Death of Mithradates VI; Lucullus celebrates triumph.
    Cicero as consul quells Catilinarian conspiracy.
    Birth of Gaius Octavius, the future Augustus.

62 Pompey's "Eastern Settlement" (Bithynia and Cilicia provinces, client-kings set up).
    Pompey returns to Italy, disbands army (December).

60 "First Triumvirate" of Caesar, Pompey, Crassus.

59 Ptolemy XII (the Piper) driven out of Alexandria, visits Cato on
    Rhodes.
    Caesar persuades Senate to recognize Ptolemy XII.
58/7 Cato annexes Cyprus to province of Cilicia.
    Ptolemy XII in Rome; death of Cleopatra V Tryphaena.
    Berenice IV (daughter of Ptolemy XII) ascends throne of Egypt,
    marries (i) Seleucus Kybiosaktes (murdered), (ii) Archelaus.
55 Aulus Gabinius restores Ptolemy XII to throne of Egypt.
    Ptolemy XII executes Berenice IV.
    Bactria lost to eastern invaders.
54 Gaius Rabirius Postumus as Ptolemy XII's finance minister; Aulus
    Gabinius recalled, prosecuted, and condemned for taking bribes
    from Ptolemy XII.
53 Crassus defeated and killed by Parthians at Carrhae (May).
    Gaius Rabirius Postumus forced to leave Egypt because of
    extortionate practices.
51 Death of Ptolemy XII (the Piper); Ptolemy XIII marries his sister
    Cleopatra VII; they become joint rulers.
    Drought in Egypt (–49); Parthians invade Syria.
50 Cleopatra VII at war with Ptolemy XIII.
    Ban on shipping grain in Egypt except to Alexandria (October).
    Cleopatra and Arsinoë leave Egypt for Thebaid and Syria.
    Pompey called on to "save the state."
49 Caesar crosses the Rubicon (January); outbreak of Roman civil war.
48 Pompey defeated by Caesar at Pharsalus; flees to Lesbos, then to
    Alexandria, murdered on arrival, head sent to Caesar (September).
    Caesar arrives in Alexandria (October), liaison with Cleopatra VII.
    Beginning of "Alexandrian War."
47 Caesar rescued by Mithradates of Pergamon (March).
    Death of Ptolemy XIII; Cleopatra and Ptolemy XIV set up as joint
    rulers.
    Caesar defeats Pharnaces at Zela (spring), returns to Rome (October).
    Birth of Caesarion to Caesar and Cleopatra (June).
46 Caesar's victory at Thapsus; Cato's suicide (April).
    Caesar's dictatorship and quadruple triumph (September/October).
    Cleopatra and entourage in Rome (–44).
45 Caesar's victory at Munda in Spain (March); Parthians invade Syria.
    Caesar returns to Rome, triumph (October).
44 Assassination of Caesar on Ides of March.
    Cleopatra returns to Alexandria, has Ptolemy XIV killed, makes
    Caesarion her co-regent.
    Arsinoë appointed ruler of Cyprus by Mark Antony.

43 Octavian's first consulship; Second Triumvirate (Antony, Octavian, Lepidus).
   Cleopatra sends four legions to Dolabella; they go to Cassius.
   Cleopatra recovers Cyprus; Arsinoë flees to Ephesus; famine in Egypt.
   The proscriptions; murder of Cicero (December 7).

42 Deification of Caesar (January).
   Battles of Philippi, suicides of Brutus and Cassius (October).
   Antony ruling eastern Roman provinces.

41 Meeting of Cleopatra and Antony at Tarsus.
   Antony executes Arsinoë, takes over Cyprus, winters in Alexandria with Cleopatra (−40).

40 Antony in Greece; Cleopatra bears him twins.
   Treaty of Brundisium; Antony marries Octavia.
   Parthians attacking Syria.

39 Agreement at Misenum between Antony, Octavian, and Sextus Pompeius.

38 Roman victories over Parthians; Octavian marries Livia (January).
   Octavia bears Antony a daughter.

37 Cleopatra promulgates the "New Era," Antony acknowledges their children.

36 Antony's disastrous Parthian campaign; Cleopatra bears him third child, rescues his army.
   Lepidus removed from Second Triumvirate.

34 Antony's Armenian campaign; the Donations of Alexandria.

32 Antony divorces Octavia; Octavian publishes Antony's will in Rome.
   Declaration of war by Rome against Cleopatra alone.
   Antony and Cleopatra winter in Greece (−31).

31 Battle of Actium (September); Antony and Cleopatra, defeated, retreat to Alexandria.

30 Suicide of Antony; Octavian enters Alexandria; suicide of Cleopatra.
   Octavian declares end of Ptolemaic empire (August 29).

Maps and Genealogies

Getae

Triballi

Odrysia

BLACK SEA

CAUCASUS

COLCHIS

PAEONIA
MACEDONIA
Pella   Amphipolis
Pydna   Philippi   Abdera
Dion   Pella   Maronea
EPIRUS

Perinthus
Byzantium

PAPHLAGONIA

PONTUS

Sestos
Abydos
Hellespont
HELLESPONTINE
PHRYGIA

Dascylium
Gordium

Ancyra

GALATIA

BITHYNIA

THESSALY
AETOLIA
Thebes   Athens
Corinth
PELOPONNESE
Sparta

Ephesus
Miletus
Halicarnassus
Xanthus

Sardis
LYDIA
CARIA
LYCIA
Phaselis

PISIDIA
Sagalassus
Aspendus
Side
CILICIA

Cilician Gates
Tarsus
Issus
Soli

CAPPADOCIA

Nisibis

ARMENIA

ASSYRIA
Gaugamela
Arbela

Syrian Gates
Thapsacus
SYRIA

MESOPOTAMIA

R. Tigris

ME

R. Euphrates

Opis

MEDITERRANEAN SEA

Arad
Tripolis
Byblos
Sidon
Tyre

PHOENICIA

Damascus

Babylon

BABYLO

CYRENAICA

Alexandria

Paraetonium   Naucratis
Memphis

(Ammon
Oasis) Siwah

Gaza

PALESTINE

Pelusium

EGYPT

R. Nile

ARABIA

RED SEA

—— Overland route
---- Sea route
······ Route taken by the
        Macedonian fleet
■ Towns founded by Alexander
● Other towns

ALEXANDER'S JOURNEY

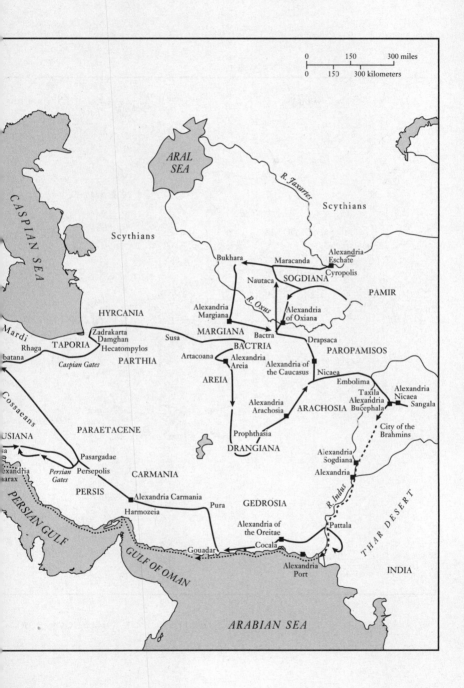

Scythians

Sarmatians

*SEA OF
AZOV*

CRIMEA

COLCHI

R. Danube

ILLYRIA

BLACK SEA

CAU

THRACE

Heracleia   Sinope

Trapezus

ITALY

Epidamnus

MACEDONIA

PAPHLAGONIA

PONTUS

Taras

THESSALY

EPIRUS

HELLESPONTINE
PHRYGIA

BITHYNIA

R. Halys

CAPPADOCIA

ARMENI

R. T

PHRYGIA

PISIDIA

LYCAONIA

MESOPOTAM

Athens

CARIA
LYCIA

PAMPHYLIA

CILICIA

Antioch

Syracuse

CRETE

RHODES

Seleucia

Apamea

R. Euphrates

MEDITERRANEAN SEA

CYPRUS

SYRIA

Sidon

Damascus

Cyrene

Tyre

Ptolemais-Ake

Jerusalem

CYRENAICA

Alexandria

Gaza

*SYRIAN
DESERT*

Naucratis

Pelusium

Petra

Siwah Oasis

Memphis

Nabataeans

R. Nile

EGYPT

ARAB

Thebes

*RED
SEA*

Syene

0   150   300 miles

0   150   300 kilometers

ALEXANDER'S EMPIRE: THE INHERITANCE OF THE SUCCESSORS

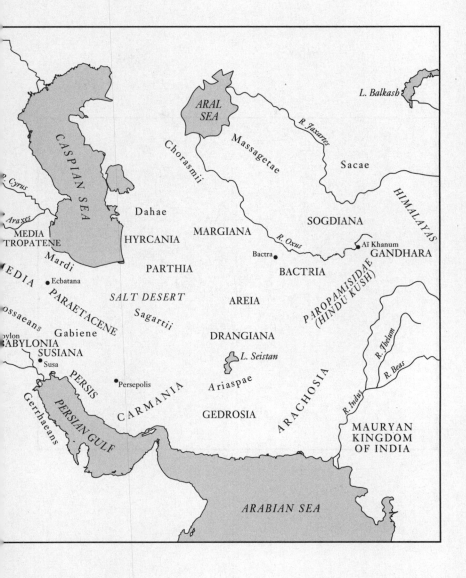

CASPIAN SEA

ARAL SEA

L. Balkash

R. Cyrus

Araxes

MEDIA TROPATENE

Mardi

Dahae

Chorasmii

Massagetae

R. Jaxartes

Sacae

MEDIA

Ecbatana

PARAETACENE

HYRCANIA

PARTHIA

MARGIANA

SALT DESERT

Sagartii

SOGDIANA

R. Oxus

Bactra

BACTRIA

Aï Khanum

GANDHARA

HIMALAYAS

PAROPAMISIDAE (HINDU KUSH)

AREIA

ossaeans

Gabiene

BABYLONIA

SUSIANA

Susa

oylon

PERSIS

Persepolis

CARMANIA

DRANGIANA

L. Seistan

Ariaspae

GEDROSIA

ARACHOSIA

R. Indus

R. Thelum

R. Beas

MAURYAN KINGDOM OF INDIA

Gerrhaeans

PERSIAN GULF

ARABIAN SEA

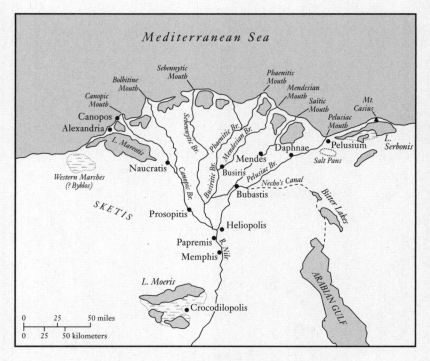

Mediterranean Sea

*Sebennytic
Mouth*

*Bolbitine
Mouth*

*Phaenitic
Mouth*

*Canopic
Mouth*

*Mendesian
Mouth*

*Saïtic
Mouth*

*Mt.
Casius*

*Pelusiac
Mouth*

Canopos

Alexandria

L. Mareotis

Pelusium

*L.
Serbonis*

Daphnae

Naucratis

Mendes

Salt Pans

*Western Marshes
(? Byblos)*

Busiris

Sebennytic Br.

Phaenitic Br.

Mendesian Br.

Busiritic Br.

Pelusiac Br.

Necho's Canal

SKETIS

Canopic Br.

Bubastis

Bitter Lakes

Prosopitis

Heliopolis

Papremis

Memphis

R. Nile

ARABIAN GULF

L. Moeris

Crocodilopolis

0   25   50 miles

0   25   50 kilometers

THE EGYPTIAN DELTA

MAINLAND GREECE AND THE AEGEAN BASIN

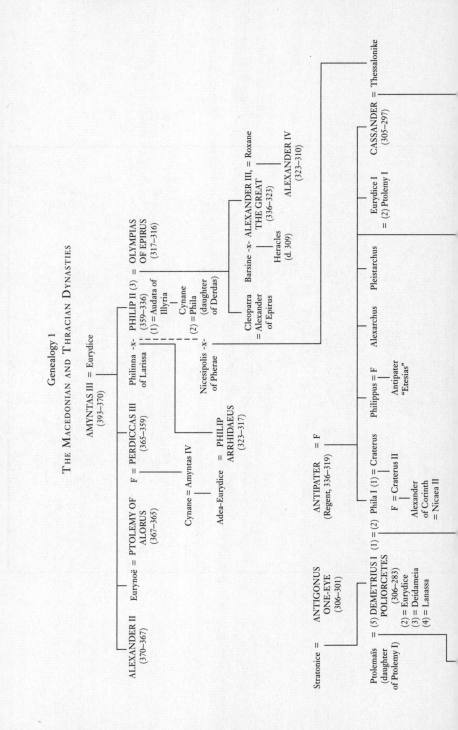

Genealogy 1

THE MACEDONIAN AND THRACIAN DYNASTIES

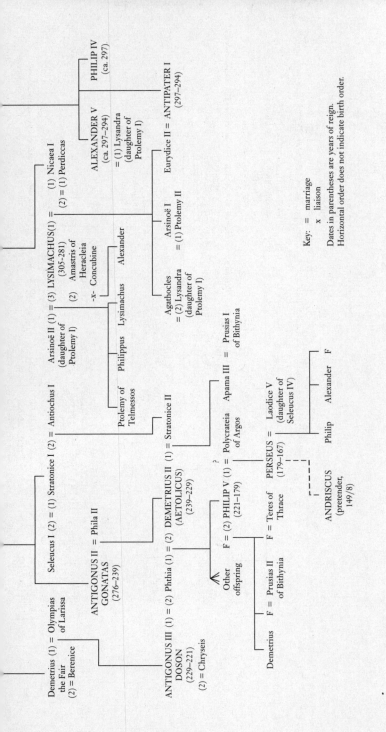

Demetrius (1) = Olympias
the Fair   of Larissa
(2) = Berenice

Seleucus I (2) = (1) Stratonice I (2) = Antiochus I

Arsinoë II (1) = (3) LYSIMACHUS(1) = (1) Nicaea I
(daughter of   (305-281)   (2) = (1) Perdiccas
Ptolemy I)   (2) Amastris of
                        Heracleia
                    -x- Concubine

PHILIP IV
(ca. 297)

ANTIGONUS II = Phila II
GONATAS
(276-239)

Ptolemy of   Philippus   Lysimachus   Alexander
Telmessos

ALEXANDER V
(ca. 297-294)

= (1) Lysandra
(daughter of
Ptolemy I)

Arsinoë I
= (1) Ptolemy II

Eurydice II = ANTIPATER I
(297-294)

Agathocles
= (2) Lysandra
(daughter of
Ptolemy I)

ANTIGONUS III (1) = (2) Phthia (1) = (2) DEMETRIUS II (1) = Stratonice II
DOSON   (AETOLICUS)
(229-221)   (239-229)
(2) = Chryseis

Apama III = Prusias I
of Bithynia

Other
offspring   F = (2) PHILIP V (1) = Polycrateia   PERSEUS = Laodice V
             (221-179)   of Argos   (179-167) (daughter of
                                                             Seleucus IV)
             F = Teres of
                 Thrace

F = Prusias II
    of Bithynia

Demetrius

Philip   Alexander   F

ANDRISCUS
(pretender,
149/8)

Key: = marriage
      x liaison

Dates in parentheses are years of reign.
Horizontal order does not indicate birth order.

Genealogy 2

THE SELEUCIDS

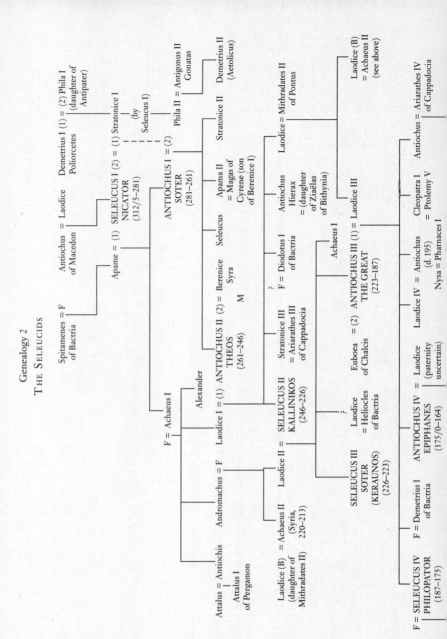

Seleucid Dynasty Genealogical Chart

Stratonice
(1) = Eumenes II
(2) = Attalus II

Antiochus (?)

Laodice V = Perseus of Macedon

DEMETRIUS I = F SOTER (162/1–151/0)

ANTIOCHUS V EUPATOR (164–162/1)

Laodice = Mithradates V of Pontus

ALEXANDER BALAS (pretender, 151/0–145) = (1) Cleopatra Thea (and see below)

DIODOTUS TRYPHON (usurper, 142/1–138)

ANTIOCHUS VI EPIPHANES DIONYSUS (145–142/1)

ALEXANDER ZABINAS (pretender, 128–123)

SELEUCUS V (126/5)

ANTIOCHUS XII (ca. 86–85)

Laodice Thea Philadelphos = Mithradates I of Commagene

Antiochus I of Commagene (69?–32)

DEMETRIUS III PHILOPATOR SOTER (EUKAIROS) (95–88)

Antigonus

ANTIOCHUS VII EUERGETES (SIDETES) (138–129) = (3) Cleopatra Thea (2) (1) = ALEXANDER BALAS (see above)

= (1) DEMETRIUS II NICATOR OF SYRIA (145–139?, 129–126/5) (2) = Rhodogune (daughter of Mithradates I of Parthia)

Offspring

Laodice = Phraates II of Parthia

ANTIOCHUS VIII PHILOMETOR (GRYPOS) (125–96) (1) = Cleopatra Tryphaena

Antiochus
Seleucus
Laodice

PHILIP I EPIPHANES PHILADELPHOS (95–83?) = F

PHILIP II PHILORHOMAIOS (66?–63)

SELEUCUS VI EPIPHANES NICATOR (96–95)

ANTIOCHUS XI EPIPHANES PHILADELPHOS (95)

F = (1) ANTIOCHUS IX PHILOPATOR (CYZICENUS) (115–95) (3) = (3) Cleopatra Selene (2) = (2) Cleopatra IV

ANTIOCHUS X EUSEBES PHILOPATOR (95–ca. 90/88) = (4)

ANTIOCHUS XIII (ASIATICUS) (69–64)

Seleucus Kybiosaktes (?) = Berenice IV

Key: = marriage   x liaison

Dates in parentheses are years of reign.
Horizontal order does not indicate birth order.

Genealogy 3

THE PTOLEMIES

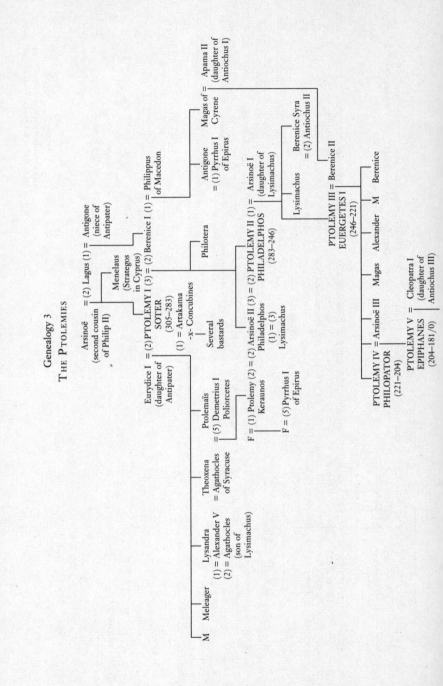

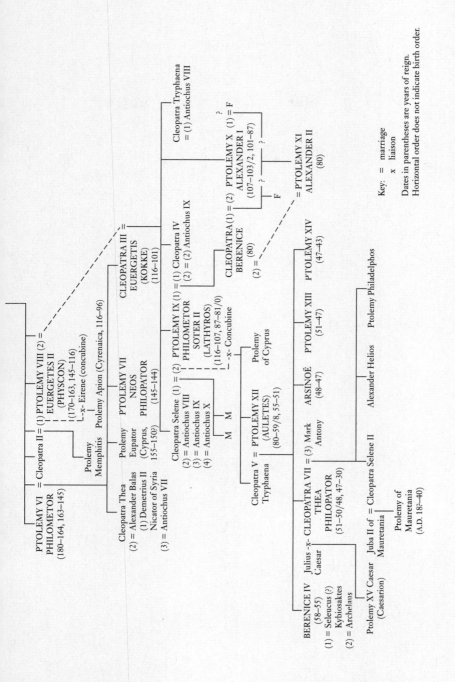

PTOLEMY VI
PHILOMETOR
(180–164, 163–145)

Cleopatra II = (1) PTOLEMY VIII = (2)
EUERGETES II
(PHYSCON)
(170–163, 145–116)
└─x─ Eirene (concubine)

Cleopatra Tryphaena
= (1) Antiochus VIII

Ptolemy
Memphitis   Ptolemy Apion (Cyrenaica, 116–96)

CLEOPATRA III =
EUERGETIS
(KOKKE)
(116–101)

Cleopatra Thea
(2) = Alexander Balas
(1) Demetrius II
Nicator of Syria
(3) = Antiochus VII

Ptolemy
Eupator
(Cyprus,
155–150?)

PTOLEMY VII
NEOS
PHILOPATOR
(145–144)

PTOLEMY IX (1) = (1) Cleopatra IV
PHILOMETOR
SOTER II
(LATHYROS)
(116–107, 87–81/0)
└──x─ Concubine

(2) = (2) Antiochus IX

PTOLEMY X   (1) = F
ALEXANDER I
(107–103/2, 101–87)
                        ?

Cleopatra Selene (1) = (2)
(2) = Antiochus VIII
(3) = Antiochus IX
(4) = Antiochus X
         M   M

Ptolemy
of Cyprus

CLEOPATRA(1) = (2) PTOLEMY XI
BERENICE   ALEXANDER II
                        (80)
(2) = (80)   ?   ?
         F   F

Cleopatra V = PTOLEMY XII
Tryphaena   (AULETES)
               (80–59/8, 55–51)

ARSINOË
(48–47)

PTOLEMY XIII
(51–47)

PTOLEMY XIV
(47–43)

BERENICE IV   Julius –x– CLEOPATRA VII – (3) = Mark
(58–55)   Caesar   THEA   Antony
(1) = Seleucus (2)   PHILOPATOR
Kybiosaktes   (51–50/48, 47–30)
(2) = Archelaus

Juba II of = Cleopatra Selene II
Mauretania

Alexander Helios   Ptolemy Philadelphos

Ptolemy XV Caesar
(Caesarion)

Ptolemy of
Mauretania
(A.D. 18–40)

Key: = marriage
      x liaison

Dates in parentheses are years of reign.
Horizontal order does not indicate birth order.

GUIDE TO FURTHER READING

In what follows, it should always be borne in mind that these are basic recommendations only, restricted to fundamental works in English. For further exploration, readers should consult the (often very comprehensive) bibliographies that the titles recommended provide. My choices are personal and highly selective: studies that I have found valuable and stimulating, sometimes to vigorous disagreement. Not every topic is itemized here, but most of those omitted can be run down in the general surveys.

CHAPTER 1

For the general history and background of Macedonia: Adams and Borza (1982), Borza (1990) and (1995), Errington (1990), Hammond (1989), Hammond and Griffith (1979). Hammond believes in a legally binding and well-ordered constitution; others (more plausibly) see Macedonia as the home of primitive and competitive warlords, where power went to the strongest. On Philip II: Cawkwell (1978), Ellis (1976), Griffith (1979), Hammond (1994), Hatzopoulos and Loukopoulos (1980). Griffith is superb, Cawkwell a good short introduction. Ellis needs background knowledge to be fully appreciated. Hammond, though the most recent, is over-eulogistic and often out-of-date. Hatzopoulos and Loukopoulos offer a wide and informative range of articles.

Works on Alexander are innumerable and of wildly varying quality. The following are recommended. General and biographical: Adams (2005), Bosworth (1988a), Cartledge (2004), Green (1991), Hammond (1981), Mossé (2004), O'Brien (1992), Stoneman (2004), Tarn (1948), Wilcken (1967), Worthington (2004). Tarn and Hammond represent the old view of Alexander as a peerless idealist seeking the Brotherhood of Man; Bosworth and Green rather emphasize the pursuit of glory through conquest and killing. The remainder occupy various points between these extremes. Adams and Stoneman both offer excellent short biographies for beginners. O'Brien ascribes all Alexander's problems to alcoholism but has the advantage of an extremely comprehensive bibliography. Useful websites are www.living.org/aj-al/alexander/alexander00.html and www.isidore-of-seville.com/alexanderama .html. For those with German who want to explore the origins of modern theory on Alexander, Droysen (2004), a well-edited reprint of volume 1 of his *Geschichte des Hellenismus,* Gotha 1877, is highly recommended.

Other useful works include Roisman (2003) and Bosworth and Baynham (2000), wide-ranging collections of articles on the background of Alexander's career; Bosworth (1988b) on interpretation of the sources; Cohen (1997) on the great Issus mosaic; Bosworth (1996) comparing Alexander's Indian campaigns with those of the Central American conquistadors; Eddy (1961) on the violent ideological resistance to Macedonian invasion; Engels (1978) for a pioneering study of Alexander's military logistics; Fraser (1996) on Alexander's founding of cities; Holt (all titles) for a fascinating glimpse of Alexander in what is modern Afghanistan and a lesson in how ancient coins can be made to yield up historical evidence; Stewart (1993) on the intersection of art and politics in Alexander's propaganda; Wood (1997) for a vivid introduction to the topography of the campaigns; and Heckel (2006) for a brilliant who's who of the age's main characters.

CHAPTERS 2–6

The Hellenistic world is a vast and initially daunting field. Fortunately, there are today several useful and reasonably up-to-date general introductions to it. A short initial survey is provided by Burstein (1996). Easiest for the beginner (though lacking a clear narrative) is Walbank (1993), naturally followed by Walbank et al. (1984). The latter, combined with essays in Erskine (2003) and Green (1993), is the best the reader can do (to date) who wants a full narrative of political events in English, still a prime desideratum. Those with French are warmly recommended to Will (1979–1982). Erskine, Green, Shipley (2000), Cartledge et al. (1997), and Ogden (2002) between them cover most of the key topics. The essays in Ogden (2000) explore the cutthroat business of dynastic politics (more seriously than his eye-catching title might suggest). Other older works sometimes provide useful insights: Chamoux (2003, translation of a 1981 original) on Cyrene and Hellenistic kingship, Tarn and Griffith (1952) on trade and exploration, Ferguson (1973) on utopias. Many areas can be explored via www.livius.org.

The history of the early Successors has now been covered in masterly fashion by Bosworth (2002), which should be read in conjunction with Heckel (1992), a thorough and wonderfully well-documented account of all Alexander's senior commanders, many of whom played key roles after his death. See also Adams and Borza (1982) and Adams in Bugh (2006) 28–51. Individual studies of Antigonus One-Eye (Billows 1990), Ptolemy I (Ellis 1994), Seleucus I (Grainger 1990), Eumenes (Anson 2004), and Lysimachus (Lund 1992) help to fill out the picture with portraits of larger-than-life-size leaders and kings who, while Alexander lived, were no more than loyal staff officers running his formidable military machine.

For Ptolemaic Egypt, readers should begin with Turner in Walbank et al. (1984), 118–174, Thompson in Crook et al. (1994), 310–326, Erskine (2003), 105–120, and Shipley (2000), 192–234. This will prepare them for the full and advanced account in Hölbl (2001) and the discursive essays of Bowman (1986) and Chauveau (2000). Though largely outdated, Bevan (1927) still offers much useful material not available elsewhere. All have ample bibliographies for further study. On the hellenizing of Egypt, see Vasunia (2001); and on the blending of cultures, Lewis (1986) and Thompson (1988), a brilliant and fascinating study. On the great Zenon archive: Pestman et al. (1981). On women in Hellenistic Egypt: Pomeroy (1984), Rowlandson (1998). On Cleopatra VII: Volkmann (1958), still the most sensible account, Whitehorne (1994), Walker and Higgs (2001), and Kleiner (2005). On Alexandria (and much else), the monumental three volumes of Fraser (1972) and "Alexander's Alexandria," in Green (2004), 172–196.

There is no full up-to-date general study of the Seleucids. The best available is Habicht in Astin et al. (1989), 324–387. See also Shipley (2000), 271–325. The most accessible short introduction is that by Austin in Erskine (2003), 121–133. Bevan (1902) remains a very readable narrative but is badly out-of-date. Sherwin-White and Kuhrt (1993) require some prior knowledge and emphasize the Persian rather than the Western perspective, sometimes at the latter's expense. Musti in Walbank et al. (1984), 175–220, contains interesting material but is, again, for advanced readers. For the early period, Grainger (1990) is valuable. On Phoenicia, see Grainger (1991). Shipley (see earlier) also discusses the Attalids, to whom the best introduction is that of Kosmetatou in Erskine (2003), 159–174. See also Allen (1983) and Hansen (1971), a full and readable account but now dated. A lively and high-level Seleucid e-mail research and discussion group is seleukids@yahoogroups.com, linked to www.seleukids.org.

For Macedonia and mainland Greece, in addition to the works cited at the beginning of chapter 1, three introductory studies are available: Walbank in Walbank et al. (1984), 446–481, Shipley (2000), 108–152, and Scholten in Erskine (2003), 134–158, all with full bibliographies. Antigonus Gonatas: Tarn (1913) and Gabbert (1997). Philip V: Walbank (1940). Aratus of Sicyon: Walbank (1933). The Argead royal women: Carney (2000), a brilliant and immensely readable study. On the Achaean and Aetolian leagues, Larsen (1968) remains a useful introduction. On Aetolia, see also now Scholten (2000). Hellenistic Sparta: Shimron (1972), Africa (1961), Piper (1986), and the excellent survey of Cartledge and Spawforth (2002). Hellenistic Athens, not surprisingly, is well documented: see Ferguson (1911), still valuable despite new epigraphic discoveries, Mossé (1973), Frösén (1997), Green (2003b), and, above all, Habicht (1997), a full, up-to-date, and judicious account.

The impact of Rome on the Greco-Macedonian world is a topic that has produced highly contrasted views: see in particular Badian (1958), Harris (1979), and Gruen (1984). The last named provides an excellent full political narrative of the last two centuries of the Hellenistic era. See also the contributions to Astin et al. (1989) by R. M. Errington, 81–106, 244–289, and P. E. Derow, 290–323; and to Crook et al. (1994) by J. G. F. Hind, 130–164, and A. N. Sherwin-White, 229–273. For Roman rule in Asia Minor, volume 1 of Magie (1950) is still an essential resource.

Much excellent work has been done on Hellenistic cities. A good recent introduction is Billows in Erskine (2003), 196–215, with a good bibliography of recent advanced studies on special areas (for instance, Syria and western Asia Minor). Shipley and Hansen in Bugh (2006) 52–72, though excessively meliorist, offer many useful insights, and also discuss the key topic of federalism. The fundamental study is still Jones (1940). See also Wycherley (1962) and Green (1993), 155–170. For Hellenistic Rhodes and its navy, see Berthold (1984) and Gabrielsen (1997). On monarchy and the concept of kingship in general two contrasting introductions, Walbank in Walbank et al. (1984) and Ma in Erskine (2003), 177–195, show how fast ideas can develop in twenty years: cf. Shipley (2000), 59–85. On the religious element in Hellenistic royalty: Green (2003a), with bibliography of recent scholarship. On the visual evidence for concepts of monarchy: Smith (1988) and Stewart (1993).

The basic text for the Hellenistic economy is still Rostovtzeff (1941), though great advances have been made since then: for a good introduction to these, see Reger in Erskine (2003), 331–353, also Davies in Walbank et al. (1984), 237–320, in Archibald et al. (2001), 11–62, with full bibliography, and most recently in Bugh (2006), 73–92. Other essays in Archibald et al. are valuable but for the most part highly specialized. A useful sourcebook: Meijer and van Nijf (1992). For the nexus between piracy and the slave-trade, Gabrielsen in Erskine (2003), 389–404, is fundamental. On piracy in general, Ormerod (1924) is still useful but has been largely superseded by de Souza (1999). On Hellenistic slavery and utopias: Green (1993), 382–395. The study of Hellenistic warfare is now analyzed in depth by Chaniotis (2005), a thorough, wide-ranging, and exhaustively documented study. Short introduction: Baker in Erskine (2003), 373–388. Military developments: Shipley (2000), 334–341. Geography: Geus in Erskine (2003), 232–245, Fraser (1972), 1.520–553, 2.750–790, Dilke (1985) on maps, Romm (1992), and especially Clarke (1999). Science and technology: short surveys, Green (1993), 453–496, Keyser and

Irby-Massie in Bugh (2006), 241–264. General introductions: Hodges (1970), Lloyd (1973), Rihll (1999). Sourcebooks: Cohen and Drabkin (1948), Irbie-Massie and Keyser (2002).

Hellenistic religion can mostly easily be approached in the first instance via Mikalson (2005), 198–219, and in Bugh (2006), 208–222, Chamoux (2003), 323–352, Green (1993), 396–413, 586–601, and Shipley (2000), 153–176. Both Mikalson (1998) and Parker (1996), 218–281, concentrate specifically on Athenian cults and beliefs. On the deification of Hellenistic rulers, see Chaniotis in Erskine (2003), 430–445, and Green (2003a). Magic: Dickie (2001), 96–123. Overviews of Hellenistic philosophy: Long (1974), Shipley (2000), 176–191, Green (1993), 602–646. For further reading, Algra et al. (1999). Medicine: Flemming in Erskine (2003), 449–463, Green (1993), 480–496, and Nutton (2004). Von Staden (1989) on Herophilus is a cornucopia of wide-ranging medical information for the Hellenistic period. On sexuality, Skinner (2005)—non-ideological, exhaustive in its examination of sources, sensible in its judgments, and equipped with a formidable bibliography—replaces all earlier works on this topic for those in search of knowledge rather than confirmation of their prejudices.

Publications on Hellenistic literature are innumerable and of very uneven quality. A good introduction, stressing the social background, is provided by Shipley (2000), 235–270. Hutchinson (1988) surveys all the poetry except for Menander, now best examined in Hunter's chapter on him in Fantuzzi and Hunter (2004), 404–443. In general, Fantuzzi and Hunter is the widest-ranging and most up-to-date study now available: Hunter's introduction in Erskine (2003), 477–493, offers a deft digest of it, with full documentation of work on individual authors. Gutzwiller (1998) on epigram is especially rewarding. On literature, see also the coverage of original texts in my introduction, pp. xxi–xxx ff. Green (1993), 92–118, 336–361, and 566–585 provides a short introduction to the Hellenistic visual arts, of which by far the best general survey is Pollitt (1986). See also Stewart (1996) and the same author in Erskine (2003), 494–514, for a simultaneously hilarious and scarifying account of the post-Renaissance scholarship on the Laocoön and other famous icons of the period.

BIBLIOGRAPHY

ADAMS (2005): W. L. Adams, *Alexander the Great: Legacy of a Conqueror.* New York.

ADAMS AND BORZA (1982): W. L. Adams, E. N. Borza (eds.), *Philip II, Alexander the Great, and the Macedonian Heritage.* Washington, D.C.

AFRICA (1961): T. W. Africa, *Phylarchos and the Spartan Revolution.* Berkeley.

ALCOCK (1994): S. E. Alcock, "Breaking Up the Hellenistic World: Survey and Society," in Morris (1994), 171–190.

ALGRA ET AL. (1999): K. Algra et al. (eds.), *The Cambridge History of Hellenistic Philosophy.* Cambridge.

ALLEN (1983): R. E. Allen, *The Attalid Kingdom: A Constitutional History.* Oxford.

ANSON (2004): E. M. Anson, *Eumenes of Cardia: A Greek among Macedonians.* Boston and Leiden.

ARAFAT (1996): K. W. Arafat, *Pausanias' Greece: Ancient Artists and Roman Rulers.* Cambridge.

ARCHIBALD ET AL. (2001): Z. H. Archibald, J. Davies, V. Gabrielsen, G. J. Oliver (eds.), *Hellenistic Economies.* New York.

ASTIN ET AL. (1989): A. E. Astin et al. (eds.), *The Cambridge Ancient History.* 2nd ed. Vol. VIII, *Rome and the Mediterranean to 133 B.C.* Cambridge.

AUSTIN (2006): M. M. Austin, *The Hellenistic World from Alexander to the Roman Conquest.* 2nd ed. Cambridge.

BABBITT ET AL. (1927–2004): F. C. Babbitt et al., *Plutarch's Moralia.* 15 vols. Cambridge, Mass.

BADIAN (1958): E. Badian, *Foreign Clientelae.* Oxford.

BADIAN (1966): E. Badian (ed.), *Ancient Society and Institutions.* Oxford.

BAGNALL (1995): R. S. Bagnall, *Reading Papyri, Writing Ancient History.* London and New York.

BAGNALL AND DEROW (2004): R. S. Bagnall and P. Derow, *The Hellenistic Period: Historical Sources in Translation.* 2nd ed. Oxford.

BARNES (1984): J. Barnes (ed.), *The Complete Works of Aristotle.* Rev. Oxford trans. Princeton.

BAYNHAM (1998): E. Baynham, *Alexander the Great: The Unique History of Quintus Curtius.* Ann Arbor, Mich.

BELLINGER (1963): A. R. Bellinger, *Essays on the Coinage of Alexander the Great.* New York.

BERTHOLD (1984): R. M. Berthold, *Rhodes in the Hellenistic Age.* Ithaca, NY.

BETTENSON (1976): H. Bettenson, *Livy: Rome and the Mediterranean.* Introduction by A. H. McDonald. Harmondsworth.

BEVAN (1902): E. R. Bevan, *The House of Seleucus.* 2 vols. London.

BEVAN (1927): E. R. Bevan, *The House of Ptolemy: A History of Egypt Under the Ptolemaic Dynasty.* London.

BICHLER (1983): R. Bichler, "*Hellenismus*": *Geschichte und Problematik eines Epochenbegriffs.* Darmstadt.

BILLOWS (1990): R. A. Billows, *Antigonos the One-Eyed and the Creation of the Hellenistic State.* Berkeley.

BIZIÈRE (1975): F. Bizière, *Diodore de Sicile, Bibliothèque Historique.* Livre XIX. Paris.

BORZA (1990): E. N. Borza, *In the Shadow of Olympus: The Emergence of Macedon.* Princeton.

BORZA (1995): E. N. Borza, *Makedonika.* Claremont, Calif.

BOSWORTH (1980): A. B. Bosworth, *A Historical Commentary on Arrian's History of Alexander.* Vol. I, Commentary on Books I–III. Oxford.

BOSWORTH (1988a): A. B. Bosworth, *Conquest and Empire: The Reign of Alexander the Great.* Cambridge.

BOSWORTH (1988b): A. B. Bosworth, *From Arrian to Alexander: Studies in Historical Interpretation.* Oxford.

BOSWORTH (1995): A. B. Bosworth, *A Historical Commentary on Arrian's History of Alexander.* Vol. II, Commentary on Books IV–V. Oxford.

BOSWORTH (1996): A. B. Bosworth, *Alexander and the East: The Tragedy of Triumph.* Oxford.

BOSWORTH (2002): A. B. Bosworth, *The Legacy of Alexander: Politics, Warfare, and Propaganda Under the Successors.* Oxford.

BOSWORTH AND BAYNHAM (2000): A. B. Bosworth and E. J. Baynham, *Alexander the Great in Fact and Fiction.* Oxford.

BOWMAN (1986): A. K. Bowman, *Egypt After the Pharaohs: 332 BC–AD 642.* Cambridge.

BRAUND AND WILKINS (2000): D. Braund and J. Wilkins (eds.), *Athenaeus and His World: Reading Greek Culture in the Roman Empire.* Exeter.

BRIANT (2002): P. Briant, *From Cyrus to Alexander: A History of the Persian Empire.* Trans. P. T. Daniels. Winona Lake, Ind.

BROWN (1958): T. S. Brown, *Timaeus of Tauromenium.* Berkeley.

BRUNT (1976): P. A. Brunt, *Arrian: Anabasis Alexandri.* Vol. I, Books I–IV. Cambridge, Mass.

BRUNT (1983): P. A. Brunt, *Arrian: Anabasis Alexandri.* Vol. II, Books V–VII. Cambridge, Mass.

BUCKLER (2003): J. Buckler, *Aegean Greece in the Fourth Century BC.* Leiden.

BUGH (2006): G. R. Bugh (ed.), *The Cambridge Companion to the Hellenistic World.* Cambridge.

BURN (1962): A. R. Burn, *Alexander the Great and the Hellenistic World.* 2nd ed. New York.

BURSTEIN (1985): S. M. Burstein, *Translated Documents of Greece and Rome 3: The Hellenistic Age from the Battle of Ipsos to the Death of Kleopatra VII.* Cambridge.

BURSTEIN (1996): S. M. Burstein, *The Hellenistic Period in World History.* Washington, D.C.

CARNEY (2000): E. D. Carney, *Women and Monarchy in Macedonia.* Norman, Okla.

CARNEY (2003): E. D. Carney, "Women in Alexander's Court," in Roisman (2003), 227–252.

CARTLEDGE (2004): P. A. Cartledge, *Alexander the Great.* Woodstock and New York.

CARTLEDGE ET AL. (1997): P. A. Cartledge, P. Garnsey, E. Gruen (eds.), *Hellenistic Constructs: Essays in Culture, History, and Historiography.* Berkeley.

CARTLEDGE AND SPAWFORTH (2002): P. A. Cartledge and A. J. Spawforth, *Hellenistic and Roman Sparta: A Tale of Two Cities.* 2nd ed. London and New York.

CARY (1914–27): E. Cary, *Dio Cassius: Roman History.* 9 vols. Cambridge, Mass.

CAWKWELL (1978): G. Cawkwell, *Philip of Macedon.* London.

CHAMOUX (2003): F. Chamoux (ed.), *Hellenistic Civilization.* Trans. M. Roussel. Oxford.

CHANIOTIS (2005): A. Chaniotis, *War in the Hellenistic World: A Social and Cultural History.* London and New York.

CHAUVEAU (2000): M. Chauveau, *Egypt in the Age of Cleopatra: History and Society Under the Ptolemies.* Ithaca and London.

CLARKE (1997): K. Clarke, "In Search of the Author of Strabo's *Geography,*" *JRS* 87 (1997): 92–110.

CLARKE (1999): K. Clarke, *Between Geography and History: Hellenistic Constructions of the Roman World,* esp. chaps. iv–vi. Oxford.

COHEN (1997): A. Cohen, *The Alexander Mosaic: Stories of Victory and Defeat.* Cambridge.

COHEN AND DRABKIN (1948): M. R. Cohen and I. E. Drabkin, *A Source Book in Greek Science.* Cambridge, Mass.

CRAWFORD (1983): M. Crawford (ed.), *Sources for Ancient History.* Cambridge.

CROOK ET AL. (1994): J. A. Crook et al. (eds.), *The Cambridge Ancient History.* 2nd ed. Vol. 9, *The Last Age of the Roman Republic, 146–43 B.C.* Cambridge.

DEPUYDT (1997): L. Depuydt, "The Time of Death of Alexander the Great: 11 June 323 BC, ca. 4.00–5.00 PM," *Die Welt des Orients* 28 (1997): 117–135.

DE SÉLINCOURT (1971): A. de Sélincourt, *Arrian: The Campaigns of Alexander.* Introduction by J. R. Hamilton. Harmondsworth.

DE SOUZA (1999): P. de Souza, *Piracy in the Graeco-Roman World.* Cambridge.

DICKIE (2001): M. Dickie, *Magic and Magicians in the Greco-Roman World.* London.

DIGGLE (2004): J. Diggle, *Theophrastus: Characters.* Cambridge.

DILKE (1985): O. A. W. Dilke, *Greek and Roman Maps.* London.

DROYSEN (1878): J. G. Droysen, *Geschichte des Hellenismus.* 2 vols. Gotha.

DROYSEN (2004): J. G. Droysen, *Geschichte Alexanders des Grossen.* Rev. ed. A. Hohlweg. Neuried.

DRYDEN ET AL. (2001): J. Dryden et al. *Plutarch's Lives.* 2 vols. New York.

DUECK (2000): D. Dueck, *Strabo of Amasia: A Greek Man of Letters in Augustan Rome.* New York.

EASTERLING AND KNOX (1985): P. E. Easterling and B. M. W. Knox (eds.), *The Cambridge History of Classical Literature I: Greek Literature.* Cambridge.

EDDY (1961): S. K. Eddy, *The King Is Dead: Studies in the Near Eastern Resistance to Hellenism, 334–31 B.C.* Lincoln, Nebr.

EDELSTEIN AND KIDD (1989): L. Edelstein and I. G. Kidd, *Posidonius.* Vol. I, *The Fragments.* 2nd ed. Cambridge.

ELLIS (1976): J. R. Ellis, *Philip II and Macedonian Imperialism.* London, 1976.

ELLIS (1994): W. M. Ellis, *Ptolemy of Egypt.* London and New York.

ENGELS (1978): D. W. Engels, *Alexander the Great and the Logistics of the Macedonian Army.* Berkeley.

ERRINGTON (1990): R. M. Errington, *A History of Macedonia.* Trans. C. Errington. Berkeley.

ERSKINE (2003): A. Erskine (ed.), *A Companion to the Hellenistic World.* Oxford.

FANTUZZI AND HUNTER (2004): M. Fantuzzi and R. Hunter, *Tradition and Innovation in Hellenistic Poetry.* Cambridge.

FERGUSON (1911): W. S. Ferguson, *Hellenistic Athens: An Historical Essay.* New York [repr. 1969].

FERGUSON (1973): J. Ferguson, *The Heritage of Hellenism.* London.

FOERSTER (1893): R. Foerster, *Scriptores physiognomonici Graeci et Latini.* Leipzig.

FRASER (1972): P. M. Fraser, *Ptolemaic Alexandria.* 3 vols. Oxford.

FRASER (1977): P. M. Fraser, *Rhodian Funerary Monuments.* Oxford.

FRASER (1996): P. M. Fraser, *Cities of Alexander the Great.* Oxford.

FRÖSÉN (1997): J. Frösén (ed.), *Early Hellenistic Athens: Symptoms of a Change.* Helsinki.

GABBERT (1997): J. J. Gabbert, *Antigonus II Gonatas: A Political Biography*. London and New York.

GABRIELSEN (1997): V. Gabrielsen, *The Naval Aristocracy of Hellenistic Rhodes*. Aarhus.

GAGER (1992): J. G. Gager, *Curse Tablets and Binding Spells from the Ancient World*. Oxford.

GEER (1947): R. M. Geer, *Diodorus of Sicily*. Vol. IX, books xviii and xix, 1–65. Cambridge, Mass.

GEER (1954): R. M. Geer, *Diodorus of Sicily*. Vol. X, books xix, 66–110, and xx. Cambridge, Mass.

GOUKOWSKY (1978): P. Goukowsky, *Diodore de Sicile, Bibliothèque Historique*. Livre XVIII. Paris.

GOUKOWSKY (1999): P. Goukowsky, *Diodore de Sicile: Bibliothèque Historique*. Livre XVII. Paris.

GRAINGER (1990): J. D. Grainger, *Seleukos Nikator: Constructing a Hellenistic Kingdom*. London.

GRAINGER (1991): J. D. Grainger, *Hellenistic Phoenicia*. Oxford.

GRAYSON (1975): A. K. Grayson, *Assyrian and Babylonian Chronicles*. New York.

GREEN (1991): P. Green, *Alexander of Macedon, 356–323 B.C.: A Historical Biography*. Rev. ed. Berkeley.

GREEN (1993): P. Green, *Alexander to Actium: The Historical Evolution of the Hellenistic Age*. Rev. ed. Berkeley.

GREEN (1997): P. Green, *The Argonautika, by Apollonios Rhodios*. Trans., with introduction, commentary, and glossary. Berkeley.

GREEN (2003a): P. Green, "Delivering the Go(o)ds: Demetrius Poliorcetes and Hellenistic Divine Kingship," in *Gestures: Essays in Ancient History, Literature, and Philosophy Presented to Alan L. Boegehold*, eds. G. W. Bakewell, J. P. Sickinger, Oxford, 258–277.

GREEN (2003b): P. Green, "Occupation and Co-existence: The Impact of Macedon on Athens, 323–307," in *The Macedonians in Athens, 322–229 B.C.*, eds. O. Palagia, S. V. Tracy, Oxford, 1–7.

GREEN (2004): P. Green, *From Ikaria to the Stars*. Austin, Tx.

GRIFFITH (1979): G. T. Griffith, "The Reign of Philip II," in Hammond and Griffith (1979), 203–646, 675–730.

GRUEN (1984): E. S. Gruen, *The Hellenistic World and the Coming of Rome*. 2 vols. Berkeley.

GULICK (1927–1941): C. B. Gulick, *Athenaeus: The Deipnosophists*. 7 vols. Cambridge, Mass.

GUTZWILLER (1998): K. Gutzwiller, *Poetic Garlands: Hellenistic Epigrams in Context*. Berkeley.

HABICHT (1985): C. Habicht, *Pausanias' Guide to Ancient Greece*. Berkeley.

HABICHT (1997): C. Habicht, *Athens from Alexander to Antony.* Trans. D. L. Schneider. Cambridge, Mass.

HAMILTON (1969): J. R. Hamilton, *Plutarch's Alexander: A Commentary.* Oxford, 1969 [rev. ed., London, 1999].

HAMMOND (1981): N. G. L. Hammond, *Alexander the Great.* London.

HAMMOND (1989): N. G. L. Hammond, *The Macedonian State: The Origins, Institutions and History.* Oxford.

HAMMOND (1994): N. G. L. Hammond, *Philip of Macedon.* London.

HAMMOND AND GRIFFITH (1979): N. G. L. Hammond and G. T. Griffith, *A History of Macedonia,* Vol. II, *550–336 B.C.* Oxford.

HAMMOND AND WALBANK (1988): N. G. L. Hammond and F. W. Walbank, *A History of Macedonia.* Vol. III, *336–167 B.C.* Oxford.

HANSEN (1971): E. V. Hansen, *The Attalids of Pergamon.* 2nd ed. Ithaca, N.Y.

HARDING (1985): P. Harding, *Translated Documents of Greece and Rome 2: From the End of the Peloponnesian War to the Battle of Ipsus.* Cambridge.

HARRIS (1979): W. V. Harris, *War and Imperialism in Republican Rome, 327–70 BC.* Oxford.

HATZOPOULOS AND LOUKOPOULOS (1980): M. B. Hatzopoulos and L. D. Loukopoulos, *Philip of Macedon.* New Rochelle, N.Y.

HECKEL (1992): W. Heckel, *The Marshals of Alexander's Empire.* New York.

HECKEL (2006): W. Heckel, *Who's Who in the Age of Alexander the Great.* Oxford.

HECKEL AND SULLIVAN (1984): W. Heckel and R. Sullivan (eds.), *Ancient Coins of the Graeco-Roman World: The Nickle Numismatic Papers.* Waterloo, Ont.

HECKEL AND YARDLEY (2004): W. Heckel and J. C. Yardley, *Alexander the Great: Historical Sources in Translation.* Oxford.

HEISSERER (1980): A. J. Heisserer, *Alexander and the Greeks: The Epigraphic Evidence.* Norman, Okla.

HICKS (1972): R. D. Hicks, *Diogenes Laertius, Lives of Eminent Philosophers.* 2 vols. Cambridge, Mass.

HODGES (1970): H. Hodges, *Technology in the Ancient World.* Harmondsworth.

HÖLBL (2001): G. Hölbl, *A History of the Ptolemaic Empire.* Trans. T. Saavedra. London and New York.

HOLFORD-STREVENS (2003): L. Holford-Strevens, *Aulus Gellius: An Antonine Scholar and His Achievement.* 2nd ed. Oxford.

HOLT (1988): F. L. Holt, *Alexander the Great and Bactria.* Leiden.

HOLT (1999): F. L. Holt, *Thundering Zeus: The Making of Hellenistic Bactria.* Berkeley.

HOLT (2003): F. L. Holt, *Alexander the Great and the Mystery of the Elephant Medallions.* Berkeley.

HOLT (2005): F. L. Holt, *Into the Land of Bones.* Berkeley.

HORNBLOWER (1981): J. Hornblower, *Hieronymus of Cardia.* Oxford.

HOWGEGO (1995): C. Howgego, *Ancient History from Coins*. New York.

HUNT AND EDGAR (1932): A. S. Hunt and C. C. Edgar, *Select Papyri I: Non-Literary Papyri, Private Affairs*. Cambridge, Mass.

HUNT AND EDGAR (1934): A. S. Hunt and C. C. Edgar, *Select Papyri II: Non-Literary Papyri, Public Documents*. Cambridge, Mass.

HUTCHINSON (1988): G. O. Hutchinson, *Hellenistic Poetry*. Oxford.

HUTTON (2005): W. Hutton, *Describing Greece: Landscape and Literature in the Periegesis of Pausanias*. Cambridge.

IRBY-MASSIE AND KEYSER (2002): G. L. Irby-Massie and P. T. Keyser, *Greek Science of the Hellenistic Era: A Sourcebook*. London and New York.

ISAAC (2004): B. Isaac, *The Invention of Racism in Classical Antiquity*. Princeton.

JONES (1917–1932): H. L. Jones, *The Geography of Strabo*. 8 vols. Cambridge, Mass.

JONES (1918–1935): W. H. S. Jones, *Pausanias: Description of Greece*. 5 vols. Cambridge, Mass.

JONES (1940): A. H. M. Jones, *The Greek City from Alexander to Justinian*. Oxford.

KEBRIC (1977): R. B. Kebric, *In the Shadow of Macedon: Duris of Samos*. Wiesbaden.

KIDD (1988): I. G. Kidd, *Posidonius*. Vol. II, *The Commentary*. 2 vols. Cambridge.

KIDD (1999): I. G. Kidd, *Posidonius*. Vol. III, *The Translation of the Fragments*. Cambridge.

KLEINER (2005): D. E. E. Kleiner, *Cleopatra and Rome*. Cambridge, Mass.

KOCK (1880–1888): T. Kock, *Comicorum Atticorum Fragmenta*. 3 vols. Leipzig.

KRAAY (1966): C. M. Kraay, *Greek Coins*. Photographs by Max Hirmer. London.

KRENTZ AND WHEELER (1994): P. Krentz, E. L. Wheeler, *Polyaenus, Stratagems of War*. 2 vols. Chicago.

KÜBLER (1888): B. Kübler, *Iuli Valeri Res Gestae Alexandri Macedonis*. Leipzig.

LARSEN (1968): J. A. O. Larsen, *Greek Federal States*. Oxford.

LEONE (1968): P. A. M. Leone, *Johannes Tzetzae Historiae*. Naples.

LEVI (1971): P. Levi, *Pausanias: Guide to Greece*. 2 vols. Harmondsworth. Rev. ed., 1979.

LEWIS (1974): N. Lewis, *Papyrus in Classical Antiquity*. Oxford.

LEWIS (1986): N. Lewis, *Greeks in Ptolemaic Egypt: Case Studies in the Social History of the Hellenistic World*. Oxford.

LEWIS ET AL. (1994): D. M. Lewis et al. (eds.), *The Cambridge Ancient History*. 2nd ed. Vol. VI, *The Fourth Century B.C.* Cambridge.

LLOYD (1973): G. E. R. Lloyd, *Greek Science After Aristotle*. New York.

LLOYD-JONES AND PARSONS (1982): H. Lloyd-Jones, P. Parsons (eds.), *Supplementum Hellenisticum*. Berlin.

LONG (1974): A. A. Long, *Hellenistic Philosophy*. London.

LONG AND SEDLEY (1987): A. A. Long and D. N. Sedley, *The Hellenistic Philosophers*. Vol. 1, *Translations of the Principal Sources, with Philosophical Commentary*; Vol. 2, *Greek and Latin Texts with Notes and Bibliography*. Cambridge.

LUND (1992): H. S. Lund, *Lysimachus: A Study in Early Hellenistic Kingship*. New York.

MAGIE (1950): D. Magie, *Roman Rule in Asia Minor*. 2 vols. Princeton.

MARTIN (1987): L. H. Martin, *Hellenistic Religions*. Oxford.

MCLEAN (2002): B. H. McLean, *An Introduction to Greek Epigraphy of the Hellenistic and Roman Periods from Alexander the Great to the Reign of Constantine (323 B.C.–A.D. 337)*. Ann Arbor, Mich.

MEIJER AND VAN NIJF (1992): F. Meijer and O. van Nijf, *Trade, Transport and Society in the Ancient World: A Sourcebook*. London and New York.

MIKALSON (1998): J. Mikalson, *Religion in Hellenistic Athens*. Berkeley.

MIKALSON (2005): J. Mikalson, *Ancient Greek Religion*. Oxford.

MOMIGLIANO (1975): A. D. Momigliano, *Alien Wisdom: The Limits of Hellenization*. Cambridge.

MØRKHOLM (1984): O. Mørkholm, "The Monetary System in the Seleucid Empire after 187 BC," in Heckel and Sullivan (1984), 93–113.

MØRKHOLM (1991): O. Mørkholm, *Early Hellenistic Coinage: From the Accession of Alexander to the Peace of Apamea (336–186 B.C.)*. Cambridge.

MORRIS (1994): I. Morris (ed.), *Classical Greece: Ancient Histories and Modern Archaeologies*. Cambridge.

MOSSÉ (1973): C. Mossé, *Athens in Decline, 404–86 BC*. Trans. J. Stewart. London.

MOSSÉ (2004): C. Mossé, *Alexander: Destiny and Myth*. Trans. J. Lloyd. Baltimore.

NUTTON (2004): V. Nutton, *Ancient Medicine*. London and New York.

O'BRIEN (1992): J. M. O'Brien, *Alexander the Great: The Invisible Enemy*. London and New York.

OCD3 (1996): S. Hornblower and A. Spawforth, *The Oxford Classical Dictionary*. 3rd ed. Oxford.

OGDEN (2000): D. Ogden, *Polygamy, Prostitutes and Death: The Hellenistic Dynasties*. London and Swansea.

OGDEN (2002): D. Ogden (ed.), *The Hellenistic World: New Perspectives*. London.

OIKONOMIDES (1981): A. N. Oikonomides, *The Coinage of Alexander the Great*. Chicago.

OLSON (2007): S. Douglas Olson, *Athenaeus I–II* [Books 1–5]. *The Learned Banqueters*. 2 vols. [Series in progress.] Cambridge, Mass.

ORMEROD (1924): H. A. Ormerod, *Piracy in the Ancient World*. Liverpool.

PAGE (1941): D. L. Page, *Select Papyri III: Literary Papyri, Poetry*. Cambridge, Mass.

PARKER (1996): R. Parker, *Athenian Religion: A History*. Oxford.

PATON (1922–1927): W. R. Paton, *Polybius: The Histories*. 6 vols. Cambridge, Mass.

PEARSON (1960): L. Pearson, *The Lost Histories of Alexander the Great*. New York.

PERRIN (1914–1926): B. Perrin, *Plutarch's Lives*. 11 vols. Cambridge, Mass.

PESTMAN ET AL. (1981): P. W. Pestman et al., *A Guide to the Zenon Archive.* 2 vols. Leiden.

PIPER (1986): L. J. Piper, *Spartan Twilight.* New Rochelle, N.Y.

POLLITT (1986): J. J. Pollitt, *Art in the Hellenistic Age.* Cambridge.

POMEROY (1984): S. B. Pomeroy, *Women in Hellenistic Egypt from Alexander to Cleopatra.* New York.

PRICE (1974): M. J. Price, *Coins of the Macedonians.* Edinburgh and London.

PRICE (1991): M. J. Price, *The Coinage in the Name of Alexander the Great and Philip Arrhidaeus.* 2 vols. Zurich and London.

RHODES AND OSBORNE (2003): P. J. Rhodes and R. Osborne, *Greek Historical Inscriptions 404–323 BC.* Oxford.

RICE (1983): E. E. Rice, *The Grand Procession of Ptolemy Philadelphus.* Oxford.

RIHLL (1999): T. E. Rihll, *Greek Science.* Oxford.

ROBINSON (1953): C. A. Robinson Jr., *The History of Alexander the Great.* Vol. I. Providence, R.I.

ROISMAN (2003): J. Roisman (ed.), *Brill's Companion to Alexander the Great.* Leiden.

ROLFE (1927–28): J. C. Rolfe, *Aulus Gellius.* 3 vols. Cambridge, Mass.

ROLFE (1929): J. C. Rolfe, *Cornelius Nepos.* Cambridge, Mass.

ROLFE (1946): J. C. Rolfe, *Quintus Curtius.* 2 vols. Cambridge, Mass.

ROMM (1992): J. S. Romm, *The Edges of the Earth in Ancient Thought: Geography, Explorations, and Fiction.* Princeton.

ROOS AND WIRTH (1967): A. G. Roos, G. Wirth, *Flavii Arriani Quae Extant Omnia.* 2 vols. Leipzig.

ROSTOVTZEFF (1941): *The Social and Economic History of the Hellenistic World.* 3 vols. Oxford.

ROWLAND (1999): I. D. Rowland, *Vitruvius' Ten Books on Architecture.* Cambridge.

ROWLANDSON (1998): J. Rowlandson, *Women and Society in Greek and Roman Egypt: A Sourcebook.* Cambridge.

RUSSELL (1993): D. A. Russell, *Plutarch: Selected Essays and Dialogues.* Oxford 1993.

RUSTEN AND CUNNINGHAM (2002): J. Rusten, I. C. Cunningham, *Theophrastus Characters, Herodas Mimes, Sophron and Other Mime Fragments.* 3rd ed. Cambridge, Mass.

SACHS AND HUNGER (1988): A. J. Sachs and H. Hunger, *Astronomical Diaries and Related Texts from Babylon.* Vienna.

SACHS AND WISEMAN (1954): A. J. Sachs and D. J. Wiseman, "A Babylonian King List of the Hellenistic Period," *Iraq* 16 (1954): 202–211.

SACKS (1990): K. Sacks, *Diodorus Siculus and the First Century.* Princeton.

SCHOLTEN (2000): J. B. Scholten, *The Politics of Plunder: Aitolians and Their Koinon in the Early Hellenistic Era, 279–217 BC.* Berkeley.

SCOTT-KILVERT (1973): I. Scott-Kilvert, *The Age of Alexander: Nine Greek Lives by Plutarch.* Harmondsworth.

SCOTT-KILVERT (1979): I. Scott-Kilvert, *Polybius: The Rise of the Roman Empire.* Harmondsworth.

SHACKLETON BAILEY (2000): D. R. Shackleton Bailey, *Valerius Maximus: Memorable Doings and Sayings.* 2 vols. Cambridge, Mass.

SHERMAN (1952): C. L. Sherman, *Diodorus of Sicily.* Vol. VII, books xv.20–xvi.65. Cambridge, Mass.

SHERWIN-WHITE AND KUHRT (1993): S. Sherwin-White and A. Kuhrt, *From Samarkand to Sardis: A New Approach to the Seleucid Empire.* Berkeley.

SHIMRON (1972): B. Shimron, *Late Sparta: The Spartan Revolution 243–146 BC.* Buffalo, N.Y.

SHIPLEY (2000): *The Greek World After Alexander 323–30 BC.* London.

SHUCKBURGH (1889): E. S. Shuckburgh, *The Histories of Polybius.* 2 vols. London, repr. Bloomington.

SHUCKBURGH (1980): E. S. Shuckburgh, *Polybius on Roman Imperialism: The Histories of Polybius,* abridged. South Bend, Ind.

SKINNER (2005): M. B. Skinner, *Sexuality in Greek and Roman Culture.* Oxford.

SMITH (1988): R. R. R. Smith, *Hellenistic Royal Portraits.* Oxford.

SMITH (1924): S. Smith, *Babylonian Historical Texts.* London.

SNODGRASS (1987): A. M. Snodgrass, *An Archaeology of Greece: The Present State and Future Scope of a Discipline.* Berkeley.

STEWART (1993): A. Stewart, *Faces of Power: Alexander's Image and Hellenistic Politics.* Berkeley.

STEWART (1996): A. Stewart, *Art, Desire and the Body in Ancient Greece.* Cambridge.

STONEMAN (1991): R. Stoneman, *The Greek Alexander Romance.* London.

STONEMAN (2004): R. Stoneman, *Alexander the Great.* 2nd ed. London and New York.

TARN (1913): W. W. Tarn, *Antigonus Gonatas.* London.

TARN (1948): W. W. Tarn, *Alexander the Great.* 2 vols. Cambridge.

TARN AND GRIFFITH (1952): W. W. Tarn and G. T. Griffith, *Hellenistic Civilization.* 3rd ed. London.

THOMPSON (1988): D. J. Thompson, *Memphis Under the Ptolemies.* Princeton.

TOD (1948): M. N. Tod, *A Selection of Greek Historical Inscriptions.* Vol. II, *From 403 to 323 B.C.* Oxford.

TRITLE (1988): L. A. Tritle, *Phocion the Good.* London and New York.

TRITLE (1997): L. A. Tritle (ed.), *The Greek World in the Fourth Century: From the Fall of the Athenian Empire to the Successors of Alexander.* New York.

TRYPANIS (1975): C. A. Trypanis, *Callimachus.* Cambridge, Mass.

TURNER (1968): E. G. Turner, *Greek Papyri: An Introduction.* Oxford.

USSHER (1960): R. G. Ussher, *The Characters of Theophrastus.* London.

VASUNIA (2001): P. Vasunia, *The Gift of the Nile: Hellenizing Egypt from Aeschylus to Alexander.* Berkeley.

VOLKMANN (1958): H. Volkmann, *Cleopatra: A Study in Politics and Propaganda.* Trans. T. J. Cadoux. London.

VON STADEN (1989): H. von Staden, *Herophilus: The Art of Medicine in Early Alexandria.* Cambridge.

WACHSMUTH AND HENSE (1884): C. Wachsmuth, O. Hense, *Ioannis Stobaei Anthologium.* Berlin (repr. 1958).

WALBANK (1933): F. W. Walbank, *Aratus of Sicyon.* Cambridge.

WALBANK (1940): F. W. Walbank, *Philip V of Macedon.* Cambridge.

WALBANK (1957–1979): F. W. Walbank, *A Historical Commentary on Polybius.* 3 vols. Oxford.

WALBANK (1972): F. W. Walbank, *Polybius.* Berkeley.

WALBANK (1993): F. W. Walbank, *The Hellenistic World.* Rev. ed. Cambridge, Mass.

WALBANK ET AL. (1984): F. W. Walbank, A. E. Astin, M. W. Frederiksen, R. M. Ogilvie (eds.), *The Cambridge Ancient History.* 2nd ed. Vol. VII, part i, *The Hellenistic World.* Cambridge.

WALKER AND HIGGS (2001): S. Walker and P. Higgs (eds.), *Cleopatra of Egypt: From History to Myth.* Princeton.

WALTON (1957): F. R. Walton, *Diodorus of Sicily.* Vol. XI, *Fragments of Books xxi–xxxii.* Cambridge, Mass.

WALTON AND GEER (1967): F. R. Walton and R. M. Geer, *Diodorus of Sicily.* Vol. XII, *Fragments of Books xxxiii–xl, General Index.* Cambridge, Mass.

WATERFIELD (1992): R. Waterfield, *Plutarch: Essays.* Introduction and Notes, I. Kidd. Harmondsworth.

WELLES (1963): C. B. Welles, *Diodorus of Sicily.* Vol. VIII, books xvi, 66–95, and xvii. Cambridge, Mass.

WESTGATE (2002): R. Westgate, "Hellenistic Mosaics," in Ogden (2002), 221–251.

WHITE (1912–1913): H. White, *Appian's Roman History.* Vols. II–IV. Cambridge, Mass.

WHITEHORNE (1994): J. Whitehorne, *Cleopatras.* London and New York.

WILCKEN (1967): U. Wilcken, *Alexander the Great.* Trans. G. C. Richards. New York.

WILL (1979–1982): E. Will, *Histoire Politique du Monde Hellénistique.* 2 vols. 2nd ed. Nancy.

WILSON (2000): N. G. Wilson, *Aelian: Historical Miscellany.* Cambridge, Mass.

WOOD (1997): M. Wood, *In the Footsteps of Alexander the Great.* Berkeley.

WOODHEAD (1981): A. G. Woodhead, *The Study of Greek Inscriptions.* 2nd ed. Cambridge.

WORTHINGTON (2003): I. Worthington (ed.), *Alexander the Great: A Reader.* New York.

WORTHINGTON (2004): I. Worthington, *Alexander the Great: Man and God.* London and New York.

WYCHERLEY (1962): R. E. Wycherley, *How the Greeks Built Cities.* 2nd ed. London and New York.

YARDLEY AND DEVELIN (1994): J. C. Yardley (trans.), R. Develin (notes), *Justin: Epitome of the Philippic History of Pompeius Trogus.* Atlanta.

YARDLEY AND HECKEL (1984): J. C. Yardley (trans.), W. Heckel (notes), *Quintus Curtius Rufus: The History of Alexander.* Harmondsworth.

YARDLEY AND HECKEL (1997): J. C. Yardley (trans. and app.), W. Heckel (comm.), *Justin: Epitome of the Philippic History of Pompeius Trogus.* Vol. I, books 11–12: *Alexander the Great.* Oxford.

Abbreviations

Adam.	Adamantius (4th cent. CE, tr. Stewart, 1993)
Physiog.	*Physiognomonicus*
AJA	*American Journal of Archaeology*
App.	Appian[us] (1/2 cent. CE, tr. White)
Arist.	Aristotle (384–322 BCE, ed./tr. Barnes)
Meteor.	*Meteorologica*
Ps.-Oecon.	*Pseudo-Oeconomica*
Arr.	Arrian[us], Lucius Flavius (c. 86–160 CE, ed. Roos and Wirth, tr. Brunt, de Sélincourt)
Succ.	*Successores*
Athen.	Athenaeus (c. 200 CE, tr. Gulick)
BM	British Museum
Callim.	Callimachus (c. 305–240 BCE, ed./tr. Trypanis)
Aet.	*Aetia*
Catull.	Catullus (c. 84–54 BCE)
ChrEg.	*Chronique d'Égypte*
Clem.	Clement of Alexandria (c. 150–c. 215 CE, tr. Stewart 1993)
Strom.	*Stromateis*
CQ	*Classical Quarterly*
Dio Cass.	Dio Cassius (c. 164–c. 235 CE, ed./tr. Cary)
Diog. Laert.	Diogenes Laertius (? 3rd cent. CE, ed./tr. Hicks)
DS	Diodorus Siculus (c. 100–c. 30 BCE, ed./tr. Welles)
Hom.	Homer (? 8th cent. BCE)
Il.	*Iliad*
Od.	*Odyssey*
Jul. Val.	Julius Valerius (4th cent. CE, tr. Stewart, 1993)
Res. Gest. Alex. Mac.	*Res Gestae Alexandri Macedonis*

Just.	Justin[us], Marcus Junianus (? 2nd cent. CE, ed./tr. Yardley and Develin)
KRS	G. S. Kirk, J. E. Raven, and M. Schofield, *The Presocratic Philosophers,* Cambridge, 1983
Paus.	Pausanias (c. 150 CE, tr. Levi)
Polyb.	Polybius (c. 200–c. 118 BCE, tr. Paton)
Plin.	Gaius Plinius Secundus (Pliny the Elder, 23/4–79 CE)
NH	*Natural History*
Plut.	Plutarch [Mestrios Ploutarchos] of Chaeronea (c. 45–c. 120 CE, tr. Scott-Kilvert, 1973; Babbitt et al.; Perrin)
Alex.	*Alexander*
Dem.	*Demosthenes*
Demetr.	*Demetrius [Poliorcetes]*
Eum.	*Eumenes*
Mor.	*Moralia*
Pyrrh.	*Pyrrhus*
Polyaen.	Polyaenus (2nd cent. CE, tr. Krentz and Wheeler)
Ps.-Call.	Pseudo-Callisthenes ([*Alexander Romance*], tr. Stoneman, 1991)
QC	Quintus Curtius Rufus (1st cent. CE, tr. Yardley, ed. Heckel, 1984)
Stob.	Stobaeus (that is, John of Stobi, ? early 5th cent. CE, ed. Wachsmuth and Hense)
Flor.	*Florilegium*
Tzetzes	Joannes Tzetzes (12th cent. CE, tr. Stewart, ed. Leone, 1993)
Hist. Var.	
Chil.	*Historiarum variarum chiliades*
Vitruv.	M. Vitruvius Pollio (1st cent. BCE, tr. Rowland)

NOTES

INTRODUCTION: BACKGROUND AND SOURCES

1. See, for instance, Austin (2006), vii–viii; Erskine (2003), 1–3; Chamoux (2003), 1–6; Ogden (2002), ix–xiv; Shipley (2000), 1–5; and particularly Cartledge in Cartledge et al. (1997), 1–15. An excellent earlier analysis is that by Claire Préaux, "Réflexions sur l'Entité Hellénistique," *ChrEg.* 40 (1965): 129–139.
2. Cartledge in Cartledge et al. (1997), 3, referring to doubts raised by Bichler (1983) and Canfora (1987). Erskine (2003), 2, argues that "the disappearance of the last of the successor kingdoms is a convenient terminal point rather than one of profound significance," but it did, in a very real sense, mark the end of an era.
3. Grote, *History of Greece* (1888 ed.), vol. 1, ix.
4. Some (for instance, Ogden, xi–xiii) would disagree, but I have yet to see any even remotely cogent evidence for such a concept in any ancient text. This includes the fragments of Timagenes and Justin's epitome of Trogus, both cited by Ogden.
5. For excellent accounts of this, see F. M. Turner, *The Greek Heritage in Victorian Britain* (New Haven and London, 1981), and R. Jenkyns, *The Victorians and Ancient Greece* (Oxford, 1980). The alleged primacy is itself, of course, a highly debatable preference.
6. Fr. 317, Lloyd-Jones and Parsons (1982).
7. Shipley (2000), 3, is characteristic of this approach.
8. Plut. *Mor.* 824C: ἐλευθερίας δ'ὅσον οἱ κρατοῦντες νέμουσι τοῖς δήμοις μέτεστι καὶ τὸ πλέον ἴσως οὐκ ἄμεινον.
9. Alcock et al., in Erskine (2003), 371.
10. I am not including here general sources for the reign of Philip II of Macedon, the father of Alexander the Great. Those interested are referred to

book 16 of Diodorus Siculus (Sherman, 1952; Welles, 1963) and the Greek orators, mainly Demosthenes (Vince, 1930; Vince and Vince, 1926) and Isocrates (Papillon, 2004), who were Philip's contemporaries.

11. Hamilton (1969), lix–lx. In general, Hamilton's introduction offers a first-rate assessment of Plutarch's approach to Alexander, and I, like most scholars, have drawn on it heavily.

12. For a thoroughgoing analysis of Arrian's historiography, see Bosworth (1988b). Bosworth is also working on the first historical commentary on Arrian, two volumes of which (Bosworth, 1980, 1995) have already been published.

13. Yardley and Develin (1994), 1.

14. Walbank in Walbank et al. (1984), 7.

15. Erskine (2003), 8, is very perceptive on this side of Plutarch's literary tastes.

16. It is often wrongly assumed that papyrus in antiquity was not unlike the brown, dried-out material rescued after more than a two-millennia interment in desert dumps (Oliver Stone's movie *Alexander* makes this error). In fact it was creamy, smooth, shiny, and flexible, like the most expensive modern writing paper: Lewis (1974), 61.

17. See, for instance, Kraay (1966), figs. 569–572 (Alexander); 580–582 (Lysimachus); 573 (Demetrius the Besieger); and 796–799 (Ptolemy I). It is worth noting that Ptolemy seems to have set a fashion among Hellenistic monarchs for unflattering realism in portraiture: his hook-nosed, prognathous profile, instantly recognizable, shows—perhaps in deliberate contrast with Alexander's portraiture—no idealizing tendencies whatsoever.

18. A. Snodgrass in Crawford (1983), 139.

19. Ibid., 144–147.

1. Alexander and His Legacy (336–323)

1. Carney (2003), 235.

2. Philip's marriage to Cleopatra and query of Alexander's legitimacy: Plut. *Alex.* 9.44–5; Arr. 3.6.5; Athen. 13.557D–E, 560C; Just. 9.5.9, 9.7.2–6, 11.11.4–5. Alexander's smart exit-line figures, not surprisingly, in both Rossen's and Stone's Alexander movies. Alexander's use of the royal "we": Plut. *Alex.* 9.3: Ἡμεῖς δέ σοι . . . νόθοι δοκοῦμεν; . . . I use the paragraphing of Perrin's Loeb edition rather than that of Ziegler's Teubner (generally preferred by scholars), since the Loeb is the text to which general readers will have access.

3. The birth (and death) of Cleopatra's son Caranus: Just. 11.2.3 and Paus. 8.7.7. Diodorus (17.2.3) records the birth a few days before Philip's as-

sassination but does not reveal the sex of the child (παιδίον). We know that Cleopatra had also borne Philip a daughter, Europa: Satyrus in Athen. 13.557E; cf. Just. 9.7.12. Caranus is commonly dismissed as a fiction on the grounds that Cleopatra did not have time for two births (Yardley and Heckel, 1997, 82). This is done by arbitrarily placing the date of her marriage to Philip in the late fall of 337. It could (as I assume) have just as easily been up to a year earlier. She would then have borne Europa in the summer of 337 and need not have become pregnant again until the end of the year: Diodorus places the second birth close to Philip's death—that is, in October 336. What Alexander feared was a rival for the throne (Just. 9.7.3, 11.2.3), a threat Europa would not have presented.

4. Achaemenid treasure: the estimate of 180,000 talents is Strabo's (15.3.9, C.731). This breaks down into 3,000–4,000 talents taken after Gaugamela (DS 17.64.3; QC 5.1.10), at Susa perhaps 49,000 talents (DS 17.66.1 with Plut. *Alex.* 36.1; Strabo, ibid.), at Persepolis 120,000 talents plus 6,000 from Pasargadae (DS 17.71.1; QC 5.6.9). The modern purchasing power would run into billions (sterling, euros, or dollars).

5. Alexander's physical appearance: texts collected in Stewart (1993), app. I, 341–358, cf. 72–78. Note especially Plut. *Alex.* 4 (general); Chrysippus ap. Athen. 13.565A, Plut. *Mor.* 180B (beardlessness); Arr. 2.12.6, DS 17.37.5, 66.3, QC 5.2.13–15 (short stature); Plut. *Mor.* 53D, *Pyrrh.* 8.1 (crooked neck, rough voice); Plut. *Mor.* 335B, Ps.-Call. 1.13, Jul. Val., *Res Gestae Alex. Mac.* 1.7, Adam. *Physiog.* 1.14, Tzetzes *Hist. Var. Chil.* 11.368.97 (melting bicolored eyes).

6. Alexander's alleged dying words: Arr. 7.26.3, DS 17.117.4. At 18.1.4, Diodorus says "to the best," as does QC 10.5.5. Just. 12.15.8 says "to the worthiest." These variants do not suggest a real difference. Augustus' comment: Plut. *Mor.* 207D 8. Arrian's assessment: 7.1.4.

2. HAWKS AND HYENAS: THE STRUGGLE FOR EMPIRE (323–276)

1. Date of Alexander's death: Depuydt (1997) is fundamental, correcting the previous assumption of the evening of June 10, with Sachs and Hunger (1988), 206–207 (BM 45962). Cf. Arr. 7.28.1; Plut. *Alex.* 75.4, 76.4, ad fin.

2. Cleopatra as a marital prize: DS 20.37.3–6. Perdiccas' marriage to Nicaea and pursuit of Cleopatra: DS 18.23.1–4; Just. 13.6.4–7. Eumenes' involvement: Arr. *Succ.* 1.21, 26; 24.7–12, 26.1–28, Roos, cf. Plut. *Eum.* 8.4. Cleopatra sent to Sardis by Olympias: Arr. *Succ.* 1.21 Roos. Marriages of Phila and Eurydice: DS 18.8.7, 19.59.3 (Phila, 322); Paus. 1.6.8 (Eurydice, 321). Cynane and Adea: Arr. *Succ.* 1.22–23 Roos; Polyaen. 8.60, cf. DS 19.52.5.

3. Demetrius Poliorcetes' siege of Rhodes: DS 20.81–88, 91–99 passim; Plut. *Demetr.* 21–22; Vitruv. 10.16.4. Cult of Ptolemy as Savior: DS 20.100.3–4; Paus. 1.8.6. The Colossus: Strabo 14.2.5 (C. 652); Plin. *NH* 34.41; Plut. *Mor.* 183B; Vitruv. 10.16.8.

3. Kings, Cities, and Culture: The Mythic Past as the Future

1. See C. P. Cavafy, *Collected Poems,* ed. G. P. Savidis, trans. E. Keeley and P. Sherrard (Princeton, 1975), 32.
2. For *isotheotês* in Homer and Sappho, see, for instance, Hom. *Od.* 8.864–868; Sappho fr. 31 L-P, 1–4. The Empedocles quotation: KRS fr. 399 = Diog. Laert. 8.62.1–10 + Clem. *Strom.* 6.30.9–11. The Eupolis quotation: fr. 117 Kock = Stob. *Flor.* 43.9; cf. Green (2003a).
3. Arist. *Ps.-Oecon.* 2.2 passim, in Barnes (1984), 2.2135–146.
4. Garlan in Walbank et al. (1984), 362.
5. On the other hand, the rhetorical, philosophical, and scientific tradition that sustained, among other things, oratory, criticism, historiography, mathematics, astronomy, and medicine—the achievements of which were, in many ways, far more characteristic of the fourth century and the Hellenistic era as a whole—owed comparatively little to any coherent mainland tradition: the stimulus here came mostly from those other early Greek colonies of east and west, in Asia Minor, Sicily, and south Italy.
6. By Herodotus, who tells the story (4.42). Ironically, what excited his incredulity—that as the Phoenicians were sailing west around the southern coast the sun was on their right—is precisely the fact that clinches the truth of the report.
7. Arist. *Meteor.* 1.13, 350a = Barnes (1984), 1.571.

4. Eastern Horizons and the Cloud in the West (276–196)

1. S. Agar in Erskine (2003), 41.
2. For this curious episode, see Callim. *Aet.* fr. 4 (Trypanis 80 ff.); Catull. 66 = Green (2005), 159–165, cf. 245–249; and Green (1993), 148–150.
3. Polyb. 36.17.5–10 = Austin (2006), 81.
4. A delightful anonymous historians' limerick (cited by P. Derow in Erskine [2003], 70, and I suspect by him) sums up the conflicting views neatly: "Badian's Romans like clients / they're not very big on alliance / for Harris they're mean / and psychotically keen / on glory, on war, and on triumphs." See Badian (1958) and Harris (1979).
5. P. Derow in Erskine (2003), 60.

5. Dynastic Troubles, Artistic and Scientific Achievements
(196–116)

1. For Polybius' tactical disquisition on phalanx vs. legion, see 18.18–27, 28–32, cf. M. Markle, "The Macedonian Sarissa, Spear, and related Armor," *AJA* 81 (1977): 323–339.
2. Polyb. 39.2.2 = Strabo 8.6.23, C. 381. One of these pictures, with symbolic aptness, depicted Heracles in agony, wearing the shirt of Nessus.
3. On this concept and the ancient sources for it, readers should consult the lapidary essay by G. E. R. Lloyd, "Saving the Appearances," *CQ* n.s., 28 (1978): 202–222.
4. See Polyb. 31.2.1–8, 11–15; and cf. Bevan (1902), 2.188–193.
5. Menecles of Barca, cited by Athen. 4.184b–c. The Greek I translate as "cultural renaissance" is "ἀνανέωσις . . . παιδείας ἁπάσης."
6. Bevan (1927), 325.

6. Sword over Pen: Rome's Final Solution (116–30)

1. Sherwin-White and Kuhrt (1993): See 217 ff., and in particular the section on "Decadence," 228–229.
2. Fr. 4 in R. Heinze, *Xenokrates* (Leipzig, 1892, repr. 1965).
3. Strabo 14.5.2, C. 668.
4. His position was precisely that of Antigonus Gonatas, when relieved in an identical fashion of the need to deal with Pyrrhus: see p. 68.

INDEX

ABOUT THE AUTHOR

PETER GREEN is James R. Dougherty, Jr., Centennial Professor of Classics Emeritus at the University of Texas at Austin. He is the author of numerous books on the ancient world, including *Alexander of Macedon, The Greco-Persian Wars,* and *Alexander to Actium.* Currently he serves as adjunct professor of classics at the University of Iowa and editor of *Syllecta Classica.*